EXPRESS TRACK

To ITALIAN

A Teach-Yourself Program

Marina Ferdeghini • Paola Niggi

English-Language Version by

Marcel Danesi, PhD

Illustrations by Giuseppe Quattrocchi,

Xavier de Sierra

BARRON'S

Graphic Design: Claudine Combalier
Cover Design: Zaü & Gaël
Picture Research: Altelier D'Image

First published in 1990
by Barron's Educational Series, Inc.

The title of the original edition is
*Voie Express: Cours Individual
D'Italien.*

All inquiries should be addressed to:
Barron's Educational Series, Inc.
250 Wireless Boulevard
Hauppauge, NY 11788

International Standard Book No. 0-8120-4573-4

Library of Congress Catalog Card No. 90-39248

Library of Congress Cataloging-in-Publication
Data

Ferdeghini, Marina.
 [Voie express, cours individuel d'italien. En-
glish]
 Express track to Italian : a teach yourself
program / Marina Ferdeghini, Paola Niggi : English language version by Marcel Danesi;
illustrations by Giuseppe Quattrocchi.
 p. cm.
 ISBN 0-8120-4573-4
 1. Italian language—Self-instruction.
2. Italian language—Textbooks for foreign
speakers—English. I. Niggi, Paola. II. Title.
PC1112.5.F3713 1990 90-39248
458.2'421—dc20 CIP

Printed in Hong Kong
3 4900 9876

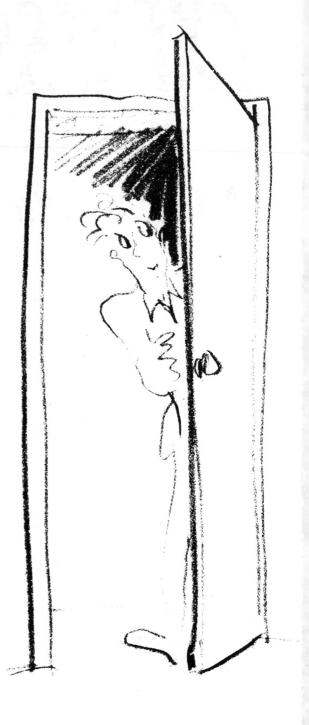

WELCOME TO EXPRESS TRACK TO ITALIAN

Maybe you have never learned Italian and feel that now is the time to start. Maybe you learned Italian years ago, and want to brush up. Maybe you're also interested in finding out about Italy and the Italians and, if you're going to the country, you'll also want to find your way around its customs and culture. Maybe you're going to work with Italians and need the basis of a business vocabulary. Maybe you're just a traveler who likes to talk. . . . Whoever you are, the authors of EXPRESS TRACK TO ITALIAN wish you a warm welcome: in Italian—Benvenuti! They have carefully thought out a complete, step-by-step guide to the Italian language.

What you will find in EXPRESS TRACK TO ITALIAN
- *THE BOOK contains dialogues, vocabulary lists, exercises, games, and commentaries on Italy.*
- *FOUR CASSETTES with dialogues, exercises, and games.*
- *A BOOKLET with a complete transcript of what's on the cassettes and translations of the dialogues.*

Now you know the basic structure; it's up to you to use EXPRESS TRACK TO ITALIAN as you wish. Depending on your time, and your preferences, you can tailor it to fit your own specific needs.

. . . For the serious student

Follow the EXPRESS TRACK TO ITALIAN method step-by-step. Each lesson begins with a dialogue. Listen to simple, practical Italian in everyday situations, practice your comprehension, and acquire vocabulary.

All the dialogues are on tape, with a selection of important phrases highlighted at the end of each dialogue. Listen for the sound signal, stop the tape, repeat, and practice your pronunciation and intonation.

Important words and expressions used in the dialogues, as well as other related vocabulary items, can be found under the headings VOCABULARY and HOW TO SAY IT. Learn them all, and you'll go a long way!

REMARKS gives you a guide to some grammatical points, and some pitfalls not to fall into! And . . .

. . . For those who want to speak fluently

ORAL PRACTICE gives you a chance to concentrate on the spoken language, with a series of structured exercises on tape (again with sound signals for you to stop the tape and speak). Grammar buffs will find explanations of all the structures in the grammar section at the back of the book.

. . . For those who like things in writing

At the end of every five units you will find a WRITTEN PRACTICE—a series of exercises on all the Italian you have acquired in the preceding five units. Extra vocabulary follows in the MORE VOCABULARY section.

. . . For the more frivolous

You will find, in each unit: short humorous accounts of all that's good and bad in Italy and what awaits the unsuspecting traveler; a selection of famous Italian songs, with their translations; listening games, as well as word puzzles, quizzes, and crosswords to fill in on the page; and a brief guide to Italian slang, so you can communicate at street level, even if you haven't grasped how to say it more formally.

Now, let's get on the EXPRESS TRACK TO ITALIAN.
Buona fortuna!

TABLE OF CONTENTS

UNIT 1

DIALOGUE

AT THE MILAN AIRPORT

The director of a business school welcomes the new students at the Milan airport.

Il responsabile : *Mi presento : sono Mario Rossi, il responsabile del Centro di formazione.*

Un corsista : *Buongiorno, mi chiamo John Miller. Sono il capo del personale della Austin Rover.*

Il responsabile : *Lei è inglese, vero?*

J. Miller : *No, non sono inglese, sono americano, ma lavoro a Londra.*

Un corsista : *E io sono Dàmaso Carrasco. Sono il direttore amministrativo della casa editrice Anagrama di Barcellona.*

Il responsabile : *Spagnolo?*

D. Carrasco : *Catalano, per la precisione!*

Una corsista : *Piacere. Il mio nome è Chantal Dulac. Sono il direttore delle vendite alla Danone.*

Il responsabile : *Molto lieto. Lei...?*

C. Dulac : *Sì, sì, sono francese!*

Un corsista : *E io sono Hans Bauer. Sono tedesco.*

Il responsabile : *Lei è della ditta...?*

H. Bauer : *Siemens. Sono il responsabile della divisione sviluppo.*

Il responsabile : *Benissimo. Ci siamo tutti? Ah, no! Manca ancora una persona. Mentre aspettiamo, andiamo a prendere un caffè.*

🔘 LISTEN AND REPEAT

You will find the translation of this dialogue on page 1 of the accompanying booklet.

The "Duomo" of Milan

NOUNS

l'aeroporto — airport
il/la corsista — enrolled student
il/la responsabile — course director
il centro — center
la formazione — training/schooling
il capo del personale — director of personnel
il direttore amministrativo — administrative/executive director
la casa editrice — publishing house
il nome — name
il direttore delle vendite — sales manager
la ditta — company
il/la responsabile della divisione sviluppo — director of development
la persona — person

---

lo stage — training period
la gestione — management
l'azienda — business/company
l'informatica — computer science
la professione — profession
il/la segretario/a — secretary
l'assistente (m/f) — assistant
l'impiegato/a — employee
l'ingegnere (m/f) — engineer

---

il paese — country
l'Italia — Italy
la Spagna — Spain
la Francia — France
la Germania — Germany
l'Inghilterra — England
il Portogallo — Portugal

la Svizzera — Switzerland
gli Stati Uniti — the United States
la nazionalità — nationality

ADJECTIVES

inglese — English
americano — American
spagnolo — Spanish
francese — French
tedesco — German

---

italiano — Italian
portoghese — Portuguese
svizzero — Swiss

VERBS

presentarsi — to introduce oneself
essere — to be
chiamarsi — to be called
lavorare — to work
mancare — to lack/be missing
aspettare — to wait for
andare — to go
prendere — to take/have something (to eat/drink)

MISCELLANEOUS

Lei — you (*pol.*) *(1)*
vero? — right?
ma — but
benissimo — very well
ancora — again/yet
mentre — while

1. INTRODUCING ONESELF

Mi presento, sono Mario Rossi — Let me introduce myself. I'm Mario Rossi.
Mi chiamo Mario Rossi — My name is Mario Rossi.
Il mio nome è Mario Rossi — My name is Mario Rossi. *(2)*

2. BEING POLITE

Piacere — A pleasure!
Molto lieto(a) — Delighted!

3. NATIONALITIES

Sono francese — I'm French. *(3)*
Non sono inglese, sono americano — I'm not English. I'm American.

4. ASKING FOR ONE'S NAME AND NATIONALITY

Come si chiama? — What's your name? *(polite) (1)*
Qual è il Suo nome? — What's your name? *(polite)*
Di che nazionalità è? — (Of) what nationality are you? *(polite)*
Qual è la Sua nazionalità? — What's your nationality? *(polite)*

5. REVEALING ONE'S PROFESSION

Sono il direttore delle vendite — I'm the sales manager. *(4)*
Sono il responsabile della divisione sviluppo — I'm the director (in charge of) the development department.

REMARKS...   REMARKS...   REMARKS...   REMARKS...

(1) Polite forms take the third-person singular of verbs. The polite subject pronoun is "Lei" (see Grammar, L. 5.) — (2) The word "nome" means both "name" in general and "first name." The word for "family name" or "surname" is "cognome." — (3) Note that the subject pronoun is missing. The information required for identifying the subject is normally found in the verb ending (see Grammar, L.) — (4) Note the use of the definite article with professions: "Sono il direttore delle vendite." = I'm (the) sales manager.

1. ANSWERING AFFIRMATIVELY

(••) LISTEN

Lei è italiano?
- *Sì, sono italiano*
Lei è tedesco?
- *Sì, sono tedesco*

Answer affirmatively, as in the model.
Lei è italiano? — Lei è tedesco? — Lei è spagnolo? — Lei è francese? — Lei è inglese? — Lei è americano? — Lei è portoghese? — Lei è svizzero?

(See Grammar, L. 4.)

2. GIVING ONE'S NATIONALITY

(••) LISTEN

Mario è italiano/Maria
- *Maria è italiana*
Jean è francese/Chantal
- *Chantal è francese*

Give the nationality of each person as in the model.
Mario è italiano/Maria — Jean è francese/Chantal — John è inglese/Mary — Carlos è spagnolo/Carmen — Hans è tedesco/Karin — Robert è americano/Jenny.

(See Grammar, C. 1.)

3. NATIONALITIES

(••) LISTEN

Di che nazionalità è Carlos?
- *Carlos è spagnolo*
Di che nazionalità è Jenny?
- *Jenny è americana*

Give the nationalities of the previous people.
Di che nazionalità è Carlos? — Di che nazionalità è Jenny? — Di che nazionalità è Chantal? — Di che nazionalità è Mario? — Di che nazionalità è Karin? — Di che nazionalità è Jean? — Di che nazionalità è Mary? — Di che nazionalità è Carmen?

(See Grammar, C. 1.)

4. GIVING ONE'S NAME

(••) LISTEN

Come si chiama?/Mario Rossi
- *Mi chiamo Mario Rossi*

Answer as if you were the following persons.
Mario Rossi — Chantal Dulac — John Miller — Carlo Bianchi — Hans Bauer — Maria Verdi — Gianni Belli.

Now give your own name.

(See Grammar, L. 3.)

5. THE VERB "TO BE"

sono, sei, è, siamo, siete, sono,

(••) LISTEN

io
- *Sono impiegato*
lui
- *È impiegato*

Give the appropriate form of the verb "to be," as in the model.
io — lui — noi — Roberto — Beatrice e Anna — lei — tu — voi — Mario e Gianni.

(See Grammar, L. 1.)

6. INTRODUCING ONESELF

(••) LISTEN

Mi presento : sono Mario Rossi/John Miller
- *Piacere. Il mio nome è John Miller.*

Imagine you are the following persons. Introduce yourself to Mario Rossi.
John Miller — Chantal Dulac — Hans Bauer — Gianni Belli — Maria Verdi — Carlo Bianchi — Jean Rollin.

Now introduce yourself.

7. PRONUNCIATION

(••) LISTEN AND REPEAT

Centro - direttore - casa editrice - responsabile - caffè - tutti - ditta - per la precisione.

IS MILAN THE CENTER OF THE WORLD?

Choosing Milan as your first stop in Italy is like hitting the bull's-eye, for it is considered the economic and cultural capital of all Italy. Bustling with life and teeming with activity, Milan often rivals Rome as a center for economic and financial decision making, as a vital communications link for northern Europe, and as a leader in fashion, design, and contemporary art. Milan is truly on top of the world.

Milan is also famous as a center for literary study. It was the favorite city of Stendhal, who found it to possess the most beautiful theater in the world, La Scala, as well as the friendliest people and the most charming women. (Would he not be equally impressed today!)

Milan and the World of Business

Milan's humid and foggy climate resembles that of Munich, rather than that of Rome or Naples. In fact, you will find a raincoat or an umbrella an absolute necessity in Milan more than anywhere else in Italy. Perhaps it is because of this climate that the Milanese—in order to stay warm—are forever keeping busy and as a result have always been consummate business people.

Milan's contribution to Italy's overall wealth is considerable: with only three percent of Italy's population, the Milanese provide over 25 percent of the Gross National Product—a sure sign of economic strength. This enormous success might also explain why misunderstandings occasionally emerge between the Milanese and other

Italians. The Milanese are often viewed as being overindustrious and unable to take it easy—veritable workaholics. And some consider the Milanese to be arrogant snobs. But then, all such things are in the mind of the perceiver.

The Beauty and Charm of Milan

The industrial aspect of Milan does not minimize its charm. First of all, there's the Duomo—one of the most Gothic cathedrals in Italy—decorated with sculptures that inspired not only Stendhal, but Napoleon as well. The Piazza del Duomo is the heart of Milan and is constantly buzzing with energy. And the famous Galleria Vittoria Emanuele, located in the Piazza, is always full of life.

Other sites to see in Milan are the Castello Sforzesco (castle of the Sforza's), the Sant'Ambrogio Basilica (Saint Ambrose is an important local saint), La Scala, the art gallery in the Brera Palace, the exclusive shops along Monte Napoleone Street, and its Navagli, which remind us that Milan was once grooved by canals.

You can even find Roman columns in Milan, in front of San Lorenzo. And of course, there is Leonardo da Vinci's "Last Supper," painted as a fresco on a wall of the church of Santa Maria delle Grazie. You will also come across a mysterious fountain attributed to Giorgio de Chirico.

But without a doubt, people are fascinated more by Milan's intellectual activity than by its monuments. The city abounds in avant-garde art galleries. This tendency toward the new and the unorthodox can also be found in its theater, il Piccolo Teatro.

Milan is also home to Italy's largest publishing houses: Mondadori, Garzanti, Rizzoli, among others. The Corriere della Sera—Italy's leading daily newspaper—is also published there.

Milan is also situated near some of Italy's most exquisite and sought-after resort centers. It is near Italy's two largest lakes—Lago di Como and Lago Maggiore—and is thus located in the heartland of Italy's "vacation land." And, of course, it is only a "stone's throw" away from the mountains of Switzerland and northern Italy. For this reason, the city becomes rather empty during the summer months, as the Milanese seek comfort and refuge from the often sweltering heat that plagues the city.

All in all, Milan can be thought of as the northern center of Italy. It attracts all kinds of visitors, both Italian and foreign, because of its unique integration of the old and the new. Like Paris, it is perceived as both a classical city and a bustling, ultramodern urban center that is leading the way into the twenty-first century. To visit Milan is a definite must the first time one goes to Italy.

N° 1 ●● LISTEN

After you have heard the following persons introduce themselves, write the number corresponding to their name in the appropriate slots.
1. *Claudio Valli* **2.** *Peter Weber* **3.** *Christiane Duval* **4.** *Carmen Vasco*

IMPIEGATA		SEGRETARIA		FRANCESE	
INGEGNERE		SPAGNOLA		ITALIANO	
DIRETTORE		TEDESCO			

Can you find these cities on the map of Europe?

Lisbona · Parigi · Londra · Roma · Bruxelles · Madrid · Atene · Bonn · Berna · Amsterdam.

PROVERBIO ●● LISTEN

Il buon giorno si vede dal mattino (lit., A good day can be seen by its morning.)

Things will go well if they start off well.

(See solutions on page 2 of the booklet.)

🔈 LISTEN

A SET-BACK

Mr. Marchi arrives at the airport, but he cannot find his suitcase.

Alla consegna dei bagagli

Sig. Marchi : *Signorina, per cortesia... Manca la mia valigia.*

L'impiegata : *Lei da dove viene?*

Sig. Marchi : *Vengo da Genova.*

L'impiegata : *Ah. Ha lo scontrino?*

Sig. Marchi : *Sì, un attimo. Ce l'ho sul biglietto. Eccolo!*

L'impiegata : *Un momento. Ora controllo. È strano! Tutti gli altri bagagli sono arrivati...*

Sig. Marchi : *Eh sì, ma la mia valigia non c'è!*

L'impiegata : *Ha fretta?*

Sig. Marchi : *Abbastanza : sono già molto in ritardo.*

L'impiegata : *Aspetti! Per caso è una valigia blu molto grande?*

Sig. Marchi : *Sì.*

L'impiegata : *Allora è in dogana. L'hanno appena trovata.*

Sig. Marchi : *Ah, per fortuna! Grazie mille.*

L'impiegata : *Di niente.*

All'appuntamento con i corsisti

Sig. Marchi : *Eccomi, scusate! Sono in ritardo! Mi chiamo Giulio Marchi. Sono il responsabile della formazione dell'Elsag di Genova.*

Il responsabile : *Noi ci conosciamo già, Dottor Marchi!*

Sig. Marchi : *Certo! Buongiorno Ingegner Rossi! Ho avuto dei problemi con i bagagli.*

Il responsabile : *Tutto a posto, adesso?*

Sig. Marchi : *Sì, sì, grazie.*

🔈 LISTEN AND REPEAT
You will find the translation on page 2 of the booklet.

*1. Piazza del Duomo
2. and 4. Galleria Vittorio Emanuele
3. The old district of Naviglio grande
5. A publishing house 6. A Milanese streetcar*

NOUNS

il contrattempo — hitch/setback
la consegna dei bagagli — baggage counter
la signorina — young lady/Miss
l'impiegato/a — clerk/employee
la valigia — suitcase
lo scontrino — stub
l'attimo — moment/minute
il biglietto — ticket
il momento — moment
il ritardo — lateness
la dogana — customs
l'appuntamento — appointment
il problema — problem *(1)*

---

la signora — madam/lady/Mrs.
il signore — gentleman/sir/Mr. *(2)*
i bagagli — baggage

ADJECTIVES

strano — strange
altro — other
blu — (dark) blue
grande — big/large
piccolo — small/little

VERBS

venire — to come
avere — to have
controllare — to check
arrivare — to arrive
avere fretta — to be in a hurry
trovare — to find
scusare/scusarsi — to excuse/excuse oneself
conoscere/conoscersi — to know (someone)/to know each other

MISCELLANEOUS

per cortesia — please
da dove — from where
eccolo — here it is
ora — now
adesso — now
c'è (non ćè) — it's there (it's not there)
abbastanza — quite/enough
già — already
molto — very/much/a lot
per caso — by chance
allora — then
per fortuna — fortunately (Thank goodness!)
certo — certainly (indeed)
tutto a posto — everything is fine

HOW TO SAY IT

1. GREETING SOMEONE

Buongiorno, Signor Verdi! — Hello/Good day/Good morning, Mr. Verdi! *(2)*
Buongiorno, Signora Verdi! — Hello/Good day/Good morning, Mrs. Verdi!
Buongiorno, Signorina Verdi! — Hello/etc., Miss/Ms. Verdi!
Buonasera, Dottor Marchi! — Hello/Good afternoon/Good evening, Dr. Marchi!
Buonasera, Ingegner Rossi! — Hello/etc., Engineer Rossi!

2. THANKING SOMEONE

Grazie! — Thank you!
Grazie mille! — Thanks a million! (*lit.*, thanks a thousand)
La ringrazio — I thank you. (polite) *(3)*

3. RESPONDING TO THANKS

Prego! — You're welcome! *(4)*
Di niente! — Don't mention it!/Think nothing of it!
Non c'è di che! — Don't mention it!

4. SAYING WHERE ONE IS COMING FROM

Vengo da Genova — I'm from Genoa./I'm coming from Genoa.
Vengo dalla Francia — I'm from France./I'm coming from France.

5. TELLING SOMEONE TO WAIT

Un momento! — One moment (please)!
Un attimo! — One minute/second (please)!
Aspetti! — Wait (please)!

6. "HERE . ."

Eccolo! — Here it is!
Eccomi! — Here I am!

REMARKS...   REMARKS...   REMARKS...   REMARKS...

(1) This is an irregular masculine noun ending in -a. Its plural is formed regularly with -i. — (2) In front of a name, masculine titles ending in -e drop this vowel — "Signor Marchi." (3) Polite form. — (4) It is always advisable to respond to thanks.

1. THE VERB "TO HAVE"

ho, hai, ha, abbiamo, avete, hanno

(• •) LISTEN

Il signor Marchi — lo scontrino
* *Il signor Marchi ha lo scontrino*
lo
* *Ho lo scontrino*

Give the correct form of the verb.
Il signor Marchi — io — noi — tu — voi — lei — loro — Marco — Francesca e Roberto — io — tu.

(See Grammar, L. 1.)

2. POSSESSIVE ADJECTIVES

(• •) LISTEN

Io ho la valigia
* *Ecco la mia valigia!*
Giulio ha il biglietto
* *Ecco il suo biglietto!*

Change the sentences as in the model.
Io ho la valigia — Marco ha il biglietto — Lei ha lo scontrino — Noi abbiamo il biglietto — Voi avete la valigia — Tu hai lo scontrino — Loro hanno il biglietto — Maria ha la valigia — Loro hanno la valigia.

(See Grammar, D. 1.)

3. PLURALS

(• •) LISTEN

Jean e Luc (francese)
* *Jean e Luc sono francesi*
Marta e Laura (italiano)
* *Marta e Laura sono italiane*

Give the nationalities of the following people.
Jean e Luc (francese) — Marta e Laura (italiano) — John e Mary (inglese) — Peter e Hans (tedesco) — Pablo e José (spagnolo) — Burt e Ron (americano) — Amelia e Carmen (portoghese) — Franka e Karin (tedesco).

(See Grammar, C. 1.)

4. THE NEGATIVE

(• •) LISTEN

John Miller è inglese? (americano)
* *No, non è inglese, è americano*
Il signor Verdi è avvocato? (ingegnere)
* *No, non è avvocato, è ingegnere*

Answer the questions as in the model.
John Miller è inglese? (americano) — Il signor Verdi è avvocato? (ingegnere) — Chantal Dulac è spagnola? (francese) — Hans Bauer è svizzero? (tedesco) — La signora Belli è segretaria? (ingegnere) — Il signor Marchi è il capo del personale? (il responsabile della formazione)

(See Grammar, L. 4.)

5. ASKING QUESTIONS

(• •) LISTEN

Il signor Marchi ha lo scontrino
* *Il signor Marchi ha lo scontrino?*
È una valigia blu
* *È una valigia blu?*

Transform the statements into questions by changing the intonation.
Il signor Marchi ha lo scontrino — É una valigia blu — Giulio è italiano — I bagagli sono arrivati — È il responsabile — Ha fretta — Marco è in ritardo — Hai il biglietto. (See Grammar, L. 4.)

6. SAYING WHERE ONE COMES FROM

(• •) LISTEN

Genova
* *Vengo da Genova*
La Francia
* *Vengo dalla Francia*

Continue, following the model.
Genova — La Francia — Parigi — Londra — Il Portogallo — La Svizzera — Madrid — L'Italia — Nantes — L'Inghilterra — Roma — Gli Stati Uniti. (See Grammar, F.)

7. PRONUNCIATION

(• •) LISTEN AND REPEAT

Il biglietto - i bagagli - la valigia - gli altri biglietti - un attimo - aspetti! - la consegna.

DO YOU HAVE YOUR RECEIPT?

Often foreigners think of Italy as a bureaucratic and an organizational mess. But this is not so. Italian bureaucracy, for such a relatively new nation (Italy became a single nation only in 1860), is imposing, highly structured, but often incredibly inflexible.

In the Realm of the Stamped Card

The longer you stay in Italy, the more you will come to understand the importance of one of the fundamental features of Italian life: the "carta bollata" (stamped card). Without this bureaucratic mark of approval, you can do virtually nothing: you cannot conduct most legal transactions, get a diploma, get a job, or apply for a visa, to name just a few.

Typical examples of how this bureaucratic mindset works can be seen in the monopolies that are controlled by the State. Italy's most popular cigarette brand, for instance, is marked M.S., which means simply "Monopolio dello Stato" (state monopoly). And, until just a few years ago salt (another state monopoly) could be bought only in tobacco stores—which to this day are called "Sali e Tabacchi."

Forms and Receipts Without End

Recent governmental measures have also made filing for income tax

incredibly difficult and may even encourage tax fraud. If one receives a salary, taxes are automatically drawn from one's salary. This stands in sharp contrast to the bureaucratic nightmare the self-employed experience. Even struggling artists and writers must fill out tax returns so complicated that they are forced to seek the help of an accountant!

Another measure that has been taken by the government to combat tax evasion requires customers of stores, restaurants, hair salons, etc., to keep their bills upon leaving. If stopped by a policeman during a routine inspection and found to be without a bill or receipt, one could easily face a fraud charge. (Fortunately, these police inspections are rare.)

Receipts ("scontrini") are also required to buy food and beverages at various eateries. At most bars, "tavole calde," "latterie," and snack bars, customers must first

pay for their order at the cashier's and then present the famous "scontrini" at the bar before being served. This is one of the first things one notices when entering the country. Faced with such practices and the ensuing chaotic line-ups at the post office, bank, bakery, etc., it is no wonder that Italians are so good at ignoring lines!

Yet, somehow, there is a kind of "hidden efficiency" in the way daily business is conducted in Italy. Visitors must simply be patient and "learn the system." (When in Rome, as the saying goes, do as the Romans do!) Although there is a tangled, bureaucratic side to the Italy of today, there is also a more personal component to the way people interact. There is a willingness in stores, offices, and service agencies to help out those who do not know the system. And with a little practice, visitors quickly learn to become efficient in the Italian way.

This hidden efficiency is one of the reasons why Italy is one of the world's leading economic powers today. In the realm of "carte bollate" and "scontrini," there is affluence and well-being. Indeed, visitors to Italy will be impressed by the fact that they will be able to purchase virtually any consumer item they desire.

●● LISTEN

Mark down the destination or point of origin of each flight, and whether it has been cancelled (annullato), is late (in ritardo), or is about to depart (in partenza).

ALITALIA	*DESTINAZIONE :*	. . . .
BRITISH AIRWAYS	*DESTINAZIONE :*	. . . .
LUFTHANSA	*PROVENIENZA :*	. . . .
AIR FRANCE	*PROVENIENZA :*	. . . .

Put each of the following groups of sentences into logical order.

1. *Allora, l'hanno appena trovata.*
2. *Manca la mia valigia...*
3. *Signorina, per cortesia!*
4. *È per caso una valigia blu?*
5. *Sì.*
6. *È in dogana.*

. . . .
. . . .

1. *Sono in ritardo.*
2. *Scusate.*
3. *Mi chiamo Giulio Marchi.*
4. *Eccomi.*

. . . .
. . . .

Rebus.

PROVERBIO 🔊 LISTEN

Chi cerca trova (lit., He who searches, will find). He who works hard will be rewarded.

(See solutions on page 3 of the booklet.)

DIALOGUE

AT THE AIRPORT ESPRESSO BAR

The students have a drink at an espresso bar.

Il responsabile : *Caffè per tutti?*

J. Miller : *Per me va bene. Io però lo vorrei lungo.*

C. Dulac : *Anch'io. Il caffè italiano è buono ma è troppo forte per me!*

G. Marchi : *Per me invece un caffè ristretto, per cortesia.*

H. Bauer : *Ah, se bevo un caffè adesso, poi questa notte non dormo. Per me è meglio una birra.*

D. Carrasco : *E io vorrei un cappuccino!*

Il responsabile : *Allora una birra, un cappuccino e quattro caffè : uno normale, due lunghi e uno ristretto.*

Il cameriere : *Ha lo scontrino?*

Il responsabile : *Ah sì! è vero : devo pagare prima?*

Il cameriere : *Sì, signore : deve pagare alla cassa.*

Il responsabile : *Va bene.*

Alla cassa

Il responsabile : *Una birra, un cappucino e quattro caffè.*

La cassiera : *Ecco lo scontrino.*

. . . .

Il cameriere : *Per chi sono i caffè?*

C. Dulac : *Per noi, grazie.*

G. Marchi : *Quanto zucchero, signora?*

C. Dulac : *Niente zucchero, grazie... Piuttosto vorrei una goccia di latte freddo.*

Il cameriere : *Eccolo.*

G. Marchi : *Lei è francese?*

C. Dulac : *Sì, sono francese.*

G. Marchi : *E di dov'è?*

C. Dulac : *Sono di Nantes, ma abito e lavoro a Parigi da anni.*

G. Marchi : *Ah, Parigi! Che bella città! La conosco bene perché vengo spesso in Francia per lavoro.*

C. Dulac : *E Lei, di dov'è?*

G. Marchi : *Io sono di Genova.*

C. Dulac : *Non conosco Genova. So solamente che è un porto importante e che si trova nel nord dell'Italia.*

G. Marchi : *È anche la città di Cristoforo Colombo!*

Il responsabile : *Bene, adesso ci siamo tutti, possiamo andare. Le macchine sono qui fuori.*

You will find the translation on page 3 of the booklet.

1. 3. 4. Espresso bars
2. An espresso bar in the bohemian Brera district

4

NOUNS

il bar — espresso bar *(1)*
il caffè — coffee *(1)*
il cameriere — waiter
la notte — night
la birra — beer
il cappuccino — cappuccino
la cassa — cashier/cashier's desk
lo zucchero — sugar
la goccia — drop
il latte — milk
l'anno — year
la città — city *(1)*
il lavoro — job/work
il porto — port
la macchina — car

ADJECTIVES

lungo/corto — long/short
lungo/ristretto — light/strong (coffee)
buono/cattivo — good/bad
forte/leggero — strong/light
freddo/caldo — cold/hot
bello/brutto — beautiful/ugly
importante — important

VERBS

volere — to want to
bere — to drink
dormire — to sleep

dovere — to have to
pagare — to pay
abitare — to live (somewhere)
sapere — to know
potere — to be able to

ADVERBS

anche — also, too
troppo — too, too much
invece — instead, rather
meglio — better
poi — then, after
prima — before, first
piuttosto — rather
bene/male — well/bad(ly)
spesso — often
solamente — only
qui/lì — here/there
fuori/dentro — inside/outside

MISCELLANEOUS

per tutti — for everyone
per me — for me
per noi — for us
però — but, however
niente (zucchero) — no (sugar)
perché — why
quanto (...)? — how much?

1. ORDERING BEVERAGES

Un caffè, per cortesia — A coffee, please!
Per me un cappucino — For me, a cappuccino!
Vorrei una birra — I would like a beer!

2. BEING FROM . . .

Di dov'è Lei? — Where are you from? *(2)*
Sono di Nantes — I'm from Nantes.

3. SAYING WHERE ONE LIVES

Dove abita? — Where do you live?
Abito a Parigi — I live in Paris.

4. FOR HOW MANY YEARS . . .

Lavoro a Parigi da anni — I've been working in Paris for years.
Sono capo del personale da cinque anni — I've been director of personnel for five years.
Abito in Francia da venti anni — I've been living in France for twenty years.

5. INDICATING PREFERENCES

Piuttosto vorrei una birra — I would like a beer instead.
Preferirei un cappuccino — I prefer a cappuccino.
Per me invece un caffè ristretto — For me, a strong coffee instead.

6. EXCLAMATIONS

Che bella città! — What a beautiful city!
Che bella donna! — What a beautiful woman!
Bene! — OK!/Fine!

| REMARKS... | REMARKS... | REMARKS... | REMARKS... |

(1) See Grammar, C. 3. — (2) Polite pronouns can be capitalized even within a word or sentence.

1. ORDERING BEVERAGES

(• •) LISTEN

un caffè

• *Un caffè, per cortesia*

Order the following things.
un caffè — un cappuccino — un tè — una birra — un caffè ristretto — un caffè lungo — un'aranciata — un apertivo — una Coca-Cola.

2. POSSESSIVES

(• •) LISTEN

Ho i biglietti

• *Ecco i miei biglietti!*

Abbiamo i biglietti

• *Ecco i nostri biglietti!*

Change the sentences as in the model.
Ho i biglietti — Abbiamo i biglietti — Ho le valigie — Abbiamo le valigie — Avete i biglietti — Hanno le valigie — Hai i biglietti — Avete le valigie — Hanno i biglietti — Hai le valigie — Ha i biglietti — Ha le valigie.

(See Grammar, D. 1.)

3. VERBS ENDING IN -ARE

(• •) LISTEN

Lei lavora alla FIAT (io)

• *Io lavoro alla FIAT*

(il signor Bianchi)

• *Il signor Bianchi lavora alla FIAT*

Change each sentence using the correct form of the verb.
io — il signor Bianchi — noi — tu — voi — io — Gianni e Paolo — Maria — Marta e Laura — noi — tu.

(See Grammar, L. 2.)

4. HOW MUCH . . . ?

(• •) LISTEN

zucchero

• *Quanto zucchero vuole, signora?*
biglietti

• *Quanta biglietti vuole, signora?*

Ask questions according to the model.
zucchero — biglietti — birra — latte — tè — aranciata — caffè — caffè (pl.) — birre — aranciate.

(See Grammar, G. 2.)

5. I LIVE IN . . .

(• •) LISTEN

Francia, Parigi

• *Abito in Francia, a Parigi*

Italia, Milano

• *Abito in Italia, a Milano*

Say where you live (as in the model.)
Francia, Parigi — Italia, Milano — Spagna, Madrid — Inghilterra, Londra — Germania, Monaco — Portogallo, Lisbona — Svizzera, Zurigo.

(See Grammar, F.)

6. "ANCHE"

(• •) LISTEN

Per me un caffè

• *Anch'io vorrei un caffè*

Per me un caffè — Per me una birra — Per me un cappuccino — Per me un tè — Per me un caffè ristretto — Per me un caffè lungo — Per me una Coca-Cola.

(See Grammar, J. 2.)

7. PRONUNCIATION

(• •) LISTEN AND REPEAT

Birra - cappuccino - spesso - troppo - vorrei - caffè - latte - notte - adesso.

LET'S HAVE SOME COFFEE!

Once you are in Italy, one of the first things that captures your attention—besides the beauty of the Italian language—is the coffee. Coffee of incomparable flavor and aroma, so the ads say. But it's true: nowhere but in Italy can one drink such good coffee.

Of course, Neopolitans would claim that only they make the "real" thing, but actually, you can't go wrong buying coffee anywhere in Italy. The secret lies in how the coffee is prepared—from the selection and roasting of the coffee bean to the type of coffee maker used.

Coffee-making has a long tradition in Italy. It was the Venetians, through their dealings with the Turks, who introduced coffee to the peninsula. Soon after, Italy became an exporter of coffee expertise. A Sicilian from Palermo, Francesco Procopio dei Coltelli, for instance, opened up the first Parisian coffee house, the now-famous Café Procope.

Coffee in the Morning, Coffee in the Evening, Coffee Anytime.

For Italians, coffee sets their daily life into motion. Indeed, it is often the only thing Italians have for breakfast. Usually it is drunk black ("espresso") or "macchiato," that is, with a drop of milk. And because it is rather bitter, most Italians add lots of sugar to sweeten it. Just notice how much sugar Italians add to their coffee. It's quite impressive! After staying awhile in Italy, you just might find yourself doing the same thing. It is little wonder that Italian life is often referred to as "la dolce vita"!

After that first morning coffee, a day is certainly long enough to lend occasion to having a few more cups, either alone or with colleagues or friends. During the morning hours, for example, one might have some with a "brioche" (in Italy, a pastry filled with jam), especially if nothing else was eaten at breakfast. And rarely does any meal end without the ever-present "tazza di espresso."

How do You Want Your Coffee?

The many ways to have coffee constitute an art. In addition to regular espresso, you can have it "ristretto"—a bit stronger (with more coffee added to the pot) or "lungo"—a bit weaker (with more water added), to name just a few. Or you might prefer the very popular "capuccino" (with steamed milk), which gets its name from the color of the hood worn by the Capuchin monks. Coffee can also be served in a variety of combinations:
"corretto" (corrected with a drop of liquor) or poured over ice cream, which is called "affogato" (drowned).

Besides the little bars where one has coffee at the bar itself, the ritual of coffee-drinking has given birth to some very well-known coffee houses such as Florian's in Venice, Pedrocchi's in Padua, and Il Greco's in Rome. These establishments play a great role in Italian culture. And visiting at least one of them is a must when you are in Italy.

N° 1   ●● LISTEN

Write down the beverages chosen by each of the persons shown below.

☐ _____

☐ _____

☐ _____

☐ _____

☐ _____

PROVERBIO   ●● LISTEN

Chi troppo vuole nulla stringe
(lit., He who wants too much gets nothing.)

Count your blessings

Complete each of the following as you wish, choosing among the cities shown on the map.

- *Lei è di Genova?*
No, non sono di Genova, sono di . . .
- *Lei è di Milano?*
No, ...
- *Lei è di Palermo?*
No, ...

- *Lei è di Reggio Calabria?*
No, ...
- *Lei è di Firenze?*
No, ...
- *Lei è di Roma?*
No, ...

(See solutions on page 5 of the booklet.)

(• •) LISTEN

AT THE HOTEL

**The course director accompanies
the students to a hotel in Milan.**

Il responsabile : *Buongiorno, ci devono
essere sei camere singole prenotate per
oggi.*

L'impiegata : *Il suo nome, per cortesia?*

Il responsabile : *La prenotazione è a nome
del Centro di formazione Michelangelo.*

L'impiegata : *Attenda un attimo. Sì, ecco.
Sono sei camere singole con bagno?*

Il responsabile : *Sì.*

L'impiegata : *Ha i documenti di queste
persone?*

Il responsabile : *Sì, ecco i passaporti.*

L'impiegata : *Bene. Questi li restituisco
domani. Le camere sono tutte al quarto
piano. Ecco le chiavi.*

G. Marchi : *È possibile avere la sveglia domani mattina?*

L'impiegata : *Certamente. A che ora?*

G. Marchi : *Alle sette e mezzo.*

L'impiegata : *Benissimo : alle sette e
mezzo, stanza 407.*

C. Dulac : *A che ora è la prima colazione?*

L'impiegata : *La colazione è servita dalle
7.30 alle 9.30 nella sala a destra in fondo
al corridoio.*

C. Dulac : *Grazie.*

H. Bauer : *Scusi, vorrei telefonare in
Germania. È possibile avere la linea in
camera?*

L'impiegata : *Naturalmente. La linea è
diretta.*

H. Bauer : *Per cortesia, qual è il prefisso
per l'estero?*

L'impiegata : *Guardi, deve fare 00, poi
aggiungere il prefisso per la Germania e
il prefisso della città, poi il numero che
vuole chiamare.*

H. Bauer : *Benissimo. Grazie mille.*

Il responsabile : *Bene. Se volete, potete
cenare qui in albergo : c'è un tavolo
prenotato per voi.*

J. Miller : *A che ora ci vediamo domani?*

Il responsabile : *L'appuntamento per
l'inizio dello stage è per domani mattina
alle dieci al Centro di formazione.
Arrivederci, a domani.*

I corsisti : *ArrivederLa.*

(• •) LISTEN AND REPEAT
You will find the translation on page 5 of the booklet.

*Milanese design 1. Hotel facade
2. and 3. Department store windows
4. An avant-garde
furniture store
5. On the Corso Vittorio Emanuele*

HOTEL EXECUTIVE

3

arflex

4

BVLGARI

5

NOUNS

l'albergo — hotel
la camera (la stanza) — room
singola — single
doppia — double
matrimoniale — matrimonial (big bed)
la prenotazione — reservation
il bagno — bath
il documento — document
il passaporto — passport
il piano — floor
la chiave — key
la sveglia — wakeup call
la mattina — morning
l'ora — time/hour
la prima colazione — breakfast
la sala — room/hall
il corridoio — corridor
la linea — line
il prefisso — area code
l'estero — abroad
il tavolo — table
l'inizio — start/beginning

il letto — bed
la carta d'identità — identity card
la patente — driver's license
l'orologio — watch/clock
il minuto — minute

il pranzo — lunch/meal
la cena — dinner
oggi — today
domani — tomorrow
ieri — yesterday
il pomeriggio — afternoon
la sera — evening
il giorno — day

ADJECTIVES

primo — first
secondo — second
terzo — third
quarto — fourth
quinto — fifth
sesto — sixth
settimo — seventh
ottavo — eighth
nono — ninth
decimo — tenth
undicesimo — eleventh
ventesimo — twentieth

VERBS

prenotare — to reserve
attendere — to wait
restituire — to give back/return
servire — to serve
telefonare — to phone
fare — to do, make
aggiungere — to add (on)
chiamare — to call
cenare — to dine/have dinner
vedere — to see
vedersi — to see each other/meet

fare colazione — to have breakfast
pranzare — to have lunch

MISCELLANEOUS

certamente (certo) — certainly
a nome di ... — made out to/under
questo — this
a destra — to the right
a sinistra — to the left
in fondo a ... — at the end of

HOW TO SAY IT

---

1. CHECKING INTO A HOTEL

Buongiorno, ci deve essere una camera singola prenotata per oggi — Hello. There should be a single room reserved for today.
La prenotazione è a nome della ditta X — The reservation is under Company X.

---

2. ASKING SOMEONE'S NAME

Il Suo nome, per cortesia? — Your name, please?
Qual è il Suo nome? — What is your name?
Come si chiama? — What is your name?

---

3. ASKING FOR A WAKE-UP CALL

Scusi, è possibile avere la sveglia domani mattina alle 7? — Excuse me, is it possible to have a wakeup call tomorrow morning at 7:00?

---

4. TELLING TIME

A che ora? — At what time?
A mezzogiorno — At noon.
A mezzanotte — At midnight.
All'una — At 1:00. *(1)*

Alle due — At two.
Alle 2 e cinque — At 2:05.
Alle 2 e un quarto — At 2:15.
Alle 2 e mezzo — At half past two/2:30.
Alle 3 meno un quarto — At a quarter to three/2:45.

---

5. FROM 7:30 TO 9:30

La colazione è servita dalle 7.30 alle 9.30 — Breakfast is served from 7:30 to 9:30.

---

6. TAKING LEAVE

ArrivederLa! — Good-bye! *(pol.)*
Arrivederci! — Good-bye! *(fam.)* *(2)*
A domani! — See you tomorrow!

A presto! — See you soon!
A stasera! — See you this evening!

REMARKS...	*REMARKS...*	*REMARKS...*	*REMARKS...*

(1) Official time (trains, planes, etc.) works on the basis of the 24-hour-clock. But in everyday conversation the tendency is to say, for instance, 4:00 in the afternoon. — (2) This is the most general form, used in both familiar and polite address.

1. NAMES AND NATIONALITIES

⊙⊙ LISTEN

Mi chiamo Giulio Marchi
* *Qual è il Suo nome?*
Sono italiano
* *Qual è la Sua nazionalità?*

Form questions as in the example.
Mi chiamo Giulio Marchi — Sono italiano — Mi chiamo Hans Bauer — Sono tedesco — Mi chiamo John Miller — Sono inglese — Mi chiamo Chantal Dulac — Sono francese — Mi chiamo Damaso Carrasco — Sono spagnolo.

(See Grammar, G. 2.)

2. TELLING TIME

⊙⊙ LISTEN

La colazione è alle 7
* *A che ora è la colazione?*
Va all'albergo alle 3
* *A che ora va all'albergo?*

Continue asking questions in the same way.
La colazione è alle 7 — Va all'albergo alle 3 — La sveglia è alle 8 — Va all'aeroporto alle 2 — Va al bar alle 11 — Ha l'appuntamento alle 10 — Va a letto a mezzanotte — Arriva a Torino alle 6.

(See Grammar, G. 2.)

3. IS IT POSSIBLE TO . . . ?

⊙⊙ LISTEN

Una camera singola
* *È possibile avere una camera singola?*
La sveglia domani mattina
* *È possibile avere la sveglia domani mattina?*

Ask questions as in the model.
Una camera singola — La sveglia domani mattina — Una camera doppia — La chiave della camera 12 — Una camera matrimoniale — La colazione in camera — Una camera con bagno.

(See Grammar, L. 1.)

4. AT WHAT TIME?

⊙⊙ LISTEN

A che ora è la colazione? (7.30/9.30)
* *La colazione è dalle 7.30 alle 9.30*

Answer the following questions.
A che ora è la colazione? (7.30/9.30) — A che ora è la cena? (19.30/21) — A che ora è il pranzo? (12.30/14) — A che ora è la colazione? (8/10) — A che ora è la cena? (20/22.30) — A che ora è il pranzo? (12/13.30).

(See Grammar, F.)

5. ORDINAL NUMBERS

⊙⊙ LISTEN

A che piano è la camera 17? (1°)
* *La camera 17 è al primo piano.*

Answer the following questions in the same way.
A che piano è la camera 17? (1°) — A che piano è la camera 16? (3°) — A che piano è la camera 21? (2°) — A che piano è la camera 19? (4°) — A che piano è la camera 28? (8°) — A che piano è la camera 51? (5°) — A che piano è la camera 60? (6°) — A che piano è la camera 70? (7°).

(See Grammar, K. 2.)

6. VERBS ENDING IN *-ERE*

⊙⊙ LISTEN

Mario prende un caffè (io)
* *Anch'io prendo un caffè*
(noi)
* *Anche noi prendiamo un caffè*

Respond by following the model.
io — noi — tu — voi — loro — Chantal — Giulio e Mario — Luisa — tu — il signor Rossi — io.

(See Grammar, L. 2.)

7. PRONUNCIATION

⊙⊙ LISTEN AND REPEAT

Prenotazione - colazione - mezzanotte - mezzogiorno - inizio - stanza - mezzo - terzo.

SOCIAL AMENITIES

Italians have the reputation of being direct and responsive. The image one commonly has of Italians is that of a happy-go-lucky people who have little use for social amenities. This is somewhat of a myth. Like people in all other cultures, Italians also have their forms of respect and a whole repertory of titles to show deference.

The forms of address are an obvious case in point. Politeness is conveyed by means of the third-person pronoun "Lei" and the verb forms that it takes. There was a period before World War II when the "voi" form (second person plural) became the one used for politeness. Since the end of the war to the present time, however, it is the third person which prevails as a sign of respect. The "tu" (second person singular) forms have always designated familiarity.

To whom have I the honor . . . ?

Titles are a way of life in Italy. "Signore" (Mr.), "Signora" (Mrs.), "Signorina" (Miss/Ms.), compete with "Dottore/Dottoressa," "Professore/Professoressa," "Architetto" (architect), "Avvocato" (lawyer), "Ingegnere" (engineer), etc. for conversational air time. Most titles today have one form for both males and females— a result of basic social changes brought about by the women's movement. So, the old Avvocatessa, for a female, is giving way to Avvocato for both sexes.

In addition to forms of respect and titles, Italian letter-writing is also proof of a deeply rooted sense of social formality. Letters can start with expressions ranging all the way from a simple "Gentile Signore" (Kind Sir) to a cumbersome "Egregio Signore" (Egregious Sir). Letter closings such as "Voglia gradire i miei più distinti saluti" (Please accept my most distinct greetings) are not unusual. But there is a growing tendency today to simplify social formulas. Italians, like others, have both a sense of formality and one of practicality in communication.

The Impact of the Media

Leading the way in the process of simplifying the ways in which Italians interact are the media. Like never before in Italy's history, the media, especially TV, have become shapers of the ways in which Italians speak to each other. The fact that newscasters use the "voi" form in addressing their audiences cannot help but have entrenched this form of address in the minds of all Italians. The fact that more and more television shows are aimed at a "general" audience with eclectic tastes, also makes the option for a more "generalized" form of address a fact of life.

The change in formality can also be seen in the print medium, which has always had a long and illustrious history in Italy. It is interesting to note that school grammars of the language are now beginning to reflect the impact of the media. In many ways, these changes in communicative style are proof that Italy is becoming more and more democratic and informal.

| N° 1 | 🔘🔘 LISTEN |

Fill out the hotel register on the basis of the information you hear.

PRENOTAZIONE	TIPO CAMERA	N° CAMERA	PIANO	CON BAGNO	SENZA BAGNO
Sarti	....	....	....	....	....
Verdi					....
Chiari					
Bianchi					....

| N° 2 | 🔘🔘 LISTEN |

Put in the missing times (writing out the hours and minutes in letters) on the basis of what you hear. Don't forget to use "alle" (alle due e mezzo = at 2:30).

Il dottor Marchi domanda la sveglia .... Poi, ...
fa colazione al bar dell'albergo e, ..., va all'appuntamento con
l'ingegner Rossi. La signora Dulac domanda la sveglia .... Fa
colazione .... e, ..., è nella hall dell'abergo.

Complete each sentence with «dalle . . . alle . . .» to specify the time periods in which the various meals are being served.

La colazione è servita . . . .

Il pranzo è servito . . . .

La cena è servita . . . .

Prima colazione
7.30 -8.00
Pranzo
12.00 -14.30
Cena
19.30 -21.30

STAGE DI GESTIONE

1° giorno
orario dei corsi mattina : 10.00/12.30
pomeriggio : 13.30/17.00
2° giorno
mattina : 9.30/12.00
pomeriggio : 15.30/19.00

1° giorno :

il corso della mattina è . . . .

il corso del pomeriggio è . . . .

2° giorno :

il corso della mattina è . . . .

il corso del pomeriggio è . . . .

PROVERBIO   ●● LISTEN

Chi tardi arriva male alloggia
(lit., He who arrives late, gets bad lodgings).   The early bird gets the worm.

(See solutions on page 6 of the booklet.)

DIALOGUE

🔊 LISTEN

A CONVERSATION AFTER DINNER

Mr. Marchi and Ms. Dulac strike up a conversation in the hotel lobby.

Sig. Marchi : *Permette? Non la disturbo?*

Sig.ra Dulac : *Prego! Si figuri!*

Sig. Marchi : *Gradisce una sigaretta?*

Sig.ra Dulac : *No, grazie. Non fumo.*

Sig. Marchi : *Anche Lei resta in albergo questa sera, eh?*

Sig.ra Dulac : *Sì, è già molto tardi e domani dobbiamo essere all'appuntamento alle 10.*

Sig. Marchi : *Conosce già Milano?*

Sig.ra Dulac : *Veramente, no.*

Sig. Marchi : *Ma, è la prima volta che viene in Italia?*

Sig.ra Dulac : *No, ci vengo spesso per ragioni di lavoro, ma vado soprattutto a Roma.*

Sig. Marchi : *Lei parla molto bene l'italiano.*

Sig.ra Dulac : *Grazie del complimento. In effetti è la lingua che preferisco.*

Sig. Marchi : *Parla anche altre lingue?*

Sig.ra Dulac : *Sì, parlo anche il tedesco e un po' di russo.*

Sig. Marchi : *Perbacco! Lei mi stupisce!*

Sig.ra Dulac : *Perché?*

Sig. Marchi : *Beh! A vederLa sembra una ragazzina! E invece...*

Sig.ra Dulac : *Eh! Mai fidarsi delle apparenze!*

Sig. Marchi : *Senta, perché invece di dire sempre Lei, Lei... non ci diamo del tu?*

Sig.ra Dulac : *Perché no? È vero che è più simpatico...*

Sig. Marchi : *Perfetto! Io mi chiamo Giulio.*

Sig.ra Dulac : *E io mi chiamo Chantal. Tu, Giulio, parli francese?*

Sig. Marchi : *Oh! Lo parlo abbastanza bene, anche perché mia moglie è francese. Tu sei sposata?*

Sig.ra Dulac : *Sì, sono sposata, e ho anche un bambino.*

Sig. Marchi : *Davvero? E quanti anni ha?*

Sig.ra Dulac : *Oh! È ancora piccolo, ha due anni e mezzo.*

Sig. Marchi : *Incredibile! Ma dove trovi il tempo di fare tutte queste cose?*

Sig.ra Dulac : *Oh, in fondo è solo una questione di organizzazione...*

🔊 LISTEN AND REPEAT
You will find the translation on page 7 of the booklet.

1. Lobby of La Scala
2. Inside La Scala
3. Michelangelo's "Pietà"
4. Brera art gallery
5. Castello art gallery

3

III

4

BELLINI

5

NOUNS

la conversazione — conversation
la prima volta — the first time
la ragione — reason
il complimento — compliment
la lingua — language
la ragazzina — little girl *(1)*
l'apparenza — appearance
la moglie — wife
il/la bambino/a (m/f) — child
il tempo — time
la cosa — thing
la questione — matter
l'organizzazione (f) — organization

la ragazza — girl
il ragazzo — boy
il ragazzino — little boy
il marito — husband

i giorni della settimana — days of the week
lunedì (m) — Monday
martedì (m) — Tuesday
mercoledì (m) — Wednesday
giovedì (m) — Thursday
venerdì (m) — Friday
sabato — Saturday
domenica — Sunday
i mesi dell anno — months of the year
gennaio — January   luglio — July
febbraio — February   agosto — August
marzo — March   settembre — September
aprile — April   ottobre — October
maggio — May   novembre — November
giugno — June   dicembre — December

ADJECTIVES

vero — true
simpatico — nice

piccolo — little, small
falso — false
antipatico — not nice
grande — big/large

VERBS

disturbare — to disturb
fumare — to smoke
restare — to remain
parlare — to talk/speak
preferire — to prefer
stupire — to surprise (stupirsi—to be surprised)
sembrare — to seem
fidarsi (di) — to trust
sentire — to hear *(2)*
dire — to say/tell
dare (darsi) del tu — to be on familiar terms
dare (darsi) del Lei — to be on polite terms
sposarsi — to get married
fare — to do/make

MISCELLANEOUS

permette? — May I?
prego — please, sure
si figuri! — not at all!
già — already
domani — tomorrow
in effetti — actually, in effect
un po' (un poco) — a bit, a little
perbacco! — Wow!
sempre — always
mai — ever (never)
perfetto! — perfect!
davvero? — really?
incredibile! — incredible!
solo — only

HOW TO SAY IT

1. PERSONAL INFORMATION (Polite form)

È la prima volta che viene in Italia? — Is this the first time that you [have] come to Italy?
È sposato/a? — Are you married?
Ha bambini? — Do you have children?
Quanti anni ha? — How old are you/is he/is she?

2. EXPRESSING ASTONISHMENT

Perbacco! — Wow!
Davvero? — Really?

Incredibile! — Incredible!
Lei mi stupisce! — You surprise/astonish me!

3. BREAKING THE ICE

Senta, perché non ci diamo del tu? — Listen, why don't we use the familiar form. *(3)*
Gradisce una sigaretta? — Would you like a cigarette?
Diamoci del tu! — Let's use the familiar form. *(3)*

4. AGREEING

Perché no? — Why not?   *Perfetto!* — Perfect!   *D'accordo!* — OK/Fine/Agreed!

5. BASIC SOCIAL CONVENTIONS

Ciao! Come stai? — Hi! How are you?
Buongiorno, Signor Rossi! Come sta? — Hello, Mr. Rossi, how are you?
Come va? — How's it going?
Bene, grazie, e tu? — Well, thanks, and you?
Non c'è male, grazie, e Lei? — Not bad, thank you, and you?
Abbastanza bene — Quite/Rather well.

6. GIVING THE DATE

Oggi è martedì — Today is Tuesday.
Oggi è il 12 settembre — Today is September 12.
Siamo nel 1989 — This is 1989. (*lit.*, We are in 1989.)

| REMARKS... | REMARKS... | REMARKS... | REMARKS... |

(1) -ino is a diminutive suffix. — *(2) The most common usage of this verb is in the expression "Senta!"* =
"Listen!" — *(3) Literally, to use the "tu" form.*

1. POLITE QUESTIONS

(••) LISTEN

Mi chiamo Giulio Marchi
- *Come si chiama?*

Ho 32 anni
- *Quanti anni ha?*

Can you form the appropriate questions? Don't forget to use "Come?" "Quanto?" "Dove?" "Perché?" and "A che ora?" when needed.
Mi chiamo Giulio Marchi — Ho 32 anni — Sono a Torino per lavoro — Abito a Parigi — Ho due bambini — Ho l'appuntamento all'aeroporto — Arrivo alle 4 — Mi chiamo Chantal Dulac — Lavoro alla FIAT — Ho 35 anni.

(See Grammar, L. 5.)

2. GIVING THE DATE

(••) LISTEN

giovedì
- *Oggi è giovedì*

12 settembre
- *Oggi è il 12 settembre*

Give the date as in the example.
giovedì — 12 settembre — sabato — 20 luglio — domenica — 1° maggio — martedì — 7 marzo — mercoledì — 28 agosto — venerdì — 15 febbraio — lunedì — 15 giugno — 7 gennaio.

3. HOW'S IT GOING?

(••) LISTEN

Mario
- *Ciao, Mario! Come stai?*

Il signor Rossi
- *Buongiorno, signor Rossi! Come sta?*

Ask the following people how they are.
Mario — Il signor Rossi — Marta — Luigi — L'ingegner Bianchi — La signora Verdi — Il professore — Il dottor Marchi — Paola.

4. "ALWAYS" AND "NEVER"

(••) LISTEN

Lavoro sempre il venerdì
- *Io invece non lavoro mai il venerdì*

Change each sentence as in the model.
Lavoro sempre il venerdì — Ceno sempre alle 8 — Prendo sempre l'aereo — Parlo sempre inglese — Parto sempre in agosto — Prendo sempre il caffè ristretto — Vado sempre in Francia per lavoro.

(See Grammar, J. 3.)

5. VERBS ENDING IN *-IRE*

(••) LISTEN

Mario dorme in albergo (io)
- *Dormo in albergo*

(lui)
- *Dorme in albergo*

Change each sentence, making sure that subject and verb agree!
Mario dorme in albergo — io — lui — il signor Rossi — voi — noi — tu — Mario e Franco — la signora Verdi — tu — noi — io.

(See Grammar, L. 2.)

6. VERBS ENDING IN *-IRE (-ISC)*

(••) LISTEN

Il signor Rossi vuole una birra
- *Il signor Rossi preferisce una birra*

Replace "volere" with "preferire."
Il signor Rossi vuole una birra — Io voglio un caffè — Noi vogliamo un caffè ristretto — Tu vuoi un'aranciata — Maria vuole un aperitivo — L'ingegnere vuole un cappuccino — Loro vogliono una Coca-Cola — Io voglio un caffè lungo — Tu vuoi una birra.

(See Grammar, L. 2.)

7. PRONUNCIATION

(••) LISTEN AND REPEAT

Tedesco - mi stupisce! - preferisco - preferisce - conoscere - conosco - finisci - capisce.

WHAT DO ITALIANS SPEAK?

One of the things you cannot help but notice when traveling throughout the peninsula is that Italy is a complex and multifaceted society, made up of several Italys that are often quite different from each other. Nowhere is this more evident than in the way the Italian language is spoken in the various parts of the country.

The inhabitants of these regions have their own manner of speaking, their "own" Italian language. There is the Italy of the Milanese, the Genoese, the Bolognese, the Venetians, the Florentines, the Romans, the Calabrians, the Sicilians, and so on.

The "Other" Italian Languages

These different languages—dialects—come as a big surprise to a foreigner just learning Italian. You will undoubtedly run into people speaking a language quite different from the one you have been studying.

Differences in language can range from the accent and sound of a word (such as the aspirated "c" of the Tuscans) to localized figurative expressions that are totally incomprehensible. But don't despair! It's not that you haven't learned anything or that your textbook is worthless. No, you have merely discovered the unexpected: a large number of Italians are actually bilingual. From one end of the

peninsula to the other, a majority of people use their respective dialect daily. This is particularly in the more rural areas of the country. And you can rest assured that Italians can have just as much difficulty as you in understanding these various dialects. It is highly unlikely, for example, that a Milanese speaking in his or her dialect would be able to communicate successfully with a Sicilian speaking his or her brand of Italian.

Compared to other countries like France, whose dialects are all but history, Italian dialects are very much alive. One's dialect is often considered more intimate and warmer, in fact even richer, than official Italian. Historically speaking, Italy has always had its share of dialects, many of which have had long and illustrious literary traditions (Neopolitan, Sicilian, Venetian, etc.). Venetian, for example, has traditionally been the language of the theater (from the days of la Commedia dell'arte and the drama-

tist Goldoni), and Roman became popular by way of the films made at Cinecittà.

Can the Dialects Survive?

The continuing use of dialects is due in part to Italy's being united only in 1860. But it is also the idea of "il campanilismo" (localism) that has kept them alive. Before being Italian, one is first Genoese, Milanese, Piedmontese, to name but a few.

However, since the Second World War and the advent of television, a "leveling" effect has been taking place. Through the mass media and standardized forms of education, Italians everywhere are learning and using a highly standardized form of Italian—the one you are learning in this book!

This standard form derives from the Tuscan spoken and written by Dante, Petrarch, and Boccaccio. For many centuries it remained a "literary" (that is, written) language in other parts of Italy. Most educated Italians read and wrote it, but spoke a dialect at home and in the immediate community.

In many ways it is sad to witness the demise of many of Italy's dialects because, like the many kinds of cuisines and local customs, dialects have always represented the heterogeneous richness that has so long been characteristic of Italy.

(● ●) LISTEN

Innamorati a Milano
(M. Remigi – A. Testa)
Sung by Memo Remigì

Lovers in Milan

Sapessi com'è strano	You can't imagine how strange it is
sentirsi innamorati	to fall in love
a Milano	in Milan
Coro : a Milano.	*Chorus:* in Milan
Senza fiori	Without flowers
senza verde	without grass (*lit.*, green)
senza cielo	without a sky
senza niente	without anything
fra la gente	among the people
Coro : tanta gente.	*Chorus:* so many people
Sapessi com'è strano	You can't imagine how strange it is
darsi appuntamenti	to go on a date
a Milano	in Milan
Coro : a Milano.	*Chorus:* in Milan
In un grande magazzino	In a department store
in piazza	in a square
o in galleria	in a "galleria"
che pazzia	what madness
Coro : che pazzia.	*Chorus:* what madness
Eppure	Still
in questo posto	in this place
impossibile	(an) impossible (place)
tu mi hai detto « ti amo »	you said "I love you"
io ti ho detto « ti amo ».	and I said "I love you."

"FIGURES" OF SPEECH

NON SBOTTONARSI
(lit., sbottonarsi: to unbutton)
To not express oneself freely

FARSI LE OSSA
(lit., to develop one's bones)
To become accustomed

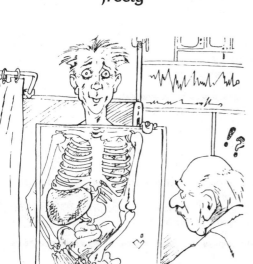

AVERE FEGATO
(lit., to have liver)
To have gall

SAPERNE UNA PIÙ DEL DIAVOLO
(lit., to know one more thing than the Devil)
To be resourceful

1.1

COMPLETE WITH THE DEFINITE ARTICLE : ... direttore — ..... segretaria — ..... impiegato — .... professione — .... ingegnere — .... stage — .... formazione — ..... ditta — ..... aeroporto — ..... nazionalità — ..... paese — ..... centro.
TRANSLATE : Jenny è americana — Chantal è francese — Carmen è spagnola.
Mr. Bauer is German. — Maria is Italian. — José is Portuguese. — John is English.

1.2

COMPLETE WITH THE APPROPRIATE POSSESSIVE ADJECTIVES : Mario ha la valigia : questa è .... valigia. — Noi abbiamo il biglietto : questo è .... biglietto. — Voi avete lo scontrino : questo è .... scontrino. — Tu hai una segretaria : questa è .... segretaria. — Loro hanno il biglietto : questo è .... biglietto. — Io ho la valigia : questa è .... valigia.
TRANSLATE : I corsisti sono al bar — Tu sei francese — Il signor Bauer e la signora Dulac hanno il biglietto. — Io sono il direttore delle vendite.
I have the ticket. — We're at the airport. — You (pol.) have a secretary. — Mr. Marchi is at the baggage counter. — We have an appointment.

1.3

PUT EACH INFINITIVE INTO ITS APPROPRIATE FORM :
Il sig. Marchi (lavorare) .... a Genova — I corsisti (aspettare) .... al bar dell'aeroporto — Io (abitare) .... a Parigi — Tu (arrivare) .... in ritardo — Voi non (trovare) .... la valigia — Noi (parlare) .... italiano.
TRANSLATE : Sono in ritardo — Lei è di Parigi? No, sono di Nantes. — La valigia è in dogana — Sono qui per lavoro.
Italian coffee is too strong for me. — I'd like a drop of milk. — I've been working in Paris for years. — I often come to France. — Where do you come from, sir? From Paris.

1.4

PUT EACH INFINITIVE INTO ITS APPROPRIATE FORM :
L'ingegner Rossi (ricevere) .... i corsisti. — Noi (prendere) .... un caffè. — Il sig. Marchi (conoscere) .... Parigi. — Io non (conoscere) .... Milano. — Tu (vivere) .... in Francia. — I corsisti (attendere) .... al bar. — Voi (vedere) .... il direttore.
TRANSLATE : A che ora è la cena? — Le camere prenotate sono al quarto piano. — Ci vediamo domani mattina alle 10.
The director accompanies the (enrolled) students to the hotel. — Breakfast is served from 7:30 to 9:30. — The rooms are on the fourth floor. — Mr. Marchi arrives at the airport.

1.5

PUT EACH INFINITIVE INTO ITS APPROPRIATE FORM :
Chantal (preferire) .... un caffè lungo. — Noi (preferire) .... un caffè ristretto. — Loro (preferire) .... una birra. — I corsisti (dormire) .... all'albergo Ambasciatori. — Io (partire) .... domani. — Voi (partire) .... alle cinque. — Lui (dormire) .... ancora! — Tu, a che ora (partire) .... ? — L'impiegato (restituire) .... i documenti.
TRANSLATE : È la prima volta che vengo in Italia. — Perché non ci diamo del tu? — Quannti anni hai?
Do you (pol.) speak Italian? — My name is John. — Are you married? — Yes, I'm married and I have two children.

(See the answers on page 36 of the booklet.)

MORE VOCABULARY

CONTINENTS

Europa — Europe
Asia — Asia
Africa — Africa
America — America
Australia — Australia
Antartico — Antarctica

COMMON MARKET COUNTRIES

Italia — Italy
Francia — France
Regno Unito — United Kingdom
Spagna — Spain
Repubblica Federale Tedesca — German Federal Republic
Portogallo — Portugal
Belgio — Belgium
Lussemburgo — Luxembourg
Paesi Bassi — Holland
Grecia — Greece
Danimarca — Denmark
Irlanda — Ireland

OTHER COUNTRIES

Svizzera — Switzerland
Austria — Austria
Polonia — Poland
Ungheria — Hungary
Romania — Roumania
Bulgaria — Bulgaria
Iugoslavia — Yugoslavia
Cecoslovacchia — Czechoslovakia
Repubblica democratica Tedesca — German Democratic Republic
Unione Sovietica — Soviet Union
Svezia — Sweden
Norvegia — Norway
Finlandia — Finland
Marocco — Morocco
Senegal — Senegal
Costa d'Avorio — Ivory Coast
Nigeria — Nigeria
Angola — Angola
Zaire — Zaire
Repubblica Sudafricana — South Africa

Mozambico — Mozambique
Kenia — Kenya
Somalia — Somalia
Etiopia — Ethiopia
Madagascar — Madagascar
Sudan — Sudan
Ciad — Chad
Algeria — Algeria
Tunisia — Tunisia
Libia — Lybia
Egitto — Egypt
Libano — Lebanon
Siria — Syria
Giordania — Jordan
Arabia Saudita — Saudi Arabia
Israele — Israel
Turchia — Turkey
Iran — Iran
Irak — Iraq
Pakistan — Pakistan
Afghanistan — Afghanistan
India — India
Cina — China
Tailandia — Thailand
Nepal — Nepal
Indonesia — Indonesia
Giappone — Japan
Corea — Korea
Viet-Nam — Vietnam
Canada — Canada
Stati Uniti — United States
Messico — Mexico
Guatemala — Guatemala
Nicaragua — Nicaragua
Antille — Antilles
Venezuela — Venezuela
Colombia — Colombia
Perù — Peru
Brasile — Brazil
Argentina — Argentina
Cile — Chile
Nuova Zelanda — New Zealand

PROFESSIONS

operaio — worker
impiegato — employee
commerciante — business
rappresentante — representative
industriale — industrialist
libero professionista — professional

ragioniere — accountant
commercialista — businessperson
fisico — physicist
biologo — biologist
chimico — chemist
geologo — geologist
chirurgo — surgeon
architetto — architect
ingegnere — engineer
avvocato — lawyer
disegnatore industriale — industrial designer
maestro — elementary school teacher
professore/professoressa — high school/university teacher
insegnante — teacher
assistente — assistant
assistente sociale — social worker
psicologo/a — psychologist
psichiatra — psychiatrist
medico — doctor
ginecologo — gynecologist
giornalista — journalist
traduttore/trice — translator
interprete — interpretor
autista — driver
fattorino — bellhop

THE WORK WORLD

salario — salary
stipendio — wage
basta-paga — take-home pay
ferie — paid holidays
tredicesima — holiday pay
anzianità — seniority
licenziamento — firing
indennità — indemnity
dipendente — salaried worker
sindacato — union
sciopero — strike
datore di lavoro — employer
capufficio — office manager
pensione — pension
pensionato/a — pensioner
dirigente — manager
casalinga — housewife
socio — member/partner
disoccupato — unemployed
disoccupazione — unemployment

I. *TEST YOURSELF*

1. PUT THE FOLLOWING SENTENCES INTO THE PLURAL

La signora è francese . . . .
L'ingegnere ha il biglietto . . . .
La mia valigia non arriva . . . .
Ecco il mio biglietto . . . .
Il viaggio è lungo . . . .
La camera singola è prenotata . . . .
Lo scontrino della valigia . . . .
Questo caffè è buono . . . .

2. COMPLETE WITH : "Quanto, Che, A che, Come, Perché, Qual, Dove"

. . . . si chiama?
. . . . zucchero, Signora?
. . . . ora è la colazione?
. . . . giorno è oggi?
. . . . anni ha?
. . . . è la sua professione?
. . . . abita?
. . . . è a Milano, per affari o per turismo?
. . . . piano è la camera?

3. WHAT WOULD YOU SAY IF YOU HAD TO...

thank someone . . . .
respond to someone who has just thanked you . . . .
greet a lady . . . .
introduce yourself . . . .
ask someone how he/she is . . . .
take leave of someone . . . .
ask for a wake-up call . . . .
order a coffee . . . .
ask someone his/her name . . . .

4. COMPLETE WITH "devono, fanno, andiamo, volete, possiamo, potete," AS THE CASE MAY BE

Se . . . ., ... cenare qui in albergo.

Il signor Marchi e la signora Dulac . . . . conoscenza.

Mentre aspettiamo, ... a prendere un caffè.

Adesso ci siamo tutti, ... andare!

Ci . . . . essere 6 camere singole prenotate.

5. ONLY ONE SENTENCE IN EACH SET IS CORRECT. CAN YOU FIND IT?

A. Questi sono i sui biglietti . . . . ☐
B. Questi sono i suoi biglietti . . . ☐
C. Questi è i suoi biglietti . . . . . . ☐

A. Ciao Mario, come stai? . . . . . ☐
B. Ciao Mario, come sta? . . . . . . ☐
C. Ciao Mario, come state? . . . . ☐

A. Il sig. Marchi viene di Genova . ☐
B. Il sig. Marchi viene per Genova ☐
C. Il sig. Marchi viene da Genova ☐

A. Hans e Karl Bauer sono tedesci ☐
B. Hans è Karl Bauer sono tedeschi ☐
C. Hans e Karl Bauer sono tedeschi ☐

A. No sono francese . . . . ☐
B. Non sono francese . . . . ☐
C. Sono non francese . . . . ☐

6. MATCH EACH QUESTION TO ITS ANSWER

A. Sono spagnola.
B. No, ci vengo spesso per ragioni di lavoro.
C. Sì, parlo anche il tedesco e un po' di russo.
D. Abbastanza, sono già molto in ritardo!

1, Ha fretta?
2. È la prima volta che viene in Italia?
3. Di che nazionalità è, signora?
4. Parla anche altre lingue?

(Check your answers on page 37 of the booklet.)

IN THE MOUTH OF THE WOLF

Even before he had time to open the door the telephone rang. There was no way out—it was Milan. Ambrose was sure of it.

Ever since he'd accepted this job in France, Ambrose hadn't had a single undisturbed evening. He would scarcely get home when he'd have to deal with the telephone again—not to hear a melodious voice making suave advances, but always, systematically, inexorably *per motivi di lavoro*. Even if he stayed in the office in front of his files, his work table, and his contracts two or three hours longer than usual, nothing helped. He couldn't avoid it.

"Why can't I have a normal employer who forgets everything after six o'clock?" he grumbled.

Right now it wasn't the case with his. *Ambrogio di qua, Ambrogio di là, mi puoi verificare quell'elenco, chiamare il tal dei tali, dare il recapito di tal altro:* It was neverending.

So, regularly, every night, Ambrose was tormented by the same doubt: Had he made a wise decision the day the director of Magagnati had proposed this job in Paris? Representing a large Italian editorial group was certainly prestigious, but it wasn't without a number of disadvantages.

Ambrose picked up the phone with a sigh—one of his everyday problems was that he never knew if he should begin immediately with "Pronto?" or simply try a prudent "Hello." This time his caller didn't leave him the time to think.

"*Pronto, Ambrogio?*" said the voice. Clearly, graciousness wasn't his style.

"*Sì, sono io.*"

"*Ce la pagherai cara.*"

And he hung up. Considering the static on the line, the call was from Italy. He didn't know what he was supposed to pay for dearly, but if he had enemies, at least they didn't live on the same floor as he did. Reassured by this observation, he let his bath run. Ten minutes later, cursing and swearing, he jumped out of the bathtub to answer the inevitable telephone call from the Milan editorial office.

Going to the office the next morning, he noticed that the water of the canal was scarcely moving. It was almost frozen. Clearly, it was going to be a hard winter. That only half pleased him. He hated to stay shut up at home. He should be used to it; he'd lived in Milan for years and had endured its fogs and frosts philosophically. He'd even come to like it.

That was why, on certain mornings in winter, when a layer of fog covered the plain of the Po from Pavia to Vigevano, he would give up the idea of taking his car because he preferred the streetcar. He would drink a *cappuccino* in a bar downstairs from his apartment and go to wait patiently beside the tracks. He liked such moments—when it was still darkest night, barely turning pale at dawn. When the streetcar came, he would pull himself up onto the step as though it were the staircase of a palace. He would go into the long orange tube, which was only modern in its looks, stamp his ticket, worm his way through the crowd pushing against each other, huddling into his coat so as to forget the absence of heat, and give himself up to the warmth of the bodies packed against him.

Through the frosted windows, Ambrose would watch the yellow reflection of the street lights: Torino Street, Plaza Cordusio, and finally Duomo Plaza where he would get off. After crossing the open space of the Cathedral, of which only the outline could be seen, he would go through the Gallery Victor Emmanuel, pass in front of La Scala, and go on foot up Via Verdi. Nothing charmed him more than the feeling of solitude imposed by the fog in the middle of Milan.

However, all that was over. Paris didn't evoke the same kind of feelings in him. Here, the least change in temperature took on the aspect of a catastrophe. All it took was a few pieces of ice drifting on the canal to create the impression of Napoleon's winter camp on the banks of the Berezina.

Ambrose was in a bad mood. This thinking about the weather had made him homesick—and his appointment book depressed him. So when Lucy, his assistant, announced with an ironic smile: "*È arrivata la Aiguement,*" his gloominess knew no limits. In all of Paris Ambrose didn't know a more impossible bore. And he believed he knew them all—*per motivo di lavoro.* that went without saying.

"*Più falsa di questa, si muore,*" he whispered to Lucy, who hurried away.

Unwilling, he stood up and went to greet his visitor.

"My dear Ambrose, how happy I am to see you again . . ."

The more he had occasion to talk to her, the more he was convinced that if she didn't actually make up stories, Mrs. Aiguement none the less cultivated a singular penchant for hypocrisy.

"So, you don't miss your beautiful country's sun too much? You're getting used to our harsh weather? Of course, at your age you'll get through the winter without any trouble."

Mrs. Aiguement liked to make platitudes with the singlemindedness that others used to do needlework.

"But you don't seem very cheerful today. You look like someone who just fell into the mouth of the wolf. And speaking of wolves, that's just what brought me here. . . that is, if I still understand my Italian. What's left of it. But when one has studied a little Latin. . ."

Ambrose agreed.

"A little Latin makes Italian seem much easier! Well, Magagnati Press has published a book which I think is called *In the Mouth of the Wolf,* or something like that. Do you know about it?"

"Certainly, *In bocca al lupo.* Milan just sent us several copies. I haven't had time to look at it yet."

"Yes, I'm sure that's it. It's the one that's the story of a killer, someone from the Mafia, and his exciting revelations on his dealings with international finance?"

"I think so. But it would be better if I made sure."

"Never mind, Ambrose dear; that's enough for me. I won't hide the fact that this book really interests us. We'd like to have an option on it. I hope that we can even sign the contract within a week."

CONTINUED . . .

UNIT 2

◉◉ LISTEN

AT THE BANK

Mr. Moreau is a tourist visiting Rome. He's in a bank to exchange some money.

Allo sportello del cambio

L'impiegata : *Buongiorno, dica!*

Sig. Moreau : *Buongiorno, vorrei sapere qual è la quotazione del franco francese.*

L'impiegata : *Dunque, oggi il franco francese è a 220 lire.*

Sig. Moreau : *Va bene. Vorrei cambiare 1.000 franchi.*

L'impiegata : *1.000 franchi a 220 lire fanno 220.000 lire. Ha un documento, per favore?*

Sig. Moreau : *Sì, eccolo.*

L'impiegata : *Attenda un attimo, per cortesia. Ecco, firmi qui.*

Sig. Moreau : *Ecco fatto.*

L'impiegata : *Benissimo, si accomodi alla cassa n° 2, in fondo al corridoio a destra.*

Sig. Moreau : *Grazie mille. Ancora una cosa. È possibile cambiare dei soldi con una carta di credito internazionale?*

L'impiegata : *Che carta di credito ha?*

Sig. Moreau : *Ho la carta VISA.*

L'impiegata : *Certamente, noi accettiamo la carta VISA, però ci vuole il libretto degli assegni e bisogna compilare un assegno.*

Sig. Moreau : *Va bene, La ringrazio... Un'ultima informazione, mi scusi.*

L'impiegata : *Sì, dica...*

Sig. Moreau : *Quali sono le condizioni per aprire un conto corrente in Italia?*

L'impiegata : *Per aprire un conto corrente, bisogna avere la residenza in Italia.*

Sig. Moreau : *Ah... Perché ho intenzione di trasferirmi in Italia l'anno prossimo...*

L'impiegata : *Allora quando Lei arriva deve fare il cambio di residenza e solo dopo può aprire un conto.*

Sig. Moreau : *Bene, grazie mille.*

L'impiegata : *Di niente, ArrivederLa.*

Sig. Moreau : *ArrivederLa.*

◉◉ LISTEN AND REPEAT
You will find the translation on page 9 of the booklet.

1. Panorama of Rome
2. The Roman Forum,
(in the heart of modern Rome)

NOUNS

la banca — bank
lo sportello — teller's window
il cambio — exchange
la quotazione — exchange rate
il franco — franc
la cassa — cash desk
i soldi — money
la carta di credito — credit card
il libretto degli assegni — checkbook
l'assegno — check
la condizione — condition
il conto corrente — current/active accounts
la residenza — residence
l'intenzione (f) — intention

———————

il denaro — money *(1)*
il franco francese — French franc
il franco svizzero — Swiss franc
il franco belga — Belgian franc
la lira italiana — Italian lira
il marco tedesco — German mark
la sterlina inglese — British pound
il dollaro USA — American dollar
lo scellino austriaco — Austrian schilling
la peseta spagnola — Spanish peseta
lo scudo portoghese — Portuguese escudo

ADVERBS

dunque — therefore/thus/OK
quando — when
dopo — after

———————

quindi — therefore/thus/OK
prima — before

VERBS

cambiare — to change/exchange
accomodarsi (alla cassa) — to go to (the cash desk) *(2)*
accettare — to accept
ci vuole — it's necessary
bisogna — it's necessary *(3)*
compilare — fill out
ringraziare — to thank
aprire — to open
chiudere — to close

MISCELLANEOUS

aver intenzione di . . . — to intend to
l'anno prossimo — next year
l'anno scorso — last year

———————

REMARKS...   REMARKS...   REMARKS...   REMARKS...

(1) "Denaro" is the general term for "money." But in common speech the plural form "i soldi" is often used. — (2) This verb is virtually untranslatable. It can be used to mean: "Go ahead," "Come in," etc. — (3) See Grammar, L.15.

HOW TO SAY IT

---

1. EXCHANGING MONEY

Vorrei sapere qual è la quotazione (del franco) — I'd like to know the exchange rate for the franc.
Vorrei sapere a quanto è (il franco) — What's the franc at?
Vorrei cambiare 1.000 franchi — I'd like to exchange 1000 francs.
Posso cambiare 1.000 franchi con la carta di credito? — Can I exchange 1000 francs with a credit card?

---

2. HOW MUCH IS . . . WORTH?

1.000 franchi a 220 lire fanno 220.000 lire — 1000 francs at 220 liras comes to 220,000 liras.

---

3. ASKING FOR MORE INFORMATION

Senta, ancora una domanda, per cortesia — Please, one more question.
Senta, ancora una cosa — One more thing.
Un'ultima informazione, mi scusi — One last bit of information, sorry.

---

4. EXPRESSING NEED

Ci vuole il libretto degli assegni — Is a checkbook needed?
Bisogna compilare un assegno — You have to make out a check.
Lei deve fare il cambio de residenza — You have to change your residence.
Bisogna avere la residenza in Italia — You must have a residence in Italy.

---

5. GIVING WHAT HAS BEEN ASKED FOR

Ha il passaporto? Sì, eccolo! — Do you have a passport? Yes, here it is!
Ha la carta d'identità? Sì, eccola! — Do you have an identity card? Yes, here it is!
Ha i franchi? Sì, eccoli! — Do you have any francs? Yes, here they are!
Ha le lire? Sì, eccole! — Do you have any liras? Yes, here they are!

---

1. ASKING WHAT THE RATE IS

(● ●) LISTEN

il marco

● *Vorrei sapere a quanto è il marco*

Continue asking what the rate is.
il marco — la sterlina — il franco — la lira — il dollaro — lo scudo — lo scellino — la peseta.

(See Grammar, G. 2.)

2. NUMBER PRACTICE

(● ●) LISTEN

1.000 franchi

● *Vorrei cambiare 1.000 franchi*

Continue saying how much money you wish to exchange.
1,000 franchi — 2.000 franchi — 300 marchi — 50 dollari — 80 sterline — 500 franchi svizzeri — 750 pesetas — 900 scellini — 600.000 lire.

(See Grammar, K. 1.)

3. GIVING WHAT HAS BEEN ASKED FOR

(● ●) LISTEN

Ha il passaporto?
● *Sì, eccolo!*
Ha la carta d'identità?
● *Sì, eccola!*

Answer the following as in the model.
Ha il passaporto? — Ha la carta d'identità? — Ha la patente? — Ha un documento? — Ha il libretto di assegni? — Ha i franchi? — Ha le lire? — Ha la chiave? — Ha i documenti? — Ha la carta di credito? — Ha i biglietti?

(See Grammar, E. 6.)

4. EXPRESSING NEED

(● ●) LISTEN

Avere un libretto di assegni
● *Bisogna avere un libretto de assegni*
Il libretto di assegni
● *Ci vuole il libretto di assegni*

Continue expressing need by using "ci vuole" or "bisogna."
Avere un libretto di assegni — Il libretto di assegni — Avere la residenza in Italia — La residenza in Italia — Avere il passaporto — Il passaporto — Avere un conto corrente — Un conto corrente — Avere la carta di credito — La carta di credito.

(See Grammar, L. 15.)

5. THE VERB "DOVERE"

(● ●) LISTEN

il sig. Moreau (compilare un assegno)
● *Il sig. Moreau deve compilare un assegno*
io
● *Devo compilare un assegno*

Continue, using the correct form of "dovere."
il sig. Moreau — io — lui — noi — Marco e Luisa — Lei — lei — voi — loro — tu — io — noi — Roberto.

(See Grammar, L. 6.)

6. THE VERB "POTERE"

(● ●) LISTEN

il sig. Moreau (cambiare con la carta di credito)
● *Il sig. Moreau può cambiare con la carta di credito*
io
● *Posso cambiare con la carta di credito*

Continue, using the correct form of "potere."
il sig. Moreau — io — tu — Franco e Mario — la signora Rossi — noi — voi — io — loro — Lei — tu.

(See Grammar, L. 6.)

7. PRONUNCIATION

(● ●) LISTEN AND REPEAT

Quotazione - franco - franchi - accettare - dunque - certamente - quale - ci vuole

POCKETS FULL OF LIRAS

Italy is one of the world's ten richest nations. Like Japan, it seems to be in a state of continual economic growth, and, like the yen, the lira has become a sought-after commodity.

Given this unprecedented prosperity, the Italian government has been seriously thinking of eliminating "three zeroes" from its currency system. Thus, 1000 liras would be transformed into a single lira. This would simply prove the growth in Italy's economic status.

More and More Liras

As it now stands, the Italian monetary system will fill your pockets with astronomical "figures." A 100,000 lira bill is not even equal to 100 American dollars. No bills are now printed below the 1000 bill and only coins of 50, 100, and 500 liras are made available for spending. There was a time when 1, 5, 10, and 20 liras were found commonly in circulation, but these have gone the way of the dinosaur. The main denominations are: "mille lire" (1000), "duemila lire" (2000), "cinquemila lire" (5000), "diecimila lire" (10,000), "cinquantamila lire" (50,000), and "centomila lire" (100,000).

Adjusting to the System

But on further reflection, it is obvious that a monetary system is just that: a monetary system! The tourist will have no difficulty in adjusting to the lira and its denominations. A few purchases and a few bills paid will quickly make one aware of the "value" of the lira in terms of its buying power. As one comes to recognize the different bills through everyday purchases, one easily comes to understand what is "expensive" or "inexpensive" in Italian monetary terms.

The visitor to Italy should also keep in mind that most stores and service agencies will accept foreign money. American currency, for instance, is accepted virtually throughout Italy. And, of course, traveler's checks (of any currency) are accepted everywhere.

So, whether one thinks in terms of single or multiple digits, the "value" of currency becomes a reality only as one uses it in daily purchasing and spending routines.

N° 1   ●● LISTEN

Write the numbers you hear.

. . . .
. . . .
. . . .

N° 2   ●● LISTEN

Circle V *if the statement is true, or* F *if it is false.*

1. *Il signore vuole cambiare dei dollari*   V   F

2. *Il cambio della sterlina oggi è 2.338 lire*   V   F

3. *Il signore vuole cambiare 50 sterline*   V   F

4. *Il signore riceve 233.800 lire*   V   F

Make out the following check, writing the numbers in letters, dating it, and signing it.

lì _____ 19 ___ lir **475.000**

BANCO^{DI} SANTO SPIRITO

FONDATO NEL 1605

A vista pagate per questo assegno bancario

lire _____

a _____

3412563 5   c/c N° 1177376

74320-8   Firma _____

Rebus.

P   🦢🦢   🎵🎵   NEL   🚪   📄

SCIOGLILINGUA *
🔊 LISTEN

Trentatrè trentini entrarono in Trento tutti e trentatrè trotterellando.

Thirty-three residents of Trento entered Trento, all thirty-three trotting.

(See solutions on page 10 of the booklet.)
*tongue twister

🔊 LISTEN

TAKING THE BUS

Mr. Moreau wants to know how to get to the Trevi Fountain.

Sig. Moreau : *Senta, scusi. Per cortesia, è lontana da qui la fontana di Trevi?*

Il passante : *Guardi, a piedi ci vuole circa mezz'ora. Però può prendere l'autobus. Con l'autobus ci vogliono solo dieci minuti.*

Sig. Moreau : *Con questo caldo preferisco prendere l'autobus. C'è una fermata qui vicino?*

Il passante : *Sì, guardi, proprio davanti al tabaccaio.*

Sig. Moreau : *Grazie mille. Per cortesia, mi sa dire anche che autobus devo prendere?*

Il passante : *Il 35.*

Sig. Moreau : *E a che fermata devo scendere?*

Il passante : *Al capolinea, cioè all'ultima fermata.*

Sig. Moreau : *Ancora una domanda, scusi : dove posso comprare il biglietto?*

Il passante : *Dal tabaccaio.*

Sig. Moreau : *Grazie mille.*

Il passante : *Di niente, si figuri!*

Il signor Moreau sale sull'autobus 35 e scende al capolinea. Qui domanda altre informazioni.

Sig. Moreau : *Senta, scusi.*

La passante : *Sì!*

Sig. Moreau : *Per cortesia, mi sa dire dov'è la fontana di Trevi?*

La passante : *Guardi, è molto facile! Vada dritto, alla prima traversa giri a destra e subito a sinistra c'è la fontana di Trevi.*

Sig. Moreau : *È lontano?*

La passante : *È molto vicino, non può sbagliare, ci vogliono due minuti.*

Sig. Moreau : *La ringrazio.*

La passante : *Non c'è di che!*

🔊 LISTEN AND REPEAT
You will find the translation on page 10 of the booklet.

1. *Piazza Navona*
2. *A Swiss Guard*
3. *Trevi Fountain*
4. *Piazza di Spagna*
5. *Four-Rivers Fountain, Piazza Navona*
6. *Piazza del Popolo*

VOCABULARY

NOUNS

l'autobus (m) — bus *(1)*
la fontana — fountain
il passante — passerby
il caldo — heat
la fermata — stop
il tabaccaio — tobacco shop
il capolinea — last stop
il biglietto — ticket *(2)*
la domanda — question
la traversa — (cross) street

———————

il freddo — cold
la risposta — answer
il treno — train
il tram — streetcar *(1)*
l'aereo — airplane
la nave — boat, ship
la macchina — car *(3)*
la bicicletta — bicycle

ADJECTIVES

ultimo — last
facile — easy
lontano — far

———————

difficile — difficult
vicino — near

VERBS

sentire — to listen/hear
scendere — to get off
comprare — to buy
salire — to go up
domandare — to ask
girare — to turn
sbagliare — to make a mistake

MISCELLANEOUS

a piedi — on foot
cioè — that is
di niente, si figuri! — Don't mention it!
dritto — straight ahead
davanti — in front
dietro — behind
vicino a/lontano da — near/far

REMARKS...   REMARKS...   REMARKS...   REMARKS...

(1) Nouns ending in a consonant are invariable. — (2) This can also mean bank note. — (3) The word "automobile" (f.) is a synonym for "macchina." — (4) "Guardi" is sometimes used just to start off a series of directional instructions. — (5) See Grammar, L. 15.

HOW TO SAY IT

1. ASKING FOR DIRECTIONS

Senta, scusi. Mi sa dire dov'è la fontana di Trevi? — Excuse me, can you tell me where the Trevi Fountain is?*(4)*
Per cortesia, è lontana da qui la fontana di Trevi? — Please, is the Trevi Fountain far from here?
Scusi, come si fa per andare al Colosseo? — Excuse me, how do you get to the Colosseum?

2. GIVING DIRECTIONS

Vada dritto — Go straight ahead.
Giri a destra — Turn right.
Giri a sinistra — Turn left.
È molto vicino — It's nearby.
È qui — It's here.
È abbastanza lontano — It's quite far.
È a 10 minuti a piedi — It's 10 minutes from here.
È proprio davanti al tabaccaio — It's right in front of the tobacco shop.

3. ASKING ABOUT BUSES

Che autobus devo prendere? — Which bus should I take?
A che fermata devo scendere? — At which stop should I get off?
C'è una fermata qui vicino? — Is there a stop nearby?
Dove posso comprare il biglietto? — Where can I buy a ticket?

4. DURATION

A piedi ci vuole circa mezz'ora — You'll need about a half hour on foot. *(5)*
Con l'autobus ci vogliono solo 10 minuti — With the bus it'll take only 10 minutes.
È molto vicino, ci vogliono due minuti — It's nearby. It takes only two minutes.

5. RESPONDING TO THANKS

(Grazie mille) — You're welcome!
Prego!
Di niente! — Don't mention it!
Si figuri! — Not at all!

1. ASKING FOR DIRECTIONS

(• •) LISTEN

La fontana di Trevi

• *Senta, scusi. Mi sa dire dov'è la fontana di Trevi?*

Continue asking for directions.
La fontana de Trevi — Il Colosseo — La fermata dell'autobus — Il tabaccaio — La stazione — L'albergo Aurora — Via Veneto — Piazza Navona — Corso Garibaldi.

2. GIVING DIRECTIONS

(• •) LISTEN

Vado dritto?

• *Sì, vada dritto!*

Continue, using the formal imperative.
Vado dritto? — Giro a destra? — Prendo l'autobus? — Scendo al capolinea? — Giro a sinistra? — Prendo via Marconi? — Vado dal tabaccaio? — Prendo il 35? — Vado dritto?

(See Grammar, L. 10.)

3. ASKING QUESTIONS

INTERROGATIVE PRONOUNS

(• •) LISTEN

Prenda l'autobus 35!

• *Che autobus devo prendere?*
Scenda alla prima fermata!

• *A che fermata devo scendere?*

Ask questions as in the model.
Prenda l'autobus 35! — Scenda alla prima fermata! — Prenda il treno per Firenze! — Scenda alla seconda fermata! — Prenda l'autobus 21 — Scenda all'ultima fermata!

(See Grammar, G. 2.)

4. HOW LONG DOES IT TAKE?

(• •) LISTEN

A piedi, mezz'ora

• *A piedu ci vuole mezz'ora*

A piedi, 10 minuti

• *A piedi ci vogliono 10 minuti*

Continue saying how long it takes.
A piedi, mezz'ora — A piedi, 10 minuti — A piedi, 1 ora — In macchina, 20 minuti — In trento, 2 ore — In aereo, 1 ora — In autobus, un quarto l'ora — A piedi, 2 minuti.

(See Grammar, L. 15.)

5. "TO GO" + PREP. + INFINITIVE

(• •) LISTEN

Prendo l'autobus

• *Vado a prendere l'autobus*
Comprano il biglietto

• *Vanno a comprare il biglietto*

Use the verb "to go" as in the model.
Prendo l'autobus — Comprano il biglietto — Vede la fontana di Trevi — Prendete un caffè — Compriamo le sigarette — Prendi il treno — Compro i fiammiferi — Mangiano al ristorante — Dormiamo in albergo.

(See Grammar, F.)

6. DIRECT OBJECT PRONOUNS

(• •) LISTEN

Conosci Mario? • *Si lo conosco*
Conosci Maria? • *Si, la conosco*
Conosci Mario e Franco? • *Si, li conosco*
Conosci Maria e Laura? • *Si, le conosco*

Answer the questions as in the model.
Conosci Mario? — Conosci Maria? — Conosci Mario e Franco? — Conosci Maria e Laura? — Conosci la città? — Conosci la fontana di Trevi? — Conosci il sig. Moreau? — Conosci la signora Dupond? — Conosci l'albergo Ligure? — Conosci queste persone? — Conosci gli amici di Mario? — Conosci le vie di Roma? — Conosci Giovanni e Filippo?

(See Grammar, E. 1.)

7. PRONUNCIATION

(• •) LISTEN AND REPEAT

Autobus - aereo - capolinea - miei - suoi - puoi - vuoi - fuori - mai - tabaccaio.

NORTH AND SOUTH

Like many nations, Italy has two main cultural areas—a North and a South. Historically, the two have had different cultural and economic fortunes—the North developing into an industrial giant, and the South struggling to make ends meet.

Both areas have contributed to the national character of Italy. Italy's writers, philosophers, and scientists have come from all over the peninsula. Local customs and dialects have always been essential components of Italy's mosaic-like identity. The great Sicilian playwright, Luigi Pirandello, is as much a symbol of Italian civilization as is the great Genoese explorer Christopher Columbus.

The "Mezzogiorno"

The Italian South has, in the past, been called Italy's "Mezzogiorno," literally, "the afternoon." This was a metaphor for the poverty and indolence (attributed to the burning afternoon sun) that have traditionally characterized southern

Italy. To rectify this situation, the government undertook various economic and political measures in the last few decades that have diminished and often eliminated differences between North and South. Today, the problem of the "Mezzogiorno" has been virtually eradicated. Economic prosperity has made all Italians equal participants in one of the world's truly great civilizations.

Tourism

Both the North and the South are blessed with beautiful areas for tourists to visit. While the North attracts tourists for its magnificent mountain and lakeside resorts, the South has become one of the major resorts of Europe. The beaches of Calabria, Sicily, and Sardinia are today among the most sought-after in the world. This fact has had obvious economic benefits for the entire South. Every summer, the whole area takes on a holiday atmosphere as visitors arrive from all over the world.

The fact that the North and the South are starting to achieve economic parity is making Italy a very stable and prosperous country. As it heads into the twenty-first century, there is no doubt that the old rift between the two Italys will only be an unfortunate memory.

N° 1 •• LISTEN

Following the directions given on the tape, indicate where the following are located: the museum, the bus stop, the bank, and the post office. Put the corresponding number in the box.

MUSEO	

BANCA	

FERMATA DELL'AUTOBUS	

POSTA	

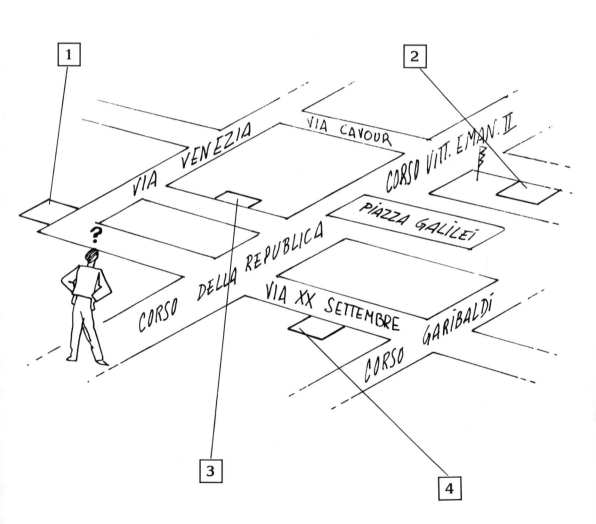

Here's a crossword puzzle for you to solve. When you have finished you will get the word for a means of transportation in the longest vertical column.

Definizioni :
1. *L'ultima fermata.*
2. *Senta, ..., mi può dire dov'è la fontana di Trevi?*
3. *Domando l'informazione a un ...*
4. *Compro il biglietto dal ...*
5. *Per prendere l'autobus ci vuole il ...*
6. *La fontana è lontano da ...*
7. *Il contrario di destra.*

PROVERBIO •• LISTEN

Tutte le strade portano a Roma.
All roads lead to Rome.

(See solutions on page 11 of the booklet.)

DIALOGUE

A PHONE CALL

Mr. Moreau phones Mr. Martini, an Italian colleague, to invite him out to dinner.

La sig.ra Martini : *Pronto?*

Il sig. Moreau : *Buongiorno. Vorrei parlare con il signor Martini per cortesia.*

La sig.ra Martini : *Chi lo desidera?*

Il sig. Moreau : *Sono François Moreau, un suo collega francese.*

La sig.ra Martini : *Mi dispiace, mio marito in questo momento non c'è. Vuole lasciar detto qualcosa?*

Il sig. Moreau : *Sì, gli dica che ho telefonato.*

La sig.ra Martini : *Mi ripete il Suo nome, per cortesia?*

Il sig. Moreau : *Moreau : Emme - o - erre - e - a - u. A che ora pensa che tornerà?*

La sig.ra Martini : *Guardi, non so di preciso. Probabilmente fra un'oretta. Se vuole può darmi il Suo numero di telefono e mio marito La richiamerà.*

Il sig. Moreau : *Sì, grazie. Il mio numero è il 48.57.46.15. Gli dica che sono all'hotel Navona e che resterò in albergo fino alle 5.*

La sig.ra Martini : *Va bene, arrivederLa.*

Il sig. Moreau : *Arrivederci.*

La centralinista dell'albergo : *Pronto, Hotel Navona, Buongiorno.*

Sig. Martini : *Buongiorno, vorrei parlare con il signor Moreau per cortesia.*

La centralinista : *Attenda in linea, prego. Ecco, Le passo la linea.*

Il sig. Moreau : *Pronto?*

Il sig. Martini : *Pronto, François? Ciao! Sono Andrea.*

Il sig. Moreau : *Ciao Andrea! Come stai?*

Il sig. Martini : *Bene, grazie. Quando sei arrivato?*

Il sig. Moreau : *Due giorni fa, e purtroppo resterò solo qualche giorno. Spero che avremo il tempo di andare a cena insieme!*

Il sig. Martini : *Con piacere! Per me va bene anche stasera.*

Il sig. Moreau : *Perfetto! Dunque, che ora è adesso?*

Il sig. Martini : *Sono quasi le cinque.*

Il sig. Moreau : *Allora ci vediamo alle 8 qui in albergo. Ti va?*

Il sig. Martini : *Benissimo. A stasera alle otto allora.*

LISTEN AND REPEAT

1. The Colosseum
2. St. Peter's (Vatican) Square

. . . .

NOUNS

la telefonata — phone call *(1)*
il/la collega — colleague/associate
il numero di telefono — phone number
la centralinista — operator
la linea — line

———————

il messaggio — message
l'elenco telefonico — phone book
il telefono — phone
la cabina telefonica — phone booth
il gettone — token
l'orologio — watch/clock

VERBS

desiderare — to desire (May I help you?)
lasciar detto qualcosa — to leave a
message
telefonare (a qualcuno) — to phone
ripetere — to repeat
pensare — to think
tornare — to return/come back
guardare — to watch/look at

richiamare — to call back
passare — to pass by/pass

———————

fare una telefonata — to call
rispondere al telefono — to answer the
phone
riattaccare — to hang up
ricevere — to receive
ripetere lettera per lettera — to spell

MISCELLANEOUS

pronto! — Hello!
mi dispiace! — I'm sorry!
probabilmente — probably
fra/tra un'ora — in an hour's time
fino alle 5 — until 5
due giorni fa — two days ago
qualche giorno — a few days *(2)*
sono quasi le 5 — it's almost 5
insieme — together

———————

REMARKS...　　*REMARKS...*　　*REMARKS...*　　*REMARKS...*

*(1) The suffix **-ata** is a common one: "telefono" = phone, telefonata = phone call. — (2) "Qualche" is always followed by a singular noun, even though its meaning is plural. — (3) In such expressions, the **-e** of the infinitive can be dropped.*

HOW TO SAY IT

---

1. PHONING

Pronto, Hotel Navona? — Hello. Is this the Hotel Navona?
Pronto, casa Martini? — Hello. Is this the Martini household?
Pronto, Signor Moreau? — Hello, Mr. Moreau?
Pronto, Andrea? — Hello, Andrea (Andrew)?

---

2. ASKING IF SOMEONE IS IN

Buongiorno, vorrei parlare con il sig. Martini, per cortesia — Hello. I'd like to speak to Mr. Martini, please.
Mi passa il sig. Moreau, per cortesia? — Can you pass me (allow me to talk) to Mr. Moreau, please?
C'è il sig. Moreau? — Is Mr. Moreau in?
Potrei parlare con Andrea? — May I speak with Andrea?

---

3. WHO IS IT?

Chi parla? — Who's speaking?
Il Suo nome, per cortesia' — Your name, please?
(Il sig. Martini) Chi lo desidera? — Who may I say wishes to speak to him?

---

4. ANSWERING THE PHONE

Sono io — This is me/It's me.
Il signor Martini non c'è — Mr. Martini is not in/here.
Attenda in linea, prego — Hold the line, please.

---

5. LEAVING A MESSAGE

Posso lasciar detto qualcosa? — May I leave a message? *(3)*
Può dire di richiamarmi? — Can you tell him/her to call me back?
Dica che ha telefonato François — Tell him/her that François called.

---

6. TEMPORAL EXPRESSIONS

In questo momento — This minute/moment
Tra un'oretta — In about an hour
Fino alle 5 — Till 5/until 5
Due giorni fa — Two days ago
Resterò qualche giorno — I'm staying a few days.

1. ASKING IF SOMEONE IS IN

(● ●) LISTEN

Il sig. Martini
* *Vorrei parlare con il sig. Martini, per cortesia*
Il direttore
* *Vorrei parlare con il direttore, per cortesia*

Say that you would like to speak to the following people.
Il sig. Martini — Il direttore — La segretaria del sig. Moreau — L'avvocato — L'ingegner Rossi — Il dotto Verde — Andrea — Il responsabile delle vendite — La signora Rossi.

2. SPELLING NAMES

(● ●) LISTEN

(a, b, c, d, e, f . . .)

LISTEN TO THE EXAMPLE

Moreau
* *emme-o-erre-e-a-u*
Martini
* *emme-a-erre-ti-i-en*

Now spell the following names.
Moreau — Martini — Jeannot — Dupleix — Goujon — Thomas — Veyrat — Khosrof — Weber.

And now try to spell your own name.

(See Grammar, A.)

3. GIVING ONE'S PHONE NUMBER

(● ●) LISTEN

640.11.26
* *Il mio numero è 6.4.0./1.1./2.6.*

These are all numbers you have! Say them.
640.11.26 — 48.57.46.15 — 54.03.27 — 79.95.84 — 43.96.17.92

Now give your real phone number.

4. TELLING TIME

(● ●) LISTEN

Sono le 16.30
* *Sono le quattro e mezzo*
Sono le 12
* *È mezzogiorno!*

Give the equivalent times as in the model.
Sono le 16.30 — Sono le 12 — Sono le 14.15 — Sono le 13 — Sono le 22.45 — Sono le 15.20 — Sono le 21.30 — Sono le 11.55.

Now tell what time it is right now.

(See Grammar, K. 3.)

5. THE FUTURE OF VERBS IN - *ARE*

(● ●) LISTEN

Il sig. Martini arriverà fra un'ora (io)
* *Arriverò fra un'ora*

Continue as in the model.
il sig. Martini — io — noi — Marco e Anna — voi — la signora Rossi — tu — il direttore — i turisti — io — il ragazzo inglese — noi.

(See Grammar, L. 8.)

6. THE FUTURE OF "TO BE" and "TO HAVE"

(● ●) LISTEN

Il signor Martini avrà un'ora di ritardo
* *Il signor Martini sarà in ritardo di un'ora*

Change the sentences as in the model.
Il signor Martini avrà un'ora di ritardo — Io avrò un'ora di ritardo — Loro avranno un'ora di ritardo — Tu avrai un'ora di ritardo — Noi avremo un'ora di ritardo — Beatrice avrà un'ora di ritardo — Voi avrete un'ora di ritardo —

(See Grammar, L. 8.)

7. PRONUNCIATION

(● ●) LISTEN AND REPEAT

Questo - qualcosa - quando - qualche - dunque - quasi - cinque - qui.

WHERE SHALL WE GO TO EAT?

Eating, to Italians, is much more than a biological necessity. It is a sort of ritual involving such factors as when a meal is eaten, what ingredients are used, and how much is prepared. And needless to say, Italians consider their cuisine second to none. They are also quite conservative with respect to what and how they eat. The idea of eating "on the run" is repugnant to most Italians, who, if at all possible, prefer to eat at home. There, they can partake in the ceremony of "il primo piatto" and "il secondo piatto," usually followed by "un dolce" (a pastry, piece of cake, etc.), and "la frutta." Wine and mineral water usually accompany the meal, and "una tazza di espresso" brings it to a dignified conclusion.

Invasion of the Fast-Food Franchises

But, as everywhere else in the world, tradition is being threatened by rapid changes. Witness the sprouting of fast-food eateries throughout the peninsula, especially in the larger cities. Places with names like "self-service" and "snack bar" have become serious contenders for the stomachs and wallets of many Italians. As a result, the traditional eating places are starting to feel threatened as never before.

A Taste for the Exotic

Recently, another trend has come forward to erode Italy's culinary rituals even further—the fad of "foreign" restaurants, especially Oriental ones. Eating Chinese or Japanese food has become a very common phenomenon in all the major Italian cities.

Just Like Mama Used to Make

But fear not! There are still plenty of places to get an authentic "Italian" meal. The choice is quite diverse: you can go to a "tavola calda," a type of self-service snack bar where you pay before eating or to a "trattoria," a small restaurant that offers traditional, simple home-style cooking (known as "la cucina casalinga") at modest prices. And of course there are the larger, more formal restaurants. In the country, you will find restaurants offering gastronomic delights at very affordable prices. These restaurants tend to specialize in dishes unique to their particular region.

When eating out, you may want to keep a few things in mind. Most eating places display their menus and price lists outside. And most will also have a "tourist" menu (which is meant to make eating out more affordable). Simply adjust your eating expectations before entering a restaurant, and you probably will manage to stay within your budget. If you still find that most eating-out places are beyond your means, then remember that grocery stores ("alimentari") have plenty of "convenience" foods (cold cuts, cheese, fresh bread, etc.) that can be bought at reasonable prices and eaten "in the park," so to speak. This is, in fact, what many tourists have started to do throughout Italy. The food is fresh, good, and affordable.

Italians take eating seriously. For this reason, whether you eat out or buy your food at a store, you simply cannot go wrong with the quality of the food. From a simple "tramezzino" (sandwich) to an elaborate meal, eating in Italy constitutes a truly satisfying "cultural experience."

N° 1 ⬤⬤ LISTEN

Complete the following sentences on the basis of the information you hear on the tape.

1. Il signore si chiama . . . .

2. Il numero del signor Rossi è . . . .

N° 2

What time is it?

Example: — È mezzogiorno (sono le dodici)   **1.** . . . .

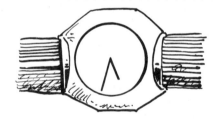

2. . . . .   **3.** . . . .

4. . . . .   **5.** . . . .

6. . . . .   **7.** . . . .

Read Mr. Rossi's daily calendar and then answer the questions that follow.

AGENDA

Lunedì. Ore 17 : *Andare dal dentista*

Martedì. Ore 10 : *Telefonare all' avvocato*

Mercoledì. Ore 18 : *Prenotare i biglietti per il Teatro*

Giovedì. Ore 15 : *accompagnare Sandra alla Stazione*

Venerdì. Ore 12 : *aprire il nuovo conto in Banca*

Sabato Ore 12 : *Prendere l'aperitivo con Mario e Franca*

Domenica Ore 17 : *richiamare Franca*

Che cosa farà il signor Rossi questa settimana?
Lunedì . . . .
Martedì . . . .
Mercoledì . . . .
Giovedì . . . .
Venerdì . . . .
Sabato . . . .
Domenica . . . .

PROVERBIO
●● LISTEN

Le ore del mattino hanno l'oro in bocca
(lit., Morning hours have gold in their mouths.)

To succeed you must always get an early start.

(See solutions on page 13 of the booklet.)

● ● ▶ LISTEN

TRATTORIA TRASTEVERE

Menù

Primi piatti
Tagliatelle alla boscaiola
Spaghetti alla carbonara
Penne all'arrabbiata
Lasagne al forno

Secondi piatti
Filetto di vitello ai ferri
Scaloppine al marsala
Pollo alla cacciatora
Sogliola alla mugnaia
Fritto misto

Contorni
Patatine fritte
Spinaci al burro
Insalata mista
Funghi trifolati

Formaggi
Gorgonzola
Mozzarella
Pecorino

Dolci
Tiramisù
Torta di fragole
Cassata siciliana

François Moreau and Andrea Martini are having dinner at a typical Roman restaurant in the Trastevere district.

Andrea : *Ci può portare il menù, per favore?*

Cameriere : *Subito, eccolo.*

Andrea : *Grazie.*

François : *Ho una fame da lupi, e tu?*

AT THE RESTAURANT

Andrea : *Anch'io ho un certo appetito, e in questo ristorante, vedrai, si mangia benissimo. Vediamo un po' che cosa c'è di buono.*

François : *Che cosa prendi di primo?*

Andrea : *Non lo so ancora : sono indeciso tra le tagliatelle alla boscaiola e le penne all'arrabbiata.*

François : *Come sono le tagliatelle alla boscaiola?*

Andrea : *Buonissime! Con la panna, i funghi e i piselli.*

François : *Ah no, i funghi non mi piacciono molto, preferisco prendere le lasagne.*

Andrea : *Io invece credo proprio che prenderò le tagliatelle.*

François : *E di secondo, prendiamo carne o pesce?*

Andrea : *Io prendo la carne, sicuramente : il pesce non mi piace, però se a te piace qui lo fanno benissimo.*

François : *Allora quasi quasi prendo una sogliola con contorno di insalata mista.*

Andrea : *E io un filetto al sangue con contorno di spinaci. E da bere, che cosa preferisci?*

François : *Vino, naturalmente! Il rosato ti piace?*

Andrea : *Sì, mi piace, allora ordiniamo una bottiglia di rosato e mezza minerale.*

● ● ▶ LISTEN AND REPEAT
You will find the translation on p. 14 of the booklet.

1. A typical restaurant
2. A hotel sign
3. Assortment of cold cuts and wines
4. A plate of "gnocchi" (dumplings)
5. Spaghetti in fish sauce
and a carafe of white
Roman wine

NOUNS

il ristorante — restaurant
il menú — menu (1)
la fame — hunger
l'appetito — appetite
il primo — first serving/dish
la panna — cream
il fungo — mushroom
i piselli — peas
il secondo — second serving/dish
la carne — meat
il pesce — fish
la sogliola — sole
il contorno — side order/dish
l'insalata — salad
il filetto — filet
il sangue — blood
gli spinaci — spinach
il vino (rosso, bianco, rosato) — wine
(red, white, rosé)
l'acqua minerale — mineral water (2)
il forno — oven
il vitello — veal
la scaloppina — scallop
il pollo — chicken
il fritto misto — fried fish
le patatine fritte — French fries
il formaggio — cheese
il dolce — sweet, dessert
la torta di fragole — strawberry cake

la bottiglia — bottle
la sete — thirst
il conto — bill/check
la mancia — tip
la pasta — pasta/pastry
la minestra — soup
la verdura — vegetables
la frutta — fruit
la carne (di vitello, di manzo, di
maiale) — meat (veal, beef, pork)

la bistecca — steak
il pomodoro — tomato
la cottura — cooked (e.g., well-cooked)
ben cotto — well-cooked
arrosto — roast
fritto — fried
il condimento — dressing
il sale — salt
il pepe — pepper
l'olio — oil
l'aceto — vinegar
la senape — mustard (3)

VERBS

portare — to bring
prendere — to take/have
piacere — to like (4)
credere — to believe
ordinare — to order
essere indesciso — to be undecided
avere una fame da lupi — to be as
hungry as a bear
avere un certo appetito — to be rather
hungry
si mangia benissimo — the food is great,
(lit., One eats well.)

pagare — to pay
scegliere — to choose

ADVERBS

proprio — really
sicuramente — surely
quasi quasi — nearly (5)
naturalmente — naturally
mezzo — half

HOW TO SAY IT

1. ASKING FOR THE MENU

Ci può portare il menù, per favore? — Can you bring us the menu, please?
Mi porta il menù, per cortesia? — Can you bring me the menu, please?

2. WHAT DISHES DO YOU HAVE?

Che cosa c'è di buono? — What's good?
Che cosa c'è di primo? — What do you have as a first dish?
Che cosa c'è di secondo? — What do you have as a second dish?
Che dolci avete? — What sweets do you have?
Che cos'è il piatto del giorno? — What's the day's special?

3. ASKING WHAT OR HOW SOMETHING IS

Che cos'è la sogliola? — What is sole?
Che cosa sono le tagliatelle alla boscaiola? — What are "tagliatelle alla boscaiola"?
Com'è la sogliola? — How's the sole?
Come sono le tagliatelle alla boscaiola? — How are the "tagliatelle alla boscaiola"?

4. EXPRESSING YOUR LIKES/DISLIKES

È buonissimo! — It's really good!
È squisito! — It's delicious!
È cattivo! — It's awful!
Mi piace molto — I like it a lot!
Non mi piace affatto — I don't like it at all!

5. BEING UNDECIDED

Sono indeciso tra la carne e il pesce — I haven't decided between meat and fish.
Quasi quasi prendo una sogliola — I think I'll have sole.

| *REMARKS...* | *REMARKS...* | *REMARKS...* | *REMARKS...* |

(1) Menus in Italy are generally a la carte. There are only a few specialized ones, such as tourist menus. — (2) When you order mineral water you will normally get the carbonated type. To get uncarbonated water, you will have to specify it: "acqua minerale naturale." — (3) Mustard is not a typical Italian condiment. You will have to order it specially. — (4) "Piacere" actually means "to be pleasing to." — (5) lack of certainty is expressed by the repeated form.

1. INDIRECT OBJECT PRONOUNS

MI, TI, GLI, LE, CI, VI, GLI

(• •) LISTEN

La cameriera porta il menù
Al sig. Rossi • *Gli porta il menù*
Alla sig.ra Rossi • *Le porta il menù*

Using pronouns, say to whom the waiter brings the menu.
Al sig. Rossi — Alla sig.ra Rossi — A noi — A me — A te — A voi — A Franco — A Maria — A Roberto e Marco — A Carlo e Gianna — A Franco e Marina — A lui.

(See Grammar, E. 1.)

2. THE VERB "PIACERE"

(• •) LISTEN

La carne • *Mi piace molto la carne*
Le tagliatelle • *Mi piacciono molto le tagliatelle*

Make "piacere" singular or plural as in the model.
La carne — Le tagliatelle — Il pesce — Le lasagne — Il vino rosso — La sogliola — Gli spinaci — I piselli — La pizza — I funghi — L'insalata — Le penne all'arrabbiata.

3. SAYING WHAT THERE IS

(• •) LISTEN

Che cosa c'è di buono?
L'arrosto di vitello • *C'è l'arrosto di vitello*
Le lasagne • *Ci sono le lasagne*

Continue as in the model.
L'arrosto di vitello — Le lasagne — Le tagliatelle alla boscaiola — La sogliola — La minestra di verdura — I funghi fritti — Gli spaghetti al pomodoro — Le patate fritte — Il filetto al pepe — Gli spinaci.

(See Grammar, L. 1.)

4. SUPERLATIVE ADJECTIVES

(• •) LISTEN

Il pesce è molto buono
• *Sì, è buonissimo*
La carne è molto buona
• *Sì, è buonissima*
Gli spaghetti sono molto buoni
• *Sì, sono buonissimi*
Le lasagne sono molto buone
• *Sì, sono buonissime*

Answer as in the model.
Il pesce è molto buono — La carne è molto buona — Gli spaghetti sono molto buoni — Le lasagne sono molto buone — I piselli sono molto buoni — Il filetto è molto buono — La pizza è molto buona — Il dolce è molto buono — La minestra è molto buona — Le tagliatelle sono molto buone — Il vino è molto buono.

(See Grammar, H. 2.)

5. WHAT IS THERE TO EAT?

(• •) LISTEN

Il primo • *Che cosa c'è di primo?*
Il formaggio • *Che cosa c'è di formaggio?*

Ask the appropriate questions as in the model.
Il primo — Il formaggio — Il secondo — L'antipasto — Il contorno — La frutta — Il dolce.

6. VERBS ENDING IN -*GARE*: PAGARE

(• •) LISTEN

Pagare il conto (io) • *Pago il conto.*
(tu) • *Paghi il conto.*

Continue conjugating, as in the model.
io — tu — noi — il sig. Moreau — Franco e Mario — voi — Lei — io — la sig.ra Rossi — noi — tu — lui — voi.

(See Grammar, L. 6.)

7. PRONUCIATION

(• •) LISTEN AND REPEAT

Menù - città - caffè - nazionalità - società pero - prenderò - perché - cioè - può.

LET'S HAVE PASTA!

So, you've been invited to dinner! Attention! In Italy you had better not be late—for two very good reasons. First, remember that most Italians do not have a big breakfast in the North American style. As a result, by the time lunch or dinnertime rolls around, you might find yourself among some very hungry people who will not take kindly to a delay in their meal. The second reason is that mealtimes adhere to a fairly strict schedule because of their major component—"la pastasciutta" (pasta).

Get Ready for Pasta!

The word "pastasciutta" actually means dry pasta. This distinguishes it from "la pasta in brodo" (in broth), which you find in soups. Minestrone, for example, is full of short or small pasta made especially for soups, and is so thick that you can almost set your spoon straight up in it. Well-known examples of "pastasciutta" are spaghetti, ravioli, lasagne, fettucine, tortellini, and tagliatelle (which means "noodles").

Pasta has to be cooked for just the right amount of time. If it's overcooked, then it tastes like mush. Italians like their pasta "al dente," that is, fairly firm. So when someone announces "a tavola!" (to the table!), be ready to go to your place and take part in a delicious meal.

Now, for the Rest of the Meal

But pasta is only the "primo piatto" of a complete Italian meal. It is preceded by an "antipasto" like "prosciutto e melone" and followed by a "secondo piatto" of meat or fish, with "contorni" of vegetables or salad. The meal is completed by fruit or "una dolce" (something sweet) and of course "una tazza di cafè."

Italian cuisine is richly varied, offering all sorts of meats and vegetables as well as cheeses, cold cuts, fish, and seafood. Just to give you an idea of what you might come across, there is "carpaccio," consisting of very thin slices of raw beef served with a wedge of lemon; "melanzane alla parmigiana" (eggplant with parmesan cheese); and lightly fried mixed vegetables ("fritto misto") or seafood ("scampi fritti"). No matter what your preference, you'll always find something to please your palate.

One more thing: the idea of a first course, then a second, and perhaps even a third draws one to the conclusion that Italians eat quite a bit. But despite the tons of pasta consumed yearly by the Italian population, Italians generally are not overweight. In fact, recent theories about diet defend the eating of pasta as part of a very healthful "Mediterranean" diet—along with olive oil, lean meat, and fresh vegetables.

How could anyone resist the temptations of Italian food? No wonder it has become one of the symbols of Italian know-how and finesse.

Indicate on the menu the dishes chosen by the two people.

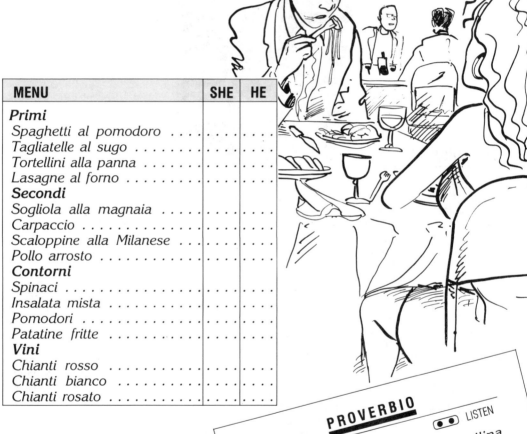

MENU	SHE	HE
Primi		
Spaghetti al pomodoro		
Tagliatelle al sugo		
Tortellini alla panna		
Lasagne al forno		
Secondi		
Sogliola alla magnaia		
Carpaccio		
Scaloppine alla Milanese		
Pollo arrosto		
Contorni		
Spinaci		
Insalata mista		
Pomodori		
Patatine fritte		
Vini		
Chianti rosso		
Chianti bianco		
Chianti rosato		

PROVERBIO
●● LISTEN

Meglio un uovo oggi che una gallina domani
(lit., Better an egg today than a chicken tomorrow).
A bird in the hand is worth two in the bush.

Match each object to its name and put the corresponding number in the box.

COLTELLO ☐	FORCHETTA ☐	CUCCHIAIO ☐
CUCCHIAINO ☐	BOTTIGLIA ☐	BICCHIERE ☐
PIATTO ☐	TOVAGLIOLO ☐	TOVAGLIA ☐

SEDIA ☐

PANE ☐

FRUTTA ☐

SALE ☐

PEPE ☐

MENÙ ☐

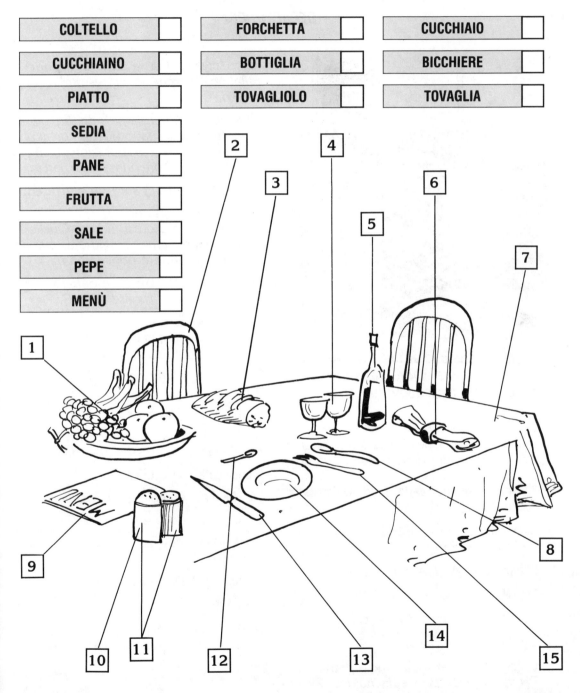

(See solutions on page 15 of the booklet.)

DEPARTURE!

Mr. Moreau is at the Termini train station in Rome where he is buying a ticket to get back home to Paris.

L'altoparlante : *L'espresso 712 proveniente da Perugia per Napoli è in arrivo al binario 18. Carrozze di prima classe in coda.*

Allo sportello della biglietteria della stazione

Sig. Moreau : *Buongiorno, vorrei un biglietto per Parigi.*

L'impiegata : *Andata e ritorno?*

Sig. Moreau : *No, sola andata.*

L'impiegata : *Di prima o di seconda classe?*

Sig. Moreau : *Di prima.*

L'impiegata : *Che treno vuole prendere? Perché lo sa che per il Palatino deve avere la prenotazione del vagone letto?*

Sig. Moreau : *Ma a che ora parte il Palatino? Perché io vorrei partire oggi stesso.*

L'impiegata : *Guardi, se non ha già la prenotazione del vagone letto non lo può prendere oggi. La prenotazione bisogna farla almeno 12 ore prima della partenza.*

Sig. Moreau : *Ma ci sarà un altro treno!*

L'impiegata : *Certamente! C'è il Napoli Express che parte tra un'ora. Quello lo può prendere perché la prenotazione del vagone letto non è obbligatoria.*

Sig. Moreau : *Ah! Benissimo. Però, corro il rischio di non trovare posto?*

L'impiegata : *Eh sì, dipende un po' dal periodo, ma in genere in prima classe si trova.*

Sig. Moreau : *Comunque a che ora arriva a Parigi?*

L'impiegata : *Alle 8 della mattina.*

Sig. Moreau : *Ma sì, mi faccia il biglietto per il Napoli Express. Quanto costa?*

L'impiegata : *190.000 lire.*

Sig. Moreau : *Eccole 200.000 lire.*

L'impiegata : *Ecco a Lei 10.000 di resto.*

Sig. Moreau : *Mi scusi, da che binario parte il treno?*

L'impiegata : *Dal binario 11.*

Sig. Moreau : *La ringrazio.*

●● LISTEN AND REPEAT
You will find the translation on page 15 of the booklet.

1. Trinità dei Monti (Rome)
2. The gardens of the Palazzo Farnese
3. Piazza Navona

3

NOUNS

la partenza — departure
l'altoparlante (m) — loudspeaker
l'espresso — express train
l'arrivo — arrival
il binario — track
la carozza — car (train)
la classe — class
la coda — line
la biglietteria — ticket counter
l'andata — "going" (ticket)
il ritorno — return (ticket)
il treno — train
il vagone — carriage/train car
il vagone letto — sleeper car
il posto da sedere — place to sit
il periodo — period
il resto — change (money)

---

la stazione — station
la coincidenza — (train) connection
la cuccetta — berth
ul vagone ristorante — restaurant car
il diretto — direct train
il rapido — rapid train
il locale — local train
il viaggiatore — traveler

VERBS

partire — to leave, depart
correre il rischio di — to run the risk of
dipendere (da) — to depend on
fare il biglietto — to purchase a ticket

MISCELLANEOUS

costare — to cost
oggi stesso — this very day
almeno — at least
in genere — in general
comunque — however
prenotazione obbligatoria — required reservation

HOW TO SAY IT

---

1. BUYING A TRAIN TICKET

Vorrei un biglietto di andata e ritorno per Roma — I'd like a round-trip ticket for Rome.
Vorrei prenotare una cuccetta sul treno per Parigi — I'd like to reserve a sleeping berth on the Paris train.
Vorrei un biglietto di seconda classe solo andata per Vienna — I'd like only a second-class one-way ticket for Vienna.

---

2. ASKING WHICH TRACK THE TRAIN IS LEAVING FROM

Scusi, da quale binario parte il treno per Parigi? — Excuse me. From what track is the train for Paris leaving?

---

3. ARRIVALS

A che ora arriva a Parigi? — At what time is it arriving in Paris?
A che stazione arriva il treno? — In what station is the train arriving?

---

4. KINDS OF TRAINS

È un treno diretto? — Is it a direct train?
Bisogna cambiare? — Is it necessary to change?
C'è la coincidenza? — Is there a connection?
È un locale? — Is it a local train?
È un espresso? — Is it an express train?
È un rapido? — Is it a rapid train?

---

5. ASKING HOW MUCH IT COSTS

Quanto costa? — How much does it cost?
Quanto costa la prenotazione? — How much does a reservation cost?
Quanto costano i biglietti? — How much are the tickets?
Quanto costa il supplemento rapido? — How much is the difference for a ticket for the rapid train?

---

6. MORE QUESTIONS ABOUT TRAINS

Quanti treni ci sono per Parigi? — How many trains for Paris are there?
C'è solo un treno diretto al giorno? — Is there only one direct train per day?
A che ora è il prossimo treno per Londra? — At what time is the next train for London?

---

1. BUYING A TRAIN TICKET

(• •) LISTEN

Andata e ritorno - Parigi
* *Vorrei un biglietto di andata e ritorno per Parigi*

Buy the following kinds of tickets.
Andata e ritorno (Parigi) — Solo andata (Milano) — Prima classe (Monaco) — Seconda classe (Bologna) — Andata e ritorno (Bruxelles) — Solo andata (Roma).

(See Grammar, F.)

2. ASKING HOW MUCH IT COSTS

(• •) LISTEN

Il vagone letto
* *Quanto costa il vagone letto?*
I biglietti
* *Quanto costano i biglietti?*

Continue asking how much things cost.
Il vagone letto — I biglietti — La prenotazione — La prima classe — Le cuccette — La seconda classe — Il taxi — Gli alberghi — Le sigarette — Una birra — Due caffè.

(See Grammar, G. 2)

3. FROM WHICH TRACK . . . ?

(• •) LISTEN

Da che binario parte il treno per Parigi? (11)
* *Il treno per Parigi parte dal binario 11*

Continue answering in this way.
Da che binario parte il treno per Parigi? (11) — Da che binario parte il treno per Londra? (8) — Da che binario parte il treno per Roma? (3) — Da che binario parte il treno per Bologna? (6) — Da che binario parte il treno per Venezia? (4)

(See Grammar, F.)

4. MAKING RESERVATIONS

(• •) LISTEN

Vagone letto/1ª classe/Parigi
* *Vorrei prenotare un vagone letto in 1ª classe per Parigi*

Continue making reservations as in the model.
Vagone letto/1ª classe/Parigi — Due cuccette/2ª classe/Roma — Un posto/2ª classe/Venezia — Una cuccetta/2ª classe/Londra — Un posto/1ª classe/Milano.

5. THE VERB "DIPENDERE (DA)"

(• •) LISTEN

Il periodo • *Dipende dal periodo*
La gente • *Dipende dalla gente*
I ragazzi • *Dipende dai ragazzi*
Le situazioni • *Dipende dalle situazioni*

Continue, as in the model, using the appropriate form of the preposition "da."
Il periodo — La gente — I ragazzi — Le situazioni — Il tempo — La sig.ra Rossi — Il momento — I treni — L'orario — Il ristorante — Le persone — L'ora.

(See Grammar, F.)

6. THE PRONOUN CI (= "THERE")

(• •) LISTEN

Andiamo alla stazione?
* *Sì, ci andiamo*

Answer, using the pronoun "ci."
Andiamo alla stazione? — Andiamo al ristorante? — Arriviamo a Parigi? — Restiamo in albergo? — Siamo al capolinea? — Ritorniamo alla biglietteria? — Restiamo a Roma?

(See Grammar, E. 2.)

7. PRONUNCIATION

(• •) LISTEN AND REPEAT

Periodo — binario — vorrei — paretenza — obbligatorio — prima — un altro treno — corro il rischio.

YOUR ATTENTION, PLEASE, THE TRAIN IS ABOUT TO LEAVE

Italian trains, which once were notorious for never being on time, have generally become dependable. Most of the better-known routes are now extremely reliable—though some continue to have terrible reputations. The famous Napoli Express, which connects Paris and Naples is one of the worst. In either direction, it frequently runs an hour or so late. So when traveling by train in Italy, be prepared for possible delays, especially if you have a connection to make.

It must be noted that, to compensate for these delays, the Italian railway system has one of the lowest fare schedules anywhere in the world. And special prices are given for round-trip excursions and other types of tickets.

The local trains—especially with names like "diretti," "direttisimi," and "espressi"–can be disappointingly slow. The InterCity lines, which are the most efficient and punctual, are indeed the most expensive. Getting somewhere quickly and on time is rather a luxury that you have to pay for.

All Aboard!

Yet despite these annoyances, taking a trip by train in Italy can be a most pleasant and unforgettable experience. Take, for example, the Paris–Venice line. If you take the night train, you are awakened in the morning by the sound of a hand-rung bell and the irresistible aroma of Italian coffee. Imagine having coffee and a pastry in the dining car or in your own seat as the train zips by cities like Verona, the home of Romeo and Juliet; Vicenza, known for the great Renaissance architect Palladio; and then Padua, which evokes such names as Giotto, Donatello (both created masterpieces there), and Saint Anthony's basilica. If you decide to stop in Mestre, the mainland station for Venice, then you can take a ferry down the Grand Canal. Nowhere else is this possible. Was it a dream? No, just another example of the wondrous possibilities when traveling by train in Italy.

Traveling "all'italiana"

Another important thing to keep in mind about the Italian railway system is that you can catch a train to almost anywhere, including out-of-the-way places and resorts. Another factor in favor of travel by train is that railway stations are also excellent places for shopping, eating, and just "browsing around." These stations are located, generally, in the heart of a city and are therefore conveniently placed for the tourist staying downtown.

If you can, take the train in Italy. If you do so, you will be taking part in a cultural tradition. The train has always been the transportation means that the Italians themselves have used to get around. Even in this day of the almighty automobile, the train stations are jammed with people traveling "all'italiana" and enjoying a more relaxed pace.

TAKE-A-BREAK

⊙⊙ LISTEN

Tintarella di luna

(B. de Filippi - F. Migliacci)
Sung by Mina
© *With permission of Edizioni Musicali/Edizoni Curci*

Moon-tanned Girl

Abbronzate, tutte chiazze	Tanned, full of spots
Pellirosse un po'paonazze	Red-skinned and a bit purplish
Son le ragazze che prendono il sol	Are the girls who get the sun
Ma ce n'è una	But there is one
Che prende la luna	Who "gets the moon"
Ritornello	Refrain
Tintarella di luna	Moon-tanned girl
Tintarella color latte	Milk-tanned girl
Tutta notte sopra al tetto	All night on top of the roof
Sopra al tetto come i gatti	On the roof like a cat
E se c'è la luna piena	And if the moon is full
Tu diventi candida	You become white
Tintarella di luna	Moon-tanned girl
Tintarella color latte	Milk-tanned girl
Che fa bianca la tua pelle	(The moon) makes your skin white
Ti fa ella tra le belle	And makes you beautiful among the beautiful
E se c'è la luna piena	And if the moon is full
Tu diventi candida	You become white.
Tin, tin, tin	Tin, tin, tin
Raggi di luna	Moon rays
Tin, tin, tin	Tin, tin, tin
baciano te	They kiss you
Al mondo nessuna è candida come te	No one in the world is as white as you
Tintarella di luna	Moon-tanned girl
Tintarella color latte	Milk-tanned girl
Tutta notte sopra al tetto	All night on top of the roof
Sopra al tetto come i gatti	On the roof like a cat
E se c'è la luna piena } ter	And if the moon is full
Tu diventi candida	You become white.

"FIGURES" OF SPEECH

AVERE UN DIAVOLO PER CAPELLO
(lit., to have a devil on every hair)
To be in a foul mood

ESSERE ALL'OSCURO DI TUTTO
To be in the dark about everything

SPUTARE IL ROSPO
(lit., to spit out a toad)
To give someone a piece of your mind

AVERE UNO CERVELLO DA GALLINA
(lit., to have the brain of a chicken)
To be really dumb

2.1

WRITE OUT IN LETTERS : *1.000, 2.000, 1.560, 730, 2.820, 14.000, 21.700, 100.000, 1.000.000*
. . . .
. . . .

TRANSLATE : *Attenda un attimo, per cortesia! — Si accomodi alla cassa. — Ci vuole il libretto degli assegni.*
I'd like to know what the exchange rate for the Italian lira is. — I'd like to exchange 5000 francs. — Do you accept an international credit card? — I thank you, sir.

2.2

COMPLETE WITH lo, la, li, le : *Mario Rossi, ... conosco bene. — Il caffè, ... prendo ristretto. — La fontana di Trevi, ... vedo domani. — I biglietti, ... compro dal tabaccaio. — Le informazioni, ... domando a un passante. — La città, ... visito oggi. — I soldi, ... cambio in banca.*

TRANSLATE : *Ritorni indietro. — Scenda al capolinea. — Domandi a un passante. — Aspetti un momento!*
Turn right! — Take bus number 53. — Go straight ahead. — Cross the square. — Go through the lights.

2.3

PUT EACH INFINITIVE INTO ITS APPROPRIATE FORM :

Io (domandare) . . . . la direzione. — Lui (prendere) . . . . l'appuntamento. — Noi (dormire) . . . . all'hotel. — Tu (andare) . . . . a Roma. — Voi (avere) . . . . molto tempo. — Loro (essere) . . . . in ritardo. — Io non (potere) . . . . venire. — Voi (dovere) . . . . cenare con noi.

TRANSLATE : *Pronto chi parla? — Posso lasciar detto qualcosa? — Gli dica di richiamarmi fra un'ora.*
I'd like to speak with Mr. Moreau. — Hello, Robert. Hi, it's me. — I'm sorry. The director isn't here today.

2.4

REPLACE EACH PHRASE IN PARENTHESES WITH ONE OF (mi, ti, gli, le, Le, ci, vi, gli) :

Io . . . . telefono (a Roberto). — Lui . . . . parla (a me). — L'ingegner Rossi . . . . prenota le camere (a voi). — Il signor Marchi . . . . . . domanda un'informazione (all'impiegata). — Signora, ... posso offrire un caffè? (a Lei). — Signor Bauer, ... posso offrire un caffè? (a Lei). — Il cameriere . . . . porta il menù (a loro). — Per cortesia, ... porta il menù? (a noi).

TRANSLATE : *Di contorno ci sono gli spinaci. — A Roma ci sono molti ristoranti caratteristici. — Come pesce c'è la sogliola.*
First, there's spinach. — For the second dish there's roast veal. — Today, there are mushrooms. — To drink there's red wine and white wine.

2.5

PUT EACH INFINITIVE INTO ITS APPROPRIATE FORM : *Il signor*
Rossi (pagare) . . . . . . con un biglietto da 100.000 lire. — Tu (cercare) . . . . . . la stazione. — Noi (pagare) . . . . con un assegno. — Voi (cercare) . . . . una segretaria bilingue. — Io (pagare) . . . . il conto dell'albergo. — Loro (cercare) . . . . un albergo vicino alla stazione. — Che cosa (tu-cercare) . . . . ?

TRANSLATE : *È possibile prenotare una cuccetta? — Quanto costa il vagone letto? — A che ora arriva a Roma?*
A round-trip ticket for Rome. — From which track is the train departing? — I'd like a first-class ticket. — The connection is in Turin.

BEVERAGES

acquavite — brandy
alcoolici — alcoholic drinks
amaro — bitter
analcoolici — nonalcoholic drinks
bevande — drinks
cognac — cognac
digestivo — digestive
gassosa — sparkling
gin — gin
grappa — "grappa"
liquore — liqueur
moscato — muscatel
spremuta d'arancia — orange juice
spremuta di limone — lemon juices
spumante — sparkling wine
succo di frutta — fruit juice
succo di pomodoro — tomato juice
vodka — vodka
whiskey — whiskey

FOODS

albicocca — apricot
ananas — pineapple
anguria — watermelon
banana — banana
cibo — food
ciliegia — cherry
fico — fig
fragola — strawberry
lampone — raspberry
mandarino — mandarin orange
mela — apple
melone — melon
mirtillo — blueberry
mora — blackberry
pera — pear
pesca — peach
prugna — prune
ribes — currant
uva — grapes
verdura — vegetables
aglio — garlic
basilico — basil
carciofo — artichoke
carota — carrot
cavolo — cabbage
cece — chick pea

cipolla — onion
fagiolino — string bean
fagiolo — bean
finocchio — fennel
lenticchia — lentil
melanzana — eggplant
menta — mint
peperone — pepperoni
porro — leek
prezzemolo — parsley
zucchino — zucchini
cacciagione — game
capriolo — deer
cinghiale — wild boar
fagiano — pheasant
lepre — jack rabbit
pernice — partridge
quaglia — quail
animali da allevamento — farm animals
anatra — duck
bue (m, plur.: buoi) — ox, oxen
capra — goat
cavallo — horse
coniglio — rabbit
gallina — chicken
maiale — pig
mucca — cow
oca — goose
pecora — sheep
pollo — fowl
toro — bull
pesce — fish
acciuga — anchovy
anguilla — eel
carpa — carp
luccio — pike
merluzzo — cod
nasello — hake
pescespada — swordfish
salmone — salmon
sardina — sardine
tinca — tench [fish]
tonno — tuna
frutti di mare — seafood
aragosta — lobster
gamberetto — small shrimp
gambero — shrimp
granchio — crab
muscolo — red meat
ostrica — ostrich
scampo — prawn
vongola — clam

molluschi — mollusks
calamaro — squid
polpo — octopus
seppia — cuttlefish
la tavola — table
bicchiere — drinking glass
coltello — knife
cucchiaino — small spoon
cucchiaio — spoon
forchetta — fork
piatto — plate
posate — tableware
tovaglia — tablecloth
tovagliolo — napkin

COLD CUTS

prosciutto — ham (*crudo*—uncooked, *cotto*—cooked)
salame — salami
pancetta — bacon
pancetta affumicata — smoked bacon
lardo — lard

WEIGHTS

grammo — gram
etto — hectogram
mezzo etto — half a hectogram
due etti — two hectograms
mezzo chilo — half a kilogram
un chilo — kilogram
due chili — two kilograms
un litro — a liter
mezzo litro — half a liter
quintale — 100 kilograms
tonnellata — ton

EATING OUT

ristorante — restaurant
trattoria — restaurant (less formal)
tavola calda — snack bar
pizzeria — pizza parlor
self-service — cafeteria
paninoteca — sandwich shop
birreria — beer house
bar — espresso bar
mensa aziendale — company cafeteria
mensa studentesca — school cafeteria

1. REPLACE EACH PHRASE WITH THE APPROPRIATE OBJECT PRONOUN

(A Paolo) . . . . *telefono alle 5.*

(Il documento) . . . . *restituisco domani.*

(I franchi) . . . . *cambierò in banca.*

(La prenotazione) . . . . *faccio subito.*

(Alla segretaria) . . . . *lascio il mio numero di telefono.*

(A noi) . . . . *piace il caffè ristretto.*

(Le tagliatelle) . . . . *mangio volentieri.*

(Ai corsisti) . . . . *do l'appuntamento alle 10.*

2. USE EITHER "TRA" OR "FA" ACCORDING TO THE MEANING

Sono arrivato a Milano due giorni . . . .

Il treno per Roma partirà . . . . *un'ora.*

Ho telefonato a Carlo 10 minuti . . . .

Gli ritelefonerò . . . . *10 minuti.*

Ho prenotato le camere una settimana . . . .

Andrò a Roma . . . . *un anno.*

Mi sono sposato 10 anni . . . .

Il signor Marchi arriverà . . . . *un attimo.*

3. GIVE THE OPPOSITE (ANTONYM) OF EACH WORD

sempre	*bello* . . . .
simpatico	*facile* . . . .
il primo	*buono* . . . .
grande	*lontano* . . . .
caldo	*forte* . . . .
l'andata	*davanti* . . . .

4. WHAT WOULD YOU SAY IF YOU . . .

wanted to exchange 100 marks in a bank . . . .
wanted to know how much time it took to get to the train station . . . .
wanted to know the time . . . .
wanted the waiter to give you a menu . . . .
wanted to know how much a ticket costs . . . .
wanted to tell someone "he's not in" . . . .

5. ONLY ONE ANSWER IN EACH SET IS CORRECT. CAN YOU FIND IT?

A. Per aprire un conto bisogna un documento . . . . ☐
B. Per aprire un conto ci vuole un documento . . . . ☐
C. Per aprire un conto ci vuole avere un documento . . . . ☐

A. Vado a comprare il biglietto . . . . ☐
B. Vado comprare il biglietto . . . . ☐
C. Vado da comprare il biglietto . . . . ☐

A. Le lasagne mi piace molto . . . . ☐
B. Le lasagne me piace molto . . . . ☐
C. Le lasagne mi piacciono molto . . . . ☐

A. Quanto costa le cuccette? . . . . ☐
B. Quanto costano le cuccette? . . . . ☐
C. Quante costano le cuccette? . . . . ☐

6. MATCH EACH QUESTION TO ITS ANSWER

A. Al capolinea.
B. Due giorni fa.
C. Vino, naturalmente!
D. Di niente!
E. Eccolo!

1. Da bere, che cosa preferisci?
2. Ha il passaporto?
3. A che fermata devo scendere?
4. Grazie mille!
5. Quando sei arrivato?

(Check your answers on page 37 of the booklet.)

IN THE MOUTH OF THE WOLF

Hardly had Mrs. Aiguement turned on her heel when Lucy came breathlessly into the office. "Ambrogio, avresti dovuto vederla quando è arrivata; sembrava fuori di testa. Cosa ti ha chiesto quella pazza?"

—Mah... Non me lo sarei immaginato. Voleva l'opzione su In bocca al lupo. Sai, la solita cosettina sulla mafia."

Lucy burst out laughing. "Ti tocca leggerlo, allora."

Ambrose groaned; he collapsed over his desk moaning and hid his face in his hands. "No, dai, Lucia! Per carità. Fammi un favore. Leggilo tu. Così mi fai un riassunto."

Lucy made a face. "Nemmeno per sogno," she replied. "Lo sai che sono impegnatissima. Poi basta darci un'occhiata, no?"

—Portamelo, almeno, se sei ancora la mia assistente."

He had regained the superior tone of an executive conscious of his responsibilities, respectful of the differences of the hierarchy. Lucy darted a murderous glance at him; "Così sei ancora più insopportabile."

"You're never satisfied."

"No! And as for your résumé, you can do it yourself. It's enough that I'm nice enough to look for the book for you."

She went out, slamming the door. Ambrose smiled. All things considered, these little multilingual blowups didn't make him unhappy. The Italian language certainly provided more room for pantomime and emoting!

Lucy returned and threw on his desk a book whose title stood out in red blood against a yellow background.

"Have fun," she said, sticking out her tongue.

Ambrose chuckled reading the name of the author: ANONYMOUS. It couldn't be otherwise when it concerned the onorata società. The anonymous author was presented as a famous journalist who had been willing to lend his pen—and only his pen—to put together the confessions of a certain Mr. S.—as in sicario—a professional killer on the verge of retirement. He wanted to reveal what he knew about a certain number of affairs that had made the news in Italy as well as all over the world. Mr. S. prided himself on having no connection of any kind with the Mafia. He had worked freelance all his life, refusing to submit to the laws of an organization as he preferred the marketplace. This had allowed him to place a high price on his services. He boasted moreover of such efficiency and speed that he rarely suffered from competition.

Mr. S.'s customers were, according to him, essentially men of politics and finance—a prestigious clientele that didn't object to paying a high price on the spot as soon as they knew they could rely totally on his professionalism. As for his clients, Mr. S. never tired of praising them: people who were discreet, extremely proper, never lacking in the smallest gesture, polite but never obsequious. In all his life only one of his clients had failed to pay him. This client, Mr. S. assured his readers, was the first to regret it. His profession was thankless and the competition was often disloyal; he couldn't allow unpleasant rumors to be spread about him—for example, that he let himself be fleeced without caring about it.

But in every respect Mr. S.'s life was irreproachable. Devoted to his work, that he practiced like a priesthood, a vocation, he hadn't hesitated to adopt a life of virtual asceticism in order to do a job of which he was proud. In this brilliant career he only regretted one thing: the secrecy to which he was obliged to submit. A man of culture, he was perfectly aware of the historical interest of certain of the affairs he had to deal with. But, as a practical man, he kept quiet. Sometimes he had the feeling that he was the hand of justice, the instrument of destiny or of a supreme order, only accomplishing on earth what had been predestined for all time. Such an idea had its seduction, but he still had a feeling of such acute frustration that he decided to take his pen in hand—or rather, that of another—in order to pass on to posterity several stories that he judged edifying.

Reading this, Ambrose couldn't help smiling. He recognized the house style of Magagnati: blood and sensationalism. And, definitely, hot air. That Aiguement went for it didn't surprise him; it was reassuring to see that she, like everyone else, put herself in the mouth of the wolf.

That same evening, Ambrose had hardly had time to hang up his coat, get his briefcase out, open it and take out, among other papers, the volume of Anonymous when the telephone rang. Certainly, he could pretend not to have come in, or to have already gone out again—wasn't it already after eight? Didn't he have a right to a private life, too? But a sense of duty always propelled him.

Through the bay window in the living room he saw snow falling in big flakes on the balcony. It made a carpet that was getting thicker and thicker and beginning to muffle the outside noises. The street lights were enough to light the room. He picked up the phone.

"Pronto, Ambrogio?"

It was the unknown voice of the evening before, still as disagreeable. Ambrose didn't bother to answer; he simply put his hand over the mouthpiece.

"Lo so che sei tu," the voice began again. "Dammi retta. Ti sei messo in bocca al lupo."

Ambrose started. "Un momento. Chi parla?"

He shouted in vain; the man had hung up. This time no noise could be heard on the line; the speaker had seemed terribly close.

CONTINUED . . .

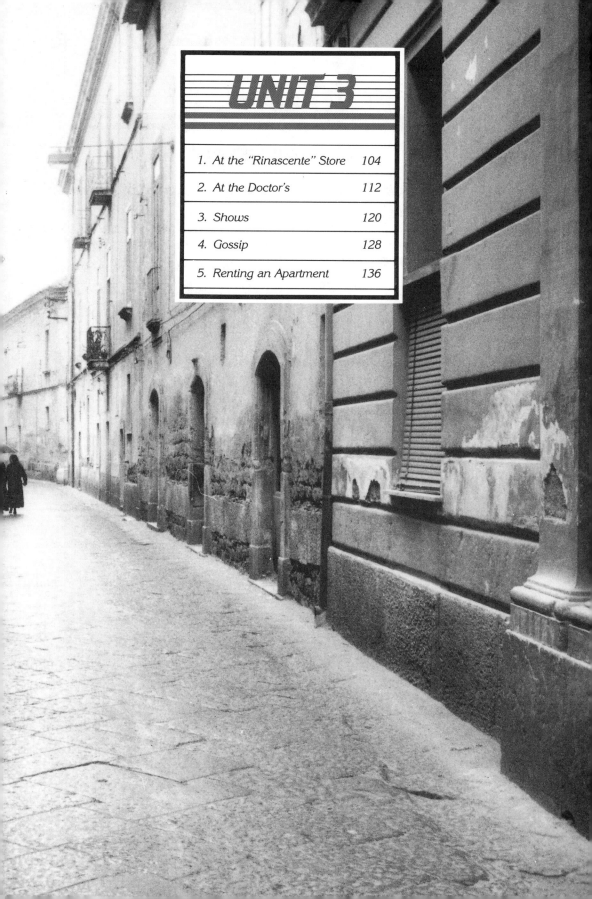

UNIT 3

(•••) LISTEN

AT THE ''RINASCENTE'' STORE

The Clerici's are a Neapolitan couple. They are shopping in a department store.

Al reparto «abbigliamento donna»

La commessa : *In che cosa posso servirLa?*

La sig.ra Clerici : *Vorrei vedere una gonna a pieghe.*

La commessa : *Ha già visto qualcosa che Le piace?*

La sig.ra Clerici : *Sì, quella gonna bianca che è in vetrina. È di seta?*

La commessa : *Sì, è di pura seta leggerissima. Vuole provarla?*

La sig.ra Clerici : *Sì, ma vorrei sapere prima quanto viene.*

La commessa : *Questo modello viene 180.000 lire, e esiste anche in nero e in azzurro.*

La sig.ra Clerici : *Va bene, allora la provo.*

La commessa : *Che taglia porta?*

La sig.ra Clerici : *La 44.*

La commessa : *Ecco : questa è la Sua taglia. Per provarla si accomodi in cabina.*

La sig.ra Clerici : *Come mi sta?*

Il marito : *Bene, ma mi sembra un po' lunga.*

La commessa : *La lunghezza non ha importanza : si può sempre accorciare.*

La sig.ra Clerici : *Sì, però forse è anche un po' larga. Quasi quasi provo la taglia più piccola.*

La commessa : *Ecco la 42.*

Il marito : *Ah, sì, questa ti sta molto meglio dell'altra!*

La sig.ra Clerici : *Sì, questa mi va bene. È proprio la mia misura.*

Il marito : *Allora cosa fai, la prendi?*

La sig.ra Clerici : *Sì, ho deciso.*

La commessa : *Mentre le faccio il pacchetto si accomodi pure alla cassa.*

Al reparto «abbigliamento uomo»

Il sig. Clerici : *Vorrei vedere una camicia sportiva, con le maniche lunghe.*

Il commesso : *Benissimo. Abbiamo parecchi modelli, tutti di puro cotone. Questa qui a quadretti, per esempio. Le piace?*

Il sig. Clerici: : *Non è male. Ma non mi piacciono i bottoncini sul colletto.*

Il commesso : *Allora c'è questo modello senza bottoncini, che esiste anche a righe e a tinta unita.*

Il sig. Clerici : *Questa qui a righe quanto viene?*

Il commesso : *72.000 lire.*

Il sig. Clerici : *Però! è un po' cara...*

Il commesso : *Sì, ma la qualità è ottima. Ci sono modelli più economici ma non sono di puro cotone.*

Il sig. Clerici: : *Mi ha convinto. La prendo.*

(•••) LISTEN AND REPEAT
You will find the translation on page 18 of the booklet.

1. The Bay of Naples
2. Downtown Naples

NOUNS

il reparto — department
l'abbigliamento — clothing
la donna — woman
l'uomo (pl. : gli uomini) — man
il commesso, la commessa — clerk
la gonna — skirt
la vetrina — store window
la seta — silk
il modello — model/style/make
la taglia — size/fit
la cabina — changing room
la lunghezza — length
la misura — size
il pacchetto — package
la camicia — shirt
la manica — sleeve
il cotone — cotton
il bottone — button
il bottoncino — small button
il colletto — collar
la qualità — quality

_____

il colore — color
il grande magazzino — department store
il negozio — store
l'acquisto — purchase
la camicetta — blouse
il vestito — dress/suit

ADJECTIVES

leggero/pesante — light/heavy (1)
largo/stretto — loose/tight
sportivo/elegante — sporty/elegant
parecchi — several
caro/economico — expensive/cheap

azzurro — blue
bianco — white
blu — dark blue
nero — black
rosso — red
verde — green
grigio — gray
giallo — yellow
rosa — pink (2)
viola — purple (2)
marrone — brown (2)
classico/di moda — classical in style

VERBS

servire — to serve
provare — to try on
esistere — to exist
sembrare — to seem
accorciare/allungare — to shorten/lengthen
decidere — to decide
convincere — to convince

MISCELLANEOUS

a pieghe — pleated
a quadretti — checked
a righe — striped
a tinta unita — one color
di lana — wool
di cotone — cotton
di seta — silk
per esempio — for example
forse — maybe
senza — without
meglio (di) — better (than) (3)
più (di) — more (than) (4)
questo — this
quello — that

HOW TO SAY IT

1. I'D LIKE TO SEE . . .

Vorrei vedere la gonna bianca a pieghe che è in vetrina — I'd like to see the white skirt with pleats that is in the window.
Vorrei vedere una camicia sportiva con le maniche lunghe — I'd like to see a sports shirt with long sleeves.

2. DESCRIBING SIZES AND FITS

Questa gonna mi sembra un po' lunga — This skirt seems to me to be a bit long.
Forse è anche un po' larga — Maybe it's even a bit large.
È un modello di ottima qualità — It's of top quality.
È propio la mia misura — It's my size./It's the right size.
Mi va bene — It fits me.
Me sta bene — It looks good (on me).
Non mi sta bene — It doesn't look good.

3. COMPARING

Questa gonna è più bella di quella — This skirt is more beautiful than that one.
Questa camicia è meno cara dell'atra — This skirt is less expensive than the other one.
Questa ti sta molto meglio dell'altra — This looks better on you than the other one.

4. PRICE, QUALITY, AND SIZES

Quanto viene quella gonna? — How much does the skirt come to (cost)?
Questo modello viene a 60.000 lire — This make costs 60,000 liras.
Costa 42.000 lire — It costs 42,000 liras.
La qualità è ottima — It's of top quality.
Porto il 44 — I wear size 44 **(5).**
È una 42 — It's a 42.

5. MAKING UP ONE'S MIND

Ho deciso, la prendo — I've decided. I'll take it.
Mi ha convinto — You've convinced me.
Va bene, allora la provo — OK, then, I'll try it on.

| REMARKS... | REMARKS... | REMARKS... | REMARKS... |

(1) This means "heavy," but can also mean "warm" for clothing. — (2) Invariable. — (3) See Grammar, H. 1. — (4) See Grammar, H. 1. — (5) Italian sizes use a different system than the American one.

1. "QUEL/QUELLA"

(••) LISTEN

La gonna • Di che colore è quella gonna
Il vestito • Di che colore è quel vestito?

Continue asking questions, using "quel" or "quella."
La gonna — Il vestito — La camicetta — Il modello — La cravatta — La valigia — La camicia — Il vestito — La gonna.

(See Grammar, D. 2.)

2. "QUESTO/QUESTA"

(••) LISTEN

Gonna/corta • Questa gonna mi sembra un po' corta
Vestito/stretto • Questo vestito mi sembra un po' stretto

Form sentences using "questo" or "questa."
Gonna/corta — Vestito/stretto — Camicetta/larga — Modello/caro — Colletto/largo — Lana/pesante — Cotone/leggero — Taglia/grande.

(See Grammar, D. 2.)

3. COMPARING

(••) LISTEN

Gonna-bella • Questa gonna è più bella di quella
Vestito-caro • Questo vestito è più caro di quello
Camicie-leggere • Queste camicie sono più leggere di quelle
Modelli-economici • Questi modelli sono più economici di quelli

Continue making comparisons, as in the model.
Gonna-bella — Vestito-caro — Camicie-leggere — Modelli-economici — Camicetta-stretta — Modello-elegante — Vestiti-classici — Cravatta-sportiva — Ristorante-caro

(See Grammar, H. 1.)

4. THE PAST TENSE

(••) LISTEN

Oggi compro una gonna
• Ieri ho comprato una gonna
Oggi bevo un caffè?
• Ieri ho bevuto un caffè
Oggi finisco alle 8 • Ieri ho finito alle 8

Continue, as in the model.
Oggi compro una gonna — Oggi bevo un caffè — Oggi finisco alle otto — Oggi telefono a Claudio — Oggi firmo il contratto — Oggi ripeto l'esercizio — Oggi non dormo — Oggi spedisco la lettera.

(See Grammar, L. 7.)

5. THE PAST TENSE AGAIN

MOVEMENT VERBS
(••) LISTEN

Sei già andato alla stazione?
• No, non ci sono ancora andato.

Continue answering negatively, using the pronoun "ci."
Sei già andato alla stazione? — Sei già ritornato a Roma? — Sei già salito al quinto piano? — Sei già stato a Napoli? — Sei già andato in ufficio? — Sei già stato in quel ristorante?

(See Grammar, L. 7.)

6. THE PAST TENSE ONE MORE TIME

A FEW IRREGULAR VERBS
(••) LISTEN

Prendere la macchina (io)
• Ho preso la macchina
Decidere subito (tu) • Hai deciso subito

Change to the past tense, as in the model.
Prendere la macchina (io) — Decidere subito (tu) — Chiudere la prota (noi) — Vedere la gonna in vetrina (la sig.ra Clerici) — Scrivere la lettera (voi) — Leggere la posta (io) — Fare una telefonata (tu).

(See Grammar, L. 7.)

SHOPPING IN ITALY

Do you want to do some shopping? Italy is a shopper's dream come true, so take advantage of it. You will find that everything is very well made and in the latest style. Who has not heard of Armani, Valentino, Capucci, Versace, or Missoni in the world of fashion; Pomellato or Bulgari of jewelry design; or Ferragamo and Fratelli Rossetti of footwear design? And versatility is the operative word: Armani and Gucci not only make stylish clothes and wonderful shoes, but perfumes as well. These names, among others, are known in all the major cities.

Luxury—at a Price

Inevitably, good things do not come cheap. Everything you buy is of top quality: "di pura seta" (pure silk), "di puro cottone" (pure cotton), "di vero cuoio" (genuine leather), and so on. And only the finest gold is used in making jewelry. In fact, Italian has two different words for jewelry: stores that sell "costume" jewelry are called "bigiotterie," whereas those that sell more "serious" articles of jewelry are known as "gioillerie." As for Italian shoes, their renown is indisputable. The better shoes, naturally, are made only of leather. However, this does not prevent Italian shoe manufacturers from producing large quantities of cheaper shoes made primarily of synthetic materials.

Quality—Within Your Budget

But your shopping need not be limited to the chic boutiques and expensive shops. You will always find fine clothing and accessories at La Rinascente, the principal department-store chain (based in Milan) in Italy. Other chain stores include La Standa and Upim, where you can buy anything from garden tools to junk food. (You will also inevitably face long lines at the cashier!) The many "saldi" (sales) and "sconti" (discounts) are certainly worth taking advantage of. There was a time in Italy when you could actually barter for a reduced price. But those days are long gone! "Prezzi fissi" are now the order of the day.

And just one more thing before you decide to start your shopping adventure. Except for the major department stores, almost all stores close down for a few hours during the afternoon. And after eight in the evening, everything is closed. Just keep this in mind and you will enjoy discovering the shopper's paradise that is Italy.

LISTEN

Indicate which of the two articles of clothing in each drawing is the one chosen by the customer.

1 | A | B

2 | A | B

PROVERBIO

 LISTEN

Chi più spende, meno spende
(lit., He who spends more, spends less).
Good things are expensive.

3 | A | B

List the ten differences (objects, articles of clothing) between the two drawings.
For appropriate vocabulary to help you with this game, see page 145.

(See solutions on page 19 of the booklet.)

DIALOGUE

(●●) LISTEN

AT THE DOCTOR'S

Mr. Clerici does not feel very well, so he has made an appointment with the doctor.

La segretaria : *Buongiorno, signor Clerici. Ha un appuntamento?*

Sig. Clerici : *Sì, alle 6. Sono un po' in anticipo...*

La segretaria : *Il dottore è ancora in visita. Si accomodi nella sala d'attesa.*

Sig. Clerici : *Va bene, grazie.*

La segretaria : *Sul tavolino ci sono delle riviste, e c'è anche il giornale di oggi, se Le interessa.*

Sig. Clerici : *Molto gentile.*

. . . .

La segretaria : *Signor Clerici, prego! Tocca a Lei: si accomodi in studio.*

Il dottore : *Buongiorno, Signor Clerici. Allora, che cosa c'è che non va?*

Sig. Clerici : *Buongiorno, dottore. Guardi, da qualche giorno non sto molto bene. Ho mal di gola e un po' di tosse e quando mi sveglio ho sempre mal di testa.*

Il dottore : *Ha la febbre?*

Sig. Clerici : *Credo di no.*

Il dottore : *Potrebbe essere un inizio di influenza. Ha già preso qualche medicina?*

Sig. Clerici : *Solo un po' di aspirina, ma non mi ha fatto niente.*

Il dottore : *Vediamo un po' quanto ha di pressione...*

Sig. Clerici : *Forse ho la pressione bassa. Mi sento piuttosto debole in questo periodo.*

Il dottore : *No, la pressione è normale. La sua debolezza è dovuta probabilmente a un po' di fatica. Lavora molto?*

Sig. Clerici : *Beh sì, ultimamente ho avuto moltissimi impegni di lavoro e ho dormito poco.*

Il dottore : *Senta, le prescrivo queste compresse : ne prenda due al giorno dopo i pasti principali. E la sera prenda un cucchiaio di questo sciroppo.*

Sig. Clerici : *Per quanto tempo devo seguire la cura?*

Il dottore : *Secondo me una settimana dovrebbe bastare. Ma ci vuole anche un po' di riposo! Ritorni martedì prossimo se vede che non va meglio.*

Sig. Clerici : *Grazie mille, dottore... ArrivederLa.*

La segretaria : *Signor Clerici! Aspetti! Ha dimenticato di prendere la ricetta!*

Sig. Clerici : *Ah, già! Che distratto!...*

(●●) LISTEN AND REPEAT

You will find the translation on page 19 of the booklet.

1. Spacca Napoli (Old Naples)
2. The coastline
3. Fish vendor
4. At a lottery shop

NOUNS

il dottore — doctor
la vista — doctor's visit
la sala d'attesa — waiting room
la rivista — magazine
il giornale — newspaper
lo studio — professional office *(1)*
la gola — throat
la tosse — cough
la testa — head
la febbre — fever/temperature
l'influenza — flu
la medicina — medicine
l'aspirina — aspirin
la pressione — blood pressure
la debolezza — weakness
la fatica — fatigue
l'impegno — obligation/thing to do
la compressa — tablet
il pasto — meal
il cucchiaio — spoon
lo sciro — syrup
la cura — cure
la ricetta — prescription *(2)*

---

il medico — doctor
la farmacia — pharmacy
il/la farmacista — pharmacist
il raffreddore — cold
l'antibiotico — antibiotic
la supposta — suppository

VERBS

interessare — to interest
stare bene/male = sentirsi
bene/male — to feel well/bad
aver mal di gola — to have a sore throat
svegliarsi — to wake up
aver mal di testa — to have a headache
dormire — to sleep
prescrivere — to prescribe
seguire — to follow
bastare — to be enough
dimenticare — to forget

---

ammalarsi — to get sick
guarire — to get better
curare — to look after/to cure

ADJECTIVES

basso — low
debole — weak
normale — normal
distratto — distracted/absent-minded

MISCELLANEOUS

tocca a Lei — it's your turn
ultimamente — lately
secondo me — according to me
due volte al giorno — twice a day
dopo i pasti — after meals
prima dei pasti — before meals
credo di no — I believe not
credo di sì — I believe so
ah già — ah, yes!

HOW TO SAY IT

---

1. WHOSE TURN IS IT?

Tocca a Lei — It's your turn!
Tocca a me! — It's my turn!

Tocca a Claudio — It's Claudio's turn!

---

2. SAYING HOW ONE FEELS

Non mi sento molto bene — I don't feel well.
Mi sento un po' debole — I feel a bit weak.
Sto male — I feel bad.
Ho il raffreddore — I have a cold.
Ho l'influenza — I have the flu.
Ho mal di testa — I have a headache.
Ho mal di schiena — I have a backache.

Ho mal di denti — I have a toothache.
Ho mal di gola — I have a sore throat.
Ho mal di stomaco — I have a stomachache.
Sto bene — I feel well.
Sono in piena forma — I'm in top shape.

---

3. EXPRESSING ONE'S OPINION

Secondo me — According to me.
A mio avviso (a mio parere) — In my opinion
Per me — For me

Credo di sì — I believe so
Credo di no — I believe not

Potrebbe essere l'influenza — It could be the flu.

---

4. HOW MANY TIMES?

Tre volte al giorno — three times a day
Una volta alla settimana — once a week

Due volte al mese — twice a month
Una volta all'anno — once a year

---

5. THE EFFECTS OF MEDICATION

Non mi ha fatto niente — Nothing happened./I didn't get any better.
Mi ha fatto bene — It helped.

Mi ha fatto male — It harmed me./It made me sick.

REMARKS...   REMARKS...   REMARKS...   REMARKS...

(1) Note that this is the word for "professional office." For other kinds of offices the word "ufficio" is used instead. — (2) This is also the word for "recipe." — (3) Note that "male" drops the final -e in expressions such as "ho mal di testa."

1. "POTERE/DOVERE/VOLERE"

FOLLOWED BY AN INFINITIVE: THE POSITION OF OBJECT PRONOUNS

(• •) LISTEN

Per la tosse, posso darLe questo sciroppo
• *Per la tosse, Le posso dare questo sciroppo*
Quando lo devo prendere?
• *Quando devo prenderlo?*

Change the following by shifting the pronoun, as in the model.
Per la tosse, posso darLe questo sciroppo — Quando lo devo prendere? — Non voglio farlo — Non lo posso dire — Non la voglio vedere — Devo prenderle 3 volte al giorno — Li posso comprare domani — Le supposte, non le voglio prendere — La camera, la devo prenotare.

(See Grammar, E. 4.)

2. THE PRONOUN "NE"

(• •) LISTEN

Hai molti amici? • *Sì, ne ho molti*
Hai molte cravatte? • *Sì, ne ho molte*

Answer the following using "ne."
Hai molti amici? — Hai molte cravatte? — Hai molti vestiti? — Hai molte valigie? — Fumi molte sigarette? — Guardi molti film? — Compri molte riviste? — Prendi molte medicine? — Scrivi molte lettere? —

(See Grammar, E. 2.)

3. THE PARTITIVE del, dello, dell', della, dei, degli, delle

(• •) LISTEN

Il vino rosso • *Vorrei del vino rosso*
Lo sciroppo per la tosse • *Vorrei dello sciroppo per la tosse*

Il vino rosso — Lo sciroppo per la tosse — Le compresse per il raffreddore — Gli antibiotici — Le riviste francesi — I francobolli da 600 lire — Le buste — La carta da lettere — Le cartoline — I giornali.

(See Grammar, B. 2.)

4. THE PREPOSITION "DA"

(• •) LISTEN

Il dottore
• *Vado dal dottore*
L'avvocato
• *Vado dall'avvocato*

Say where you are going, using the preposition "da" and the article when necessary.
Il dottore — L'avvocato — Roberto — Il medico — La segretaria — L'architetto — I miei amici — Le mie amiche — La sig.ra Rossi — Il direttore — Gli amici di Mario.

(See Grammar, F.)

5. "DA" AGAIN

(• •) LISTEN

Lavorare qui/2 anni
• *Lavoro qui da due anni*
Abitare a Roma/il 1° agosto
• *Abito a Roma dal 1° agosto*

Form sentences by using "da," as in the example.
Lavorare qui/2 anni — Abitare a Roma/il 1° agosto — Parlare l'italiano/qualche mese — Vivere in Francia/molti anni — Conoscere la sig.ra Clerici/poco tempo — Essere sposato/12 anni — Non stare bene/qualche giorno.

(See Grammar, F.)

6. AGREEMENT WITH THE OBJECT PRONOUN

IN THE PAST TENSE

(• •) LISTEN

Hai preso la medicina?
• *Sì, l'ho presa*

Answer the following, making sure the past participle agrees with the object.
Hai preso la medicina? — Hai letto il libro? — Hai seguito la cura? — Hai cambiato i dollari? — Hai scritto le cartoline? — Hai preso l'appuntamento? — Hai fatto gli esercizi? — Hai ripetuto le frasi?

(See Grammar, E. 3.)

READING IN ITALY

If you like to read, then Italy is the place for you. Every street corner has a newspaper and magazine kiosk, "un'edicola," where you can buy such highly informative magazines as Panorama, L'Espresso, Il Mondo, and L'Europeo. You will also find several nationwide and local newspapers.

The Italian press offers its readers an incredibly rich choice: in addition to the major newspapers, Il Corriere della Sera, La Stampa, La Repubblica, and Il Giorno, there are nearly eighty papers that hit the stands daily. These include papers from large cities and small towns, as well as papers speaking for the different political parties. Add to this the sports, fashion, women's, art, scientific, and other specialized magazines (stamp collecting, crossword puzzles, etc.). There is something for everyone!

Despite this abundance of printed media, complain the publishers, Italians read very little. This explains the continual effort on the part of certain magazine publishers to entice the public with splashy, often daring photos on the covers.

And often the magazine you buy is in a plastic wrap in which you will also find a small gift of sorts—a tourist guide, road map, calendar, even a paperback novel! There seems to be no limit to devices for attracting more readers.

What's on TV?

What is happening in Italy is occurring elsewhere throughout the industrialized nations: the literary world must now compete with the almighty TV (pronounced "tee voo"). Depending on the region you live in and the size of your television set, you can get up to twenty channels. Most of these are private, but there are also State-owned stations that provide excellent programming and also produces some excellent films. With such a variety of programs to choose from, Italians are fast becoming a nation of TV addicts. "Fotoromanzi" (soap operas in print) are losing the battle to the Italian versions of "Dallas" and "The Young and the Restless." And Guida TV (TV Guide) now outsells crossword puzzle magazines and romantic novels.

But to make matters worse, unlike French television and very much like American television, Italian programming is continuously interrupted by messages from the sponsor—usually without any noticeable transition between the show and the commercial. Airing a film 100 minutes long actually takes an additional hour because of commercials! With the same commercial appearing several times during the film, it is certain that by the end of the film the viewer will be more impressed by the sponsor's message than by anything the film's director tried to convey!

The fact is that, for better or worse, television has become an integral part of many Italians' daily life. They eat while watching it, watch it after eating, and fall asleep in front of it. Like a disease, "la teledipendenza" is spreading throughout Italy, as it is in many other parts of the world.

N° 1 •• LISTEN

Listen to the patients tell the doctor what's wrong with them. Then under each medication write down the symptom/sickness each patient has.

1. . . . . 2. . . . .

3. . . . . 4. . . . . 5. . . . .

The human body. Match each body part to its name.

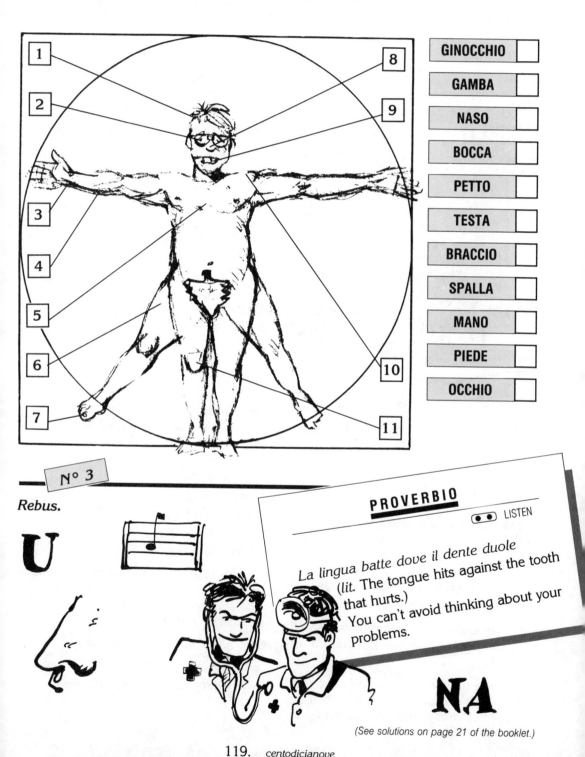

GINOCCHIO ☐

GAMBA ☐

NASO ☐

BOCCA ☐

PETTO ☐

TESTA ☐

BRACCIO ☐

SPALLA ☐

MANO ☐

PIEDE ☐

OCCHIO ☐

N° 3

Rebus.

PROVERBIO 🔊 LISTEN

La lingua batte dove il dente duole
(*lit.* The tongue hits against the tooth that hurts.)
You can't avoid thinking about your problems.

(See solutions on page 21 of the booklet.)

⊙⊙ LISTEN

SHOWS

The Clerici's are making plans for the evening.

Lui : *Che ne dici di uscire stasera?*

Lei : *Sì, usciamo! Non ho proprio voglia di stare a casa. Che cosa mi proponi di bello?*

Lui : *Andiamo a ballare!*

Lei : *Ma sei matto! Proprio tu che non hai mai messo piede in una discoteca!*

Lui : *Sto scherzando, naturalmente! Se ti va, potremmo andare al cinema o a un concerto...*

Lei : *No, a un concerto non mi va. L'ultima volta, ti ricordi, mi sono annoiata da morire! Piuttosto potremmo guardare che cosa c'è a teatro.*

Lui : : *Ho già guardato sul giornale e non c'è praticamente niente. Quasi tutti i teatri sono chiusi per ferie.*

Lei : *E al cinema che cosa danno?*

Lui : *Ma, l'unico film che vale la pena e che non abbiamo ancora visto è « Il Nome della rosa ».*

Lei : *Ah, il film tratto dal romanzo di Umberto Eco! Sarei curiosa di vederlo perchè ho letto il libro e mi è piaciuto molto. Chi è il regista?*

Lui : *È un francese, Jean-Jacques Annaud. Il protagonista è Sean Connery, quello che è diventato famoso con la serie di James Bond.*

Lei : *Ah, già, è un bravissimo attore...*

Lui : *Guarda però che il film è un po' lungo.*

Lei : : *Andiamo allo spettacolo delle otto allora. Non vorrei andare a letto troppo tardi. In quale cinema lo danno?*

Lui : : *Al Cannon Odeon. Non è troppo lontano. Se ci sbrighiamo facciamo in tempo: il film comincia alle 20.10.*

Lei : *Va bene. Mi preparo in due minuti e ceneremo dopo il film.*

Lui : *Non più di due minuti, mi raccomando... Altrimenti rischiamo di arrivare a film già cominciato. Lo sai che odio perdere le prime scene!*

Lei : *Sarò pronta in un attimo!*

⊙⊙ LISTEN AND REPEAT
You will find the translation on page 21 of the booklet.

1. A sculpture (Naples)
2. Traditional living quarters
3. Neighbors

3

NOUNS

lo spettacolo — show
la discoteca — disco
il cinema — movies *(1)*
il concerto — concert
il teatro — theater
le ferie — paid holidays *(2)*
il film — movie
il romanzo — novel
il libro — book
il regista — movie director
il protagonista — main actor
la serie — series *(3)*
l'attore/l'attrice — actor/actress
la scena — scene

---

il programma — program
la serata — evening
la commedia — comedy
la tragedia — tragedy
il dramma — drama
lo scrittore/la scrittrice — writer

ADJECTIVES

curioso — curious
famoso — famous, well-known
bravo — good
violento — violent
psicologico — psychological
drammatico — dramatic
brillante — brilliant

VERBS

uscire — to go out
proporre — to propose/suggest *(4)*
ballare — to dance
scherzare — to joke
ricordarsi — to remember
annoiarsi — to become bored
divertirsi — to enjoy oneself
diventare — to become
andare a letto — to go to bed
sbrigarsi — to hurry
fare in tempo — to make it on time
prepararsi — to get ready
mi raccomando — I mean it
rischiare — to risk
odiare — to hate
amare — to love
essere pronto — to be ready

MISCELLANEOUS

stare a casa — to stay at home *(5)*
mettere piede — to set foot in
avere voglia — to feel like
vale la pena — it's worthwhile
essere matto — to be crazy
da morire — to die
altrimenti — otherwise
tardi/presto — late/early
andare a teatro — to go to the theater
al cinema — to the movies
al concerto — to the concert
in campagna — to the country
in montagna — to the mountains
al mare — to the sea

HOW TO SAY IT

---

1. GOING OUT

Che ne dici di uscire? — What about going?
Andiamo a ballare? — Shall we go dancing?
Ti va di andare al cinema? — Do you feel like going to the movies?
Potremmo andare a teatro! — We could go to the theater!
Hai voglia di andare a un concerto? — Do you feel like going to a concert?
Usciamo insieme stasera? — Shall we go out together this evening?

---

2. FINDING OUT WHAT'S PLAYING

Che cosa c'è a teatro? — What's on at the theater?
Che cosa danno al cinema? — What's playing at the movies?
In quale cinema danno questo film? — In which theater is this movie playing?
Che film danno alla televisione? — What movie is on TV?
Quanto dura lo spettacolo? — How long does the show last?
A che ora comincia (finisce) il film? — At what time does the movie start (end)?

---

3. TALKING ABOUT ENTERTAINMENT

Lo spettacolo mi è piaciuto molto — I liked the show a lot.
Il protagonista è un bravissimo attore — The main actor is a very good actor.
Il regista è un francese — The director is French.
Lo spettacolo è stato un po' lungo — The show lasted a bit too long.
È stato molto interessante — It was very interesting.
È stato molto noioso — It was very boring.
Non mi è piaciuto affatto — I didn't like it at all.
È una discoteca di moda — It's a fashionable disco.

---

4. HURRYING UP

Presto! — Hurry up! *(6)*
Sbrigati! — Hurry up! Be quick!
Se ci sbrighiamo facciamo in tempo — If we hurry, we'll make it on time. *(7)*
Facciamo in fretta! — Let's hurry up!

| REMARKS... | REMARKS... | REMARKS... | REMARKS... |

(1) Invariable (See Grammar, C. 3.). — (2) "Ferie" are "paid holidays." — (3) Invariable. — (4) See Grammar, L. 8. — (5) "Casa" means both "house" and "home." — (6) Literally, this means "Quick!" — (7) Note that both verbs, unlike English, are in the present indicative tense.

1. REFLEXIVE VERBS IN THE PAST

(••) LISTEN

Lei si annoia al concerto
* *Lei si è annoiata al concerto*

Continue putting the sentences in the past.
Lei si annoia al concerto — Io mi diverto molto — I signori Clerici si preparano in due minuti — Tu ti preoccupi per niente — Laura si sente male — Noi ci vediamo spesso — Maria e Francesca si sbagliano — Il ragazzo si scusa.

(See Grammar, L. 7.)

2. THE VERB "PIACERE" IN THE PAST

(••) LISTEN

Il film
* *Il film mi è piaciuto*
La commedia
* *La commedia mi è piaciuta*

Say that you liked the following.
Il film — La commedia — Lo spettacolo — La tragedia — Il romanzo — La serata — Il libro — La carne — Il concerto — La scena — La discoteca — Il programma

(See Grammar, L. 7.)

3. "TO BE" IN THE PAST

(••) LISTEN

Il film — lungo
* *Il film è stato lungo*
La commedia — interessante
* *La commedia è stata interessante*

Form sentences as in the model.
Il film - lungo — La commedia - interessante — Il concerto - noioso — La scena - violenta — L'attore - bravissimo — La serata - divertente — Il viaggio - bello — Il lavoro - pesante — Lo spettacolo - simpatico.

(See Grammar, L. 7.)

4. THE INTERROGATIVE FORM "CHI"

(••) LISTEN

Il regista
* *Chi è il regista?*
Gli attori
* *Chi sono gli attori?*

Continue asking questions in this way.
Il regista — Gli attori — Il protagonista — L'autore — Le attrici — L'attore — Il direttore — I protagonisti — Il presidente — I responsabili.

(See Grammar, G. 2.)

5. THE RELATIVE PRONOUN "CHE"

(••) LISTEN

Il regista ha fatto il film — Il regista è molto bravo
* *Il regista che ha fatto il film è molto bravo*
Ho visto lo spettacolo — Lo spettacolo è lungo
* *Lo spettacolo che ho visto è lungo*

Combine the two sentences into one by using "che."
Il regista ha fatto il film - Il regista è molto bravo — Ho visto lo spettacolo - Lo spettacolo è lungo — Il ragazzo compra il giornale - Il ragazzo è americano — Ho letto il libro - Il libro è di Umberto Eco — La signora parla con il direttore - La signora è la moglie del sig. Rossi — Ho comprato una gonna - La gonna è bianca.

(See Grammar, G. 1.)

6. THE VERB "USCIRE"

(••) LISTEN

Io
* *Esco dall'ufficio alle 5*
Noi
* *Usciamo dall'ufficio alle 5*

Conjugate "uscire" as in the model.
Io — Noi — Il direttore — Tu — La segretaria — Voi — Noi — I signori Clerici — Io — Claudio — Francesco e Marco — Il responsabile — Voi.

(See Grammar, L. 6.)

EXAGGERATION, ITALIAN STYLE

It goes without saying that the idea of spectacle is an intrinsic feature of Italian culture. After all, Italy is the birthplace of opera, and this certainly did not happen by mere chance. First, there is the unquestionable musicality of the Italian language. Just listen to Italian opera. You will be struck by how the words and music merge into an inseparable whole. Maybe this is aided by the fact that Italian words end, by and large, with a vowel. And perhaps the accompanying gesticulations that go along with singing in Italian also help endow musical performances with expressive qualities.

"Lo Spettacolo"

Italians do seem to possess an innate feeling for "lo spettacolo." This is frequently manifested in the way Italians dress. To some this may appear as merely showing off. But the fact remains that many Italians have a talent for dressing impeccably and with great taste and creativity. This ability to create style has put Italy at the forefront of the fashion world.

Another example of this ability to draw attention is the exaggerated manner in which Italians speak and their dexterity in using hand gestures to express themselves more fully when words no longer suffice.

But along with this somewhat flamboyant style, one cannot deny the sincerity and friendliness of most Italians. Just look at their magnanimous displays of affection! People talk to each other on buses, in stores, and on the street. And Italians are extremely hospitable to foreigners. Always willing to be sociable, they are more than ready to have coffee with anyone at the nearest bar. From the soccer match, to the opera, to the ways an Italian dresses, there is forever the feeling and experience of "lo spettacolo" in Italy.

The Grand Scale

Exaggeration, Italian style, can perhaps also be seen in the very architecture of Italian cities. But, then, who would normally call this "exaggeration"? Yet, the grand palaces, magnificent villas, and the many other architectural displays found throughout Italy all bear witness to a cultural tendency—the need to embellish and refine one's possessions. In fact, Italy has always been a country to emulate in this area. The buildings, cars, clothes, and many other artifacts that Italian culture is famous for, all have a tinge of exaggeration in them. But this is exactly what is so appealing and unique about them.

⦿⦿ LISTEN

Circle V *if the statement is true, or* F *if it is false.*

1. Carla vuole vedere un film nuovo   V   F

2. A Carla non piacciono i film gialli   V   F

3. Carla è indecisa tra una commedia all'italiana e un vecchio western   V   F

4. Alla fine vanno a vedere "C'era una volta l'West"   V   F

Anagram. The following two clues will give you, respectively, the names of a famous movie director and his favorite actor.

1. Lei mi offende, Ric!
2. Maestro, rimani con la «L».

PROVERBIO ⦿⦿ LISTEN

Chi tardi arriva male alloggia
(lit., He who arrives late finds poor lodgings").
The last to finish will never get anywhere.

Match each kind of film (as shown in the separate drawings) with its name.

1. Comico   **2.** Giallo   **3.** Western   **4.** Drammatico
5. Fantascienza   **6.** Sentimentale

A ☐ ☐

C ☐ ☐

B ☐ ☐

D ☐ ☐

E ☐ ☐   F ☐ ☐

(See solutions on page 22 of the booklet.)

(•• ▶) LISTEN   **GOSSIP**

Mario and Luisa Clerici chat in front of a movie theater.

Luisa : *Hai visto chi c'era nella fila davanti alla nostra?*

Mario : *No. Perché? Chi c'era?*

Luisa : *Ma dai! Tu non vedi mai niente! Era la signora Calvi, sai, quella del quarto piano...*

Mario : *La signora Calvi... È quella signora che ha divorziato due anni fa?*

Luisa : *Esatto, quell'antipatica, che non mi saluta mai quando ci incontriamo per strada.*

Mario : *E allora?*

Luisa : *Non hai visto se era con qualcuno?*

Mario : *Io, a dire il vero, non ho visto proprio nessuno, e poi in fondo sono affari suoi, no?*

Luisa : *Con te non si può proprio parlare...*

Mario : *So benissimo che non la puoi soffrire ma a me sembra una persona a modo.*

Luisa : *Figurati! Si dà un sacco di arie e si veste in un modo ridicolo per la sua età.*

Mario : *Quanti anni avrà?*

Luisa : *Avrà almeno cinquantacinque anni...*

Mario : *Beh, non li dimostra.*

Luisa : *Per forza, non hai visto come è truccata?*

Mario : *Sarà, comunque è una bella donna.*

Luisa : *Bella lei?*

Mario : *Io trovo in lei un certo fascino.*

Luisa : *Per carità!*

Mario : *Ma non si è risposata recentemente?*

Luisa : *Sì, tre mesi fa, e pensa che ha sposato un uomo che avrà almeno vent'anni più di lei... Un grande industriale napoletano, ricchissimo, naturalmente...*

Mario : *Ma sai veramente tutto!*

(•• ▶) LISTEN AND REPEAT
You will find the translation on page 23 of the booklet.

1. A religious procession
2. A "scopa" card game
3. Women in a typical Neapolitan city district
4. Gesturing
5. Reading the newspaper
6. Teenagers

NOUNS

il pettegolezzo — gossip
la fila — line
l'età — age
il fascino — appeal/fascination
l'industriale — industrialist

---

il divorzio — divorce
il matrimonio — marriage/matrimony
il trucco — makeup
il rossetto — lipstick
il profumo — perfume
la crema di bellezza — beauty cream

ADJECTIVES

ridicolo — ridiculous
truccato — with make-up on
napoletano — Neapolitan
ricco — rich

---

povero — poor
agiato — calm, relaxed

VERBS

divorziare — to divorce
salutare — to greet
incontrarsi — to meet/run into
soffrire — to suffer
darsi delle arie — to give oneself airs
vestirsi — to dress oneself
dimostrare — to show/demonstrate
sposarsi — to get married
risposarsi — to remarry
non poter soffrire qualcuno — to be unable to stand someone
dimostrare l'età — to show one's age
truccarsi — to put on make-up

MISCELLANEOUS

ma dai! — come on!
esatto! — exactly!
qualcuno — someone
nessuno — no one
a dire il vero — to say the truth
sono affari miei (suoi ecc.) — it's my own business (his own, etc.)
una persona a modo — a decent person
un sacco di — a pile of
per forza! — of course!
comunque — however
per carità! — Come off it!
recentemente — recently

1. PROBABILITY

Avrà almeno 45 anni — She must be at least 45 years old. *(1)*
Avrà 20 anni più di lei — He must be 20 years older than she.
Sarà uscito — He must have gone out. *Dormirà ancora* — He must still be sleeping.

2. . . . AGO

Ha divorziato 2 anni fa — She was divorced 2 years ago.
Si è risposata 3 mesi fa — She remarried 3 months ago.
Ho visto Franco due ore fa — I saw Franco two hours ago.
Sono arrivato due minuti fa — I arrived two minutes ago.

3. SOMEONE/NO ONE

C'è qualcuno? — Is there someone here?
No, non c'è nessuno — No, there's no one.
Hai visto qualcuno? — Did you see someone?

No, non ho visto nessuno — No, I didn't see anyone.

4. SOMETHING/NOTHING

C'è qualche cosa di bello? — Is there something nice?
No, non c'è niente — No, there's nothing.

Hai visto qualcosa di bello? — Did you see something nice?
No, non ho visto niente — No, I didn't see anything.

5. COMMENTING ON OTHERS

Quella signora è antipatica — That lady is not nice.
Non la posso soffrire — I can't stand her.
Si da un sacco di arie — She is full of herself.
Si veste male — She dresses poorly/badly.

A me sembra simpatica — She seems nice to me.
È una persona a modo — She's a decent person.
È una bella donna (è un bell'uomo) — She's a beautiful woman. (He's a handsome man.)
Ha un certo fascino — She has a certain appeal/charm.

6. A FEW EXCLAMATIONS

Dai! — Come on! *Ma dai!* — Come now! *Figurati!* — Not at all! *Per carità!* — Come off it!

REMARKS...   *REMARKS...*   *REMARKS...*   *REMARKS...*

(1) The future tense is used often to express probability.

1. ANSWERING NEGATIVELY

USING "NESSUNO"

(• •) LISTEN

Ha telefonato qualcuno?
- *No, non ha telefonato nessuno*

Hai visto qualcuno?
- *No, non ho visto nessuno*

Continue answering in the negative.
Ha telefonato qualcuno? — Hai visto qualcuno? — È venuto qualcuno? — Hai incontrato qualcuno? — Hai conosciuto qualcuno? — Hai parlato con qualcuno? — Hai scritto a qualcuno? — Hai salutato qualcuno? — Hai pensato a qualcuno?

(See Grammar, I.)

2. ANSWERING NEGATIVELY

USING "NIENTE"

(• •) LISTEN

Fai qualcosa stasera?
- *No, non faccio niente*

Continue answering in the negative.
Fai qualcosa stasera? — Prendi qualcosa? — Mangi qualcosa? — Bevi qualcosa? — Desideri qualcosa? — Vedi qualcosa? — Senti qualcosa? — Compri qualcosa? — Dici qualcosa?

(See Grammar, I.)

3. . . . AGO

(• •) LISTEN

Quando sei arrivato? — due mesi
- *Sono arrivato due mesi fa*

Answer each question as indicated.
Quando sei arrivato? - due mesi — Quando hai visto Claudio? - un'ora — Quando sei ritornato? - una settimana — Quando hai cominciato a lavorare? - quattro anni — Quando ti sei sposato? - 12 anni — Quando hai telefonato? - due minuti.

(See Grammar, F.)

4. PROBABILITY

USING THE FUTURE TENSE

(• •) LISTEN

Forse dorme ancora
- *Dormirà ancora*

Forse è uscito
- *Sarà uscito*

Change the sentences as in the model.
Forse dorme ancora — Forse è uscito — Forse lavora ancora — Forse è ritornato — Forse ha telefonato — Forse è in vacanza — Forse ha 40 anni — Forse è al cinema — Forse non può venire.

(See Grammar, L. 8.)

5. HOW MUCH/HOW MANY

(• •) LISTEN

Claudio ha 5 cravatte
- *Quante cravatte ha?*

Maria ha molti vestiti
- *Quanti vestiti ha?*

Continue asking questions in this way.
Claudio ha 5 cravatte — Maria ha molti vestiti — La signora Calvi ha 55 anni — Il sig. Clerici ha due macchine — La valigia ha una sola chiave — Quel ragazzo ha molti libri — L'albergo ha quaranta stanze — Il sig. Bauer ha mille dollari.

(See Grammar, G. 2.)

6. THE IMPERFECT

"ESSERE" & "AVERE"

(• •) LISTEN

Sono occupato
- *Ero occupato*

Ho mal di testa
- *Avevo mal di testa*

Change the following sentences from the present to the future.
Sono occupato — Ho mal di testa — Sono in vacanza — Siamo in vacanza — Abbiamo un appuntamento — Hai un appuntamento — Siete in ritardo — Loro sono in anticipo — Hanno la chiave — Avete il libro — Ho 20 anni — Sono al bar.

(See Grammar, L. 9.)

DIVORCE AND THE ITALIAN FAMILY

Although divorce is a frequent subject of conversation and films (especially in the famous Italian comedies), it was legalized only in 1969. But not until after the referendum in 1974, did it become a part of daily life in Italy. Divorce, then, is relatively new, and for a country in which Catholicism is the State religion, its legalization, in a sense, started a revolution. The law, vigorously opposed by the Church, barely got through, and because of this opposition a divorce can be obtained only after five years of separation.

But despite the law and the change in attitude toward divorce, the family remains the heart and soul of Italian society. Without a doubt, marriage is still considered a positive value to which many young Italians still aspire. And despite what appears to be a decline in church attendance, the majority of Italians seek the blessings of the Church when they marry. Some municipal weddings are performed, mainly in the cities, but rarely in the country.

The Changing Family

Yet the idea of the "traditional" Italian family is indeed changing, as it is elsewhere in the industrialized countries. On one hand, a couple has fewer children; on the other hand, the extended family, which included everyone—grandparents, uncles, aunts, cousins, daughters- and sons-in-law, etc.—is gradually becoming a thing of the past. In the cities, the nuclear family—father, mother, children—is becoming the norm. And divorce in such families is increasing dramatically.

It can be said that the role of the family in Italy has always been a primary factor in ensuring Italy's social cohesiveness. Traditionally, the husband has always been the breadwinner, but in the last few decades, this also has changed drastically. Economic changes and the fight for women's rights have made husband and wife equal partners in the world of work. Very few families now have a single breadwinner.

Toward the Twenty-first Century

Though the Italian family has changed and will continue to change, the feeling that one's family is more important than anything else continues to be an essential component of Italian society. A recent survey found, in fact, that most Italians aspire to traditional family values. Even though, most also would like to live a more "independent" life, there is still a feeling that the family lies at the core of Italian life and culture.

The challenge for the twenty-first century will, in fact, be how to reconcile new personal demands with traditional ways of family life. But, as in most other areas, the Italian "ingegno" will come forward to seek and find a solution that makes it possible to amalgamate the old with the new. This has always been Italy's greatest strength—the ability to compromise creatively!

Identify the trait (positive or negative) not mentioned on the tape for each of the following people.

1. Marta è . . . .

A. simpatica   C. riservata
B. allegra   D. depressa

2. L'ingegner Verdi è . . . .
A. disonesto
B. onesto
C. serio

3. La signora Belli è . . . .
A. dinamica
B. intelligente
C. intraprendente

4. Il figlio della signora
Carmeli è . . . .
A. affettuoso   C. maleducato
B. vivace   D. insopportabile

Find the words listed in the following "word search" puzzle. Words can read from left to right, right to left in either a straight line or diagonally.

P	O	S	O	I	O	N	O
S	V	O	L	O	R	A	C
I	I	B	O	U	O	O	I
M	T	R	C	T	R	B	T
P	T	U	C	T	E	E	A
A	A	T	I	C	N	L	P
T	C	T	P	A	C	L	I
I	P	O	V	E	R	O	T
C	F	O	R	T	E	M	N
O	I	O	V	A	R	B	A
G	V	E	C	C	H	I	O

Antipatico · bravo · brutto · caro · cattivo · corti · forte · giovane · nero · noioso · piccolo · **povero** · simpatico · tuoi · vecchio.

PROVERBIO   LISTEN

Il silenzio è d'oro e la parola è d'argento (lit., Silence is gold; words are silver). Sometimes, it's better not to say anything.

Rébus.

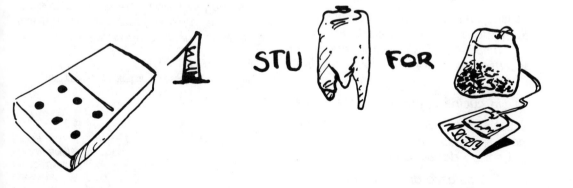

STU   FOR

(See solutions on page 24 of the booklet.)

DIALOGUE

RENTING AN APARTMENT

The Clerici's want to move, so they pay a visit to a real estate agent in Naples.

L'agente immobiliare : *Buongiorno. I Signori desiderano?*

Lui : *Buongiorno. Senta, cerchiamo un appartamento in affitto, possibilmente abbastanza grande e vicino al centro.*

L'agente imm. : *Quanti vani dovrebbe avere?*

Lui : *Quattro vani.*

L'agente imm. : *Quindi quattro stanze più i servizi. Va bene. E quanto ·vogliono spendere d'affitto?*

Lui : *Sulle sette-ottocentomila lire.*

L'agente imm. : *Vediamo un po'. Sì, su questo prezzo ne ho due che potrebbero andare bene : uno è proprio nel centro. L'altro è un po' più decentrato.*

Lei : *Com'è quello in centro?*

L'agente imm. : *Dunque... Come superficie fa 80 m². Non è grandissimo ma è ben disposto. È al settimo piano con ascensore, e ci sono anche la cantina e il box.*

Lei : *In cucina si può mangiare?*

L'agente imm. : *Non credo, perché non è molto spaziosa. Però c'è un bel soggiorno e ci sono i doppi servizi.*

Lui : *E il palazzo di che anno è?*

L'agente imm. : *Degli anni trenta, è un bel palazzo con la portineria e il citofono.*

Lei : *Il riscaldamento è centrale?*

L'agente imm. : *Sì, e le spese di amministrazione non sono troppo.elevate.*

Lui : *L'altro appartamento è più grande?*

L'agente imm. : *Sì, è circa 100 m², ma è da rinfrescare, mentre il primo di cui vi ho parlato è appena stato rimesso a nuovo.*

Lei : *Ah, e come è esposto il primo?*

L'agente imm. : *Ha un'ottima esposizione : il salotto e una delle camere da letto sono ad est, e il resto a sud.*

Lei : *Non mi sembra male! Si può visitare?*

L'agente imm. : *Certo. Quando vuole! Anche subito.*

Lui : *Per me va bene. Che ne dici, cara?*

Lei : *Oh, sì. Non vedo l'ora di vederlo!*

Lui : *Ancora una cosa : bisogna versare una cauzione?*

L'agente imm. : *Sì, alla firma del contratto deve pagare il primo mese di affitto e versare due mesi di cauzione più naturalmente le spese di agenzia.*

◉◉ LISTEN AND REPEAT
You will find the translation on page 24 of the booklet.

1. Procida
2. The old port (Naples)
3. The Posillipo district
4. A 17th-century villa
5. Wall of an old building
6. A religious statue on a street corner

NOUNS

l'appartamento — apartment
l'agenzia immobiliare — real estate agency
l'agente immobiliare — real estate agent
l'affitto — rent
il vano — room
i doppi servizi — two bathrooms (1)
la superficie — area
la cantina — basement/storage
il box — garage/parking spot
la cucina — kitchen
il soggiorno, il salotto — living room
il palazzo — building (2)
la portineria — superintendant's office
il citofono — intercom
il riscaldamento — heating
le spese di amministrazione — maintenance costs
l'esposizione — exposure
la camera da letto — bedroom
la cauzione — down payment/deposit
la firma — signature
il contratto d'affitto — rental agreement
i punti cardinali — cardinal directions
est — east
ovest — west
sud — south
nord — north

il trasloco — moving (house)
l'inquilino — tenant
il padrone di casa — house owner (3)
il portinaio — doorman
il termosifone — radiator
l'ingresso — entrance
la finestra — window

ADJECTIVES

decentrato — out/away from downtown
centrale — central
elevato — elevated
spazioso — spacious
luminoso — (with lots of) light
buio — dark

VERBS

cercare — to search/look for
affittare — to rent
spendere — to spend
disporre — to have available
rinfrescare — to renew
rimettere a nuovo — to remodel/renovate
non vedere l'ora (di) — to be unable to wait (can't wait to)
versare — to put down (a deposit)
traslocare — to move

1. RENTING AN APARTMENT/A ROOM

Cerco un appartamento in affitto — I am looking for an apartment to rent.
Vorrei affittare una camera ammobiliata per un mese — I'd like to rent a furnished room for a month.
Vorrei affittare un appartamento di tre vani più servizi. — I'd like to rent an apartment with three rooms plus a bathroom.

2. APARTMENT SHOPPING

Quant'è l'affitto? — What's the rent?
Le spese di amministrazione sono comprese? — Are maintenance costs included?
Qual è la superficie? — How big is it? (What's its area?)
Il riscaldamento è centrale (a gas, elettrico, individuale)? — Does it have central (gas, electric, localized) heating?
A che piano è? — What floor is it on?
C'è l'ascensore (il citofono, la portineria)? — Does it have an elevator (intercom, superintendent's office)?
Com'è esposto? — Which way does it face?
Il palazzo di che anno è? — How old is the building?

3. RENTING

Bisogna versare una cauzione? — Is a deposit necessary?
Quanto dura il contratto d'affitto? — How long does the rental agreement last?
Ci sono delle spese di agenzia? — Are there any real estate expenses?
L'assicurazione è obbligatoria? — Is insurance required?

4. DESCRIBING THE APARTMENT

È un po' decentrato — It's a bit out of town.
È in periferia — It's in the suburbs.
È centralissimo — It's right downtown.
È ben disposto — It's well situated.
Le finestre danno sulla strada (sul cortile) — The windows look out onto the street (yard).
Ha un'ottima esposizione — It has excellent exposure.
È un'occasione — It's a deal.
È da rinfrescare — It has to be renovated.
È rimesso a nuovo — It's been renovated.
Ci sono i doppi servizi — There are two bathrooms.

REMARKS...   REMARKS...   REMARKS...   REMARKS...

(1) "Servizi" designates "bathrooms" as well as "kitchen," "laundry room," and "entrance." — (2) A synonym is "edificio." — (3) A synonym is "proprietario."

1. THE RELATIVE PRONOUN "CUI"

(● ●) LISTEN

Vi ho parlato di un appartamento
* *Ecco l'appartamento di cui vi ho parlato*
Ho parlato con una signora
* *Ecco la signora con cui ho parlato*

Change the sentences by using "cui" with the prepositions "di, da, con, a, per," as in the model.
Vi ho parlato di un appartamento — Ho parlato con una signora — Sono venuto per un motivo — Sono andato da un agente immobiliare — Ho dato il libro a una ragazza — Ti ho parlato di una persona — Sono uscito con un amico.

(See Grammar, G. 1.)

2. THE CONDITIONAL

THE VERB "VOLERE"

(● ●) LISTEN

Io
* *Vorrei affittare un appartamento*
Tu
* *Vorresti affittare un appartamento*

Conjugate "volere" as in the model.
Io — Tu — I signori Clerici — Mario — Noi — I nostri amici — Voi — Lei — Io — Marina.

(See Grammar, L. 8.)

3. THE CONDITIONAL

THE VERB "POTERE"

(● ●) LISTEN

Visitare l'appartamento - io
* *Potrei visitare l'appartamento?*
Fare una telefonata - noi
* *Potremmo fare una telefonata?*

Continue forming questions in this way.
Visitare l'appartamento - io — Fare una telefonata - noi — Aprire la finestra - tu — Telefonare a Mario - voi — Parlare con il direttore - io — Spedire il curriculum vitae - loro.

(See Grammar, L. 8.)

4. THE IMPERSONAL "SI"

(● ●) LISTEN

È possibile entrare
* *Si può entrare*
Bisogna firmare
* *Si deve firmare*

Change each sentence as in the model.
È possibile entrare — Bisogna firmare — Non è possibile fumare — Non bisogna prenotare — È possibile pagare in due volte — Non è possibile avera la linea — Bisogna versare una cauzione.

(See Grammar, L. 15.)

5. ADJECTIVES

(● ●) LISTEN

È grande l'appartamento?
* *No, è piccolo*
È luminosa la cucina?
* *No, è buia*

Continue answering with the opposite (antonym) of the adjective given.
È grande l'appartamento? — È luminosa la cucina? — È lungo il corridoio? — È nuovo il palazzo? — È largo l'ingresso? — È divertente lo spettacolo? — È buono il pesce?

6. COMPARISON

(● ●) LISTEN

Rapido — Prendere il treno/prendere l'aereo
* *È più rapido prendere l'aereo che prendere il treno*

Make comparisons, as in the model.
Rapido - Prendere il treno/prendere l'aereo — Caro - Mangiare al ristorante/mangiare a casa — Divertente - Andare in vacanza/restare in città — Importante - Essere in buona forma/avere molti soldi.

(See Grammar, H. 1.)

FINDING A HOME IN ITALY

Are you thinking of buying a house or renting an apartment in Italy? Finding either is becoming rather difficult. Not only is the price of real estate rising, but real estate itself is getting harder to find.

Something for Everyone

What type of living quarters are you looking for? Something original? Let's start with the Matera district in the mountainous region of La Basilicata. But this might not appeal to you because the whole area is cluttered with characteristic huts. Let's go a little further south, below Bari; something there might suit your needs: the "trulli" houses of Alberobello. These houses are indeed original in design, with conical-shaped roofs topped off with a button, much like a witch's or fairy's hat. The only problem is that there is not much going on in this area. Perhaps something a little more cosmopolitan and definitely chic? Try the Navagli district of Milan or a villa in Portofino on the Isle of Capri. Or take a look at that Venetian palace located on the Grand Canal. Perhaps you could even turn it into a foundation, like the Peggy Guggenheim Museum! As far as apartments go, nothing could be finer than one that looks out onto the famous Piazza del Campo in Siena, where you can have a privileged view of the famous "Palio" horse race. And there are the magnificent Tuscan palatial homes in Fiesole, located near the European Institute (a perfect place for studying).

The Old and the New

You seem rather difficult to please. Then for you, there is a Renaissance villa in the region of Venetia in the northeast. A creation of Palladio, the great Renaissance architect, this treasure will only cost about three billion lire. What do you think of that prospect? It's yours, as long as nothing is touched or disturbed and you are willing to devote your whole life to maintaining it.

Let's go to Venice to look at something simpler. Forget your car, the train, and hop onto a "va-poretto" (steamboat). After going down the Grand Canal, passing San Marco, taking yet another "vaporetto" from Murano, stop off in Burano. This large aquatic village, with houses painted in every color would make anyone happy. But then again, you would have to buy a motor launch to make life easier!

Palaces, famous villas, and medieval and Renaissance apartments combine with ultramodern villas and homes to make Italy a dream world for anyone looking for a place to live. And then let's not forget the Italian home away from home—the apartment or villa by the sea. It you prefer clean mountain air, how about a chalet or cottage in the Alps, the Apennines, or the Dolomites? Remarkably, there are very few shanty towns to spoil the scenery. Even in the inner city, slums are comparatively rare. By and large, Italians cherish their homes, looking after them with great pride and devotion.

● ● LISTEN

L'Italiano
(C. Minellono—S. Cutugno)
Sung by Toto Cutugno
© *Number Two Edizioni/Edizioni Curci SRL/Star Edizioni*

	The Italian
Lasciatemi cantare con la chitarra in mano	Let me sing with my guitar in my hands
Lasciatemi cantare, sono un italiano	Let me sing, I'm Italian
Buongiorno Italia, gli spaghetti al dente	Good morning, Italy, spaghetti al dente
e un partigiano come Presidente	And a partisan as President
con l'autoradio sempre nella mano destra	With a car radio always in my right hand
e un canarino sopra la finestra.	and a canary on top of my window.
Buongiorno Italia con i tuoi artisti	Good morning, Italy, with all your artists
con troppa America sui manifesti	with too much America in your ads
con le canzoni, con amore, con il cuore,	with songs, love, heart,
con più donne, sempre meno suore.	with always more women and fewer nuns.
Buongiorno Italia, buongiorno Maria	Good morning, Italy, good morning, Mary
con gli occhi pieni di malinconia	with eyes full of melancholy
Buongiorno Dio	Good morning God
lo sai che ci sono anch'io.	You know that I am here too.
Lasciatemi cantare con la chitarra in mano	Let me sing with my guitar in my hands
Lasciatemi cantare una canzone piano piano	Let me sing a song softly softly
Lasciatemi cantare perché ne sono fiero	Let me sing because I'm proud
Sono un italiano, un italiano vero.	to be an Italian, a true Italian.
Buongiorno Italia che non si spaventa	Good morning fearless Italy
e con la crema da barba alla menta	with mint shaving cream
con un vestito gessato sul blu	and a chalk-blue suit
e la moviola la domenica in TV.	and moviola on Sunday TV
Buongiorno Italia col caffè ristretto	Good morning Italy with ''ristretto'' coffee
le calze nuove nel primo cassetto	new socks in the top drawer
con la bandiera in tintoria	with your flag at the laundry
e una 600 giù di carrozzeria.	and your FIAT 600 at the body shop.

"FIGURES" OF SPEECH

MANGIARE LA FOGLIA
(lit., to eat the leaf)
To figure out what's really going on

NASCERE CON LA CAMICIA
(lit., to be born with a shirt)
To be born with a silver spoon in your mouth

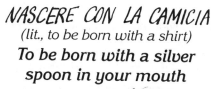

AVERE L'ACQUA ALLA GOLA
(lit., to have water at your throat)
To be drowning

ESSERE UN PALLONE GONFIATO
(lit., to be an inflated balloon)
To be full of oneself

3. *WRITTEN PRACTICE*

3.1

FILL IN THE BLANKS WITH "quel/quei/quella/quelle" : . . . . *vestito è troppo corto.* — . . . . *camicia è sportiva.* — . . . . *pantaloni sono di lana.* — . . . . *cravatte sono troppo vivaci.* — . . . . *gonna le sta molto bene.* — . . . . *modello è molto elegante.*

TRANSLATE : *Vuole provare la taglia più grande? — Quella di seta è più cara dell'altra. — Il cappotto rosso non ti sta molto bene.*
Mr. and Mrs. Clerici went to the Rinascente. — Have you already seen something in the window? — Do you like this shirt, madam? — What's your size?

3.2

ANSWER EACH QUESTION, ALWAYS USING "ne" OR "ci" AS EACH CASE REQUIRES.
Sei andato alla stazione? Sì, ...
Conosci molte persone? Sì, ...
Vieni anche tu al ristorante? Sì, ... *anch'io.*
Quante medicine prendi al giorno? . . . . *molte.*
Quando vai dal dottore? . . . . *domani.*

TRANSLATE : *Devo prendere questa medicina tre volte alla settimana. — Il dottore mi ha misurato la pressione. — Ho dimenticato di prendere la ricetta.*
Today I have a dentist appointment. — Here we are. It's my turn. — I have a headache. — I'm not sure, but I believe so.

3.3

FILL IN THE BLANKS
WITH "che" OR "chi" : *Il regista* . . . *ha fatto il film è molto famoso.* — . . . *è il protagonista?* — . . . . . . *film danno al cinema?* — *L'attore* . . . . . . *interpreta il film è un tipo affascinante.* — . . . . *ha comprato il giornale?* — . . . . *ne dici di uscire stasera?* — *La commedia* . . . . *ho visto ieri mi è piaciuta molto.*

TRANSLATE : *Il film mi è piaciuto molto. — Ti va di andare a teatro? — Sei pronta? — È una bravissima attrice.*
Shall we go out together this evening? — What movie is being shown on TV? — I didn't like the concert at all. — I hate going dancing.

3.4

ANSWER THE FOLLOWING QUESTIONS: *Ha telefonato qualcuno? No,* . . . .
Hai visto qualcuno? No, ... *C'è qualcosa al cinema? No,* . . . .
Hai fatto qualcosa di bello? No, ... ? *C'è qualcuno qui che parla il russo? No,* . . . .

TRANSLATE : *Suo marito ha dieci anni più di lei. — È sempre elegantissima! — Non si trucca mai.*
Was there someone with her? — No, there was no one. — I said nothing. — She remarried six months ago.

3.5

FILL IN THE BLANKS WITH
"cui" OR "che" AS EACH CASE REQUIRES: *Il film di* . . . . *ti ho parlato è uscito ieri.* — *La ragazza con* . . . . . *ho cenato è molto simpatica.* — *L'attore* . . . . . *preferisco è italiano.* — *Il libro da* . . . . . . *è tratto il film è un celebre romanzo di Eco. Questa è la ragione per* . . . . . . *ti scrivo.* — *Il cinema* . . . . . . *dà il nome della rosa è in centro.* — *La signora* . . . . . . *abbiamo incontrato è la vicina del 4° piano.*

TRANSLATE : *L'affitto non è troppo caro. — Il riscaldamento è individuale. — Non vedo l'ora di cambiare casa!*
The Clerici's would like to rent an apartment. — The building I talked to you about is very modern. — One can eat in the kitchen.

(Check your answers on page 36 of the booklet.)

MORE VOCABULARY

CLOTHING

accapatoio — robe
berretto — cap
calze — stockings
calze di nylon — nylons
camicia da notte — nightshirt
canottier — undershirt
cappello — hat
cappotto — coat
cintura — belt
costume da bagno — bathing suit
giacca — jacket
giubbotto — big jacket
golf — golf sweater
guanti — gloves
maglietta — undershirt
mutandine — underwear
ombrello — umbrella
pantaloncini — shorts
pantalori — pants
pelliccia — fur coat
pigiama — pajamas
reggiseno — brassiere
scarpe — shoes
scialle — shawl
sciarpa — scarf
stivali — boots

THE HUMAN BODY

capelli — hair
faccia — face
viso — face
fronte — forehead
occhi — eyes
naso — nose
bocca — mouth
labbra — lips
denti — teeth
mento — chin
orecchi — ears
collo — neck
spalle — shoulders
braccio — arm
braccia — arms
gomito — elbow
gambe — legs
coscia — thigh
ginocchio — knee
polpaccio — calf
mani — hands
ploso — wrist
piedi — feet
dito — finger
dita — fingers
schiena — back
petto — chest
seno — breast

STORES

calzoleria — shoe store
calzolaio — shoemaker
drogheria — grocery store
droghiere — grocer
farmacia — pharmacy
farmacista — pharmacist
frutta e verdura — grocery
fruttivendolo — fruit vendor
gelateria — ice cream parlor
gelataio — ice cream maker
gioielleria — jewelry shop
gioielliere — jeweler
latteria — milk store, dairy
lattaio — milk producer
macelleria — butcher shop
macellaio — butcher
panetteria — bakery
panettiere — baker
pasticceria — pastry shop
pasticcere — pastry maker
pescheria — fish store
pescivendolo — fish vendor
rosticceria — take-out
rosticcere — take-out vendor
salumeria — delicatessen
salumiere — delicatessen vendor

JOBS/PROFESSIONS

elettricista — electrician
fabbro — blacksmith
falegname — carpenter
fotografo — photographer
giornalaio — newspaper vendor
idraulico — plumber
meccanico — mechanic
orologiaio — watchmaker
parrucchiere — hairdresser
barbiere — barber

THE HOUSE

ingresso — entrance
corridoio — corridor
stanza — room
camera — bedroom
camera da letto — bedroom
sala da pranzo — dining room
salone (salotto), soggiorno — living room
cucina — kitchen
ripostiglio — closet
balcone (terrazzo) — terrace window
terrazza — terrace
bagno — bath
gabinetto — washroom
pavimento — floor
soffitto — ceiling
finestra — window
porta — door

FURNITURE

armadio — armoire
tavolo — table
sedia (seggiola) — chair
poltrona — armchair
divano (sofà) — sofa
scaffale — shelf/bookcase

3. TEST YOURSELF

1. PUT INTO THE PAST TENSE

Dico a Mario di venire . . . .
Prendiamo l'autobus . . . .
Bevono una birra . . . .
La commedia mi piace molto . . . .
Luisa si annoia al concerto . . . .
Non faccio niente . . . .
Scrivo una lettera a Mario . . . .

2. FILL IN THE BLANKS WITH "DI" OR "CHE" AS REQUIRED

Questo vestito è meno caro . . . . quello.
È meglio andare in montagna . . . . restare in città.
È più facile capire . . . . parlare una lingua straniera.
Quest'appartamento è più grande . . . . quello.
Maria è più alta . . . . Carlo.

3. GIVE THE OPPOSITE (ANTONYM) OF EACH VERB

aprire . . . .   divertirsi . . . .
entrare . . . .   accorciare . . . .
salire . . . .   cominciare . . . .
ricordare . . . .   domandare . . . .
andare . . . .   essere in anticipo . . . .

4. WHAT WOULD YOU SAY IF YOU . . .

wanted to know the color of something . . . .
wanted to say that it was your size . . . .
wanted to say that you didn't feel very well . . . .

wanted to ask a friend to go out with you . . . .
wanted to ask what's playing at a movie theater . . . .
wanted to ask how much the rent is . . . .
wanted to ask which floor the apartment is on . . . .

5. ONLY ONE SENTENCE IN EACH SET IS CORRECT. CAN YOU FIND IT?

A. *Qui si non può fumare* . . . . □
B. *Qui non si può fumare* . . . . □
C. *Qui non si può di fumare* . . . . □

A. *Le posso dare questo sciroppo* . . . . □
B. *Posso Le dare questo sciroppo* . . . . □
C. *La posso dare questo sciroppo* . . . . □

A. *Questa sera uscio con Francesco* . . . . □
B. *Questa sera uscito con Francesco* . . . . □
C. *Questa sera esco con Francesco* . . . . □

A. *Ha divorziato due anni fa* . . . . □
B. *Ha divorziato fa due anni* . . . . □
C. *Ha divorziato fra due anni* . . . . □

6. MATCH EACH QUESTION TO ITS ANSWER

A. *Molto bene : è proprio la tua misura!*
B. *Solo un po' di aspirina.*
C. *Perché no? Potremmo andare a teatro...*
D. *Non lo so di preciso... forse 45.*
E. *Sulle sette-ottocentomila lire.*

1. *Ha già preso qualche medicina?*
2. *Quanti anni avrà quella signora?*
3. *Quanto vogliono spendere d'affitto?*
4. *Come mi sta questo vestito?*
5. *Che ne diresti di uscire stasera?*

(Check your answers on page 37 of the booklet.)

IN THE MOUTH OF THE WOLF

That night Ambrose had trouble getting to sleep. This insistence on making cryptic remarks to him on the phone threw him off balance. He couldn't understand the pleasure that some people got out of making such bad jokes. These two phone calls seemed to open a chasm under his feet and he feared that he would be dragged into it. He tried to reason with himself. "In the nature of things my name gets around; it could have come to the attention of the first idiot who came along, as much in Italy as in France. Someone's trying to frighten me."

And, in fact, they were succeeding. The possibility that his mysterious caller had been able to come closer since the previous night unnerved him. But maybe it was only an illusion. After all, *in bocca al lupo* was an overused expression, perfectly common, any imbecile could readily use it. But no reasoning, even the most logical, the most perfect, could calm him. He looked at the cover of the book but didn't dare to touch it, open it, leaf through it. He had the impression that if he risked it, the most awful catastrophe would fall on his head.

It was only later in the night, when the snow already blocked the window on his balcony, that Ambrose slept.

Lucy burst out laughing when she saw his drawn face with the dark rings under his eyes. "*Come ti sei ridotto! Ma con chi hai passato la notte?*" And she added, raising her eyebrows, "*Ti sei anche tagliato.*"

"*Lo so. Non c'è niente da ridere.*"

"*Insomma, non si può piu scherzare. Sai che ho dato un'occhiata al famigerato in bocca al lupo?*"

Ambrose paled. "*Ah si?*"

"*Dai, Ambrogio, non fare questa faccia! I only looked at the table of contents. Ma forse l'avrai già consultata?*"

"*No.*" Ambrose took a serious tone. "*Come dicevi tu, sono stato molto occupato questa notte, non ho avuto un minuto da dedicare alle scemenze della Aiguement.*"

"*Allora non avrai visto che uno dei capitoli s'intitola 'Gelsi in via Pioppette.' A Milano, non abitavi in via Pioppette? Li hai visti, i gelsi, in via Pioppette?*"

Indeed; Ambrose had lived for several years in Piopette Street, that's why he used to take the streetcar in front of the Roman columns of San Lorenzo—they were one block from his house. But never—he was ready to swear by anything—had he seen mulberries on the street. Nowhere else in Milan, moreover. After all, nobody raised silkworms in the middle of town. It seemed absurd to title the chapter of a book that pretended to be a documentary "The Mulberries in Pioppete Street." Ambrose felt reassured. It reduced his worries to zero.

So it was that, sitting at his desk, he got ready to check what Lucia had told him about in Anonymous' book when she announced: "La Aiguement al telefono; te la passo? Sai, lupo non mangia lupo."

"Molto divertente."

He picked up the phone.

"Hello, Ambrose dear? I'm sorry to call you at the crack of dawn..."

"Not at all, dear Mrs. Aiguement. It's a pleasure."

Ambrose always felt a little ripple of satisfaction when he himself had to resort to hypocrisy.

"You know," she said, "I spoke to you about that book yesterday—In the Mouth of the Wolf, or whatever its title is. Well, I'm afraid I acted a little too quickly. You know how it is. I'm afraid the work doesn't interest us after all. I wanted to let you know so that you could propose it to other French editors. I'm really very sorry. I liked it a lot."

"Ma va' a quel paese," he thought. And aloud, "That's perfectly all right. Things like that happen. I understand perfectly. It'll be for another time.

At least he wouldn't have to read it so that he could talk about it—there was that much gained. The only thing that intrigued him was the nervousness that he was aware of in Mrs. Aiguement's voice. She wasn't in the habit of hurrying, and even less of excusing herself and pretending to want to be helpful. An attitude so proper on her part was surprising.

He picked up the book again. The chapter "Gelsi in via Pioppette" really existed. He looked at it and understood his error right away. It wasn't mulberries—or "gelsi"—that was found on Pioppette Street,

but bankers. Or, more specifically, a certain banker: the problematic Dr. Gelsi, financier of grand theft and corrupt businesses. One night a patrol of vigili urbani had found him hanging from a tree at the corner of Pioppette Street and Vetra Plaza. It was winter and the fog was so thick that from a distance the policemen had taken his body for a plastic bag. Under the affable pen of Anonymous, Mr. S. commented on the affair in these terms:

"Nessuno si stupì di una cosi squallida fine. Tutti sapevano delle traversie che aveva conosciuto il banchiere Gelsi, dei complotti in cui era stato coinvolto, delle colpe di cui si era macchiato. Però ci si aspettava una morte più discreta, una sparizione nel nulla, qualcosa che non destasse scalpore. Infatti, la cosa fu subito messa a tacere. Pochi giornali riferirono la notizia, e quelli che lo fecero le dedicarono appena un piccolo trafiletto. Chiaramente, i mandanti dell'omicidio volevano dare l'esempio, mandare una specie di ammonimento a certe persone di cui non farò i nomi. Insomma, tutto sarebbe andato a buon porto se non ci fosse stato un inghippo: qualcuno della zona aveva visto tutto."

CONTINUED . . .

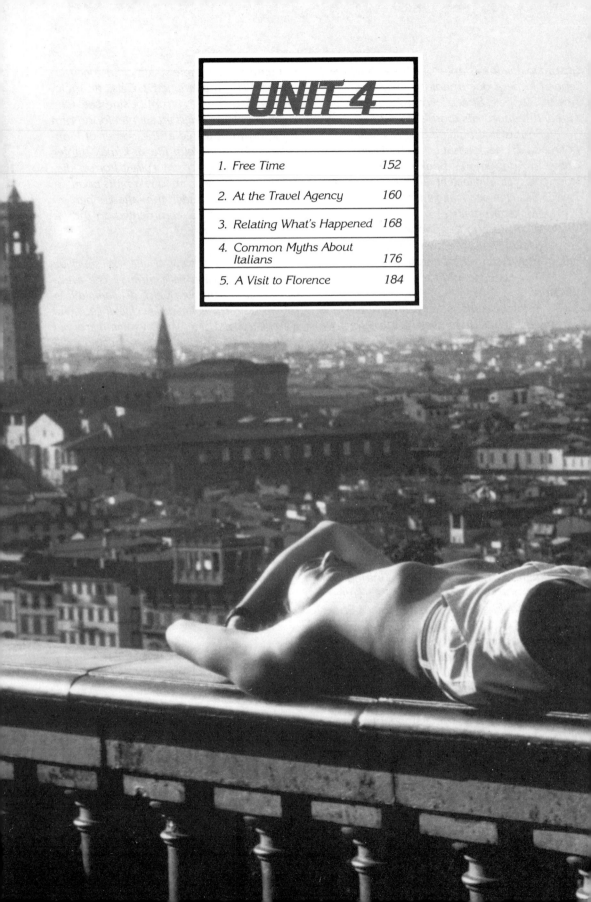

UNIT 4

⊙⊙ LISTEN

FREE TIME

Here we are in Florence where Mrs. Rizzi and Mrs. Gili are having tea.

Signora Gili : *Ieri sono andata a iscrivere mia figlia a un corso di nuoto.*

Signora Rizzi : *Anche mia figlia fa nuoto. Va in piscina due o tre volte alla settimana.*

Signora Gili : *E Suo figlio?*

Signora Rizzi : *Mio figlio invece non è per niente sportivo, ma suona molto bene il violino.*

Signora Gili : *Davvero? Ah, la musica non è il nostro forte. In famiglia siamo tutti stonati! Però la mia figlia maggiore fa danza classica.*

Signora Rizzi : *Ma guarda! Anch'io quando ero giovane facevo danza e sognavo di diventare una grande ballerina!*

Signora Gili : *E come mai non ha continuato?*

Signora Rizzi : *Eh! I miei genitori non approvavano la mia scelta. Ma è sempre stato un mio grande rimpianto.*

Signora Gili : *A volte è difficile essere genitori! Me ne rendo conto adesso che i miei figli stanno crescendo...*

Signora Rizzi : *Non me ne parli!*

Signora Gili : *Gradisce un'altra tazza di tè, signora?*

Signora Rizzi : *Grazie, volentieri.*

Signora Gili : *Allora, avete poi deciso che cosa farete questo fine settimana?*

Signora Rizzi : *Come al solito andremo in montagna. Mio marito è un appassionato di sci.*

Signora Gili : *Noi, invece, andremo in campagna dai miei.*

Signora Rizzi : *E per le vacanze che cosa fate?*

Signora Gili : *Non abbiamo ancora un programma preciso. Ci piacerebbe fare un viaggio...*

Signora Rizzi : *Noi volevamo andare in Sicilia : non ci siamo mai stati e sarebbe un'occasione per andare un po' alla spiaggia e nello stesso tempo fare anche del turismo.*

Signora Gili : *Perché non viene con me domani all'agenzia? Potremmo intanto informarci sui viaggi organizzati e farci un'idea dei prezzi.*

Signora Gili : *Con piacere.*

⊙⊙ LISTEN AND REPEAT
You will find the translation on page 27 of the booklet.

A panorama of Florence
(foreground: Badia church)
(background: Bargello Museum)

NOUNS

il tempo libero — free time
la corsa — racing
il nuoto — swimming
la piscina — swimming pool
il violino — violin
la musica — music
la danza (classica, moderna) — dance/ballet
la ballerina — ballerina
la scelta — choice
il rimpianto — regret
il fine-settimana — weekend
l'appassionato — lover of (dance, etc.)
lo sci — skiing
la vacanza — vacation
l'occasione (f) — occasion/opportunity
la spiaggia — beach
il turismo — tourism
l'agenzia — agency
il viaggio organizzato — organized tour
la famiglia — family
i genitori — parents
i miei (i tuoi, i suoi, ecc.) — mine (yours, hers, etc.)
il padre — father
la madre — mother
il figlio maggiore — oldest son
il figlio minore — youngest son
il fratello — brother
la sorella — sister
il suocero — father-in-law
la suocera — mother-in-law

---

l'hobby — hobby
lo sport — sport

il tennis — tennis
la vela — boating
la ginnastica — gymnastics
l'equitazione — horseback riding
la scherma — fencing

VERBS

iscrivere (/si) — to enroll/register
suonare (uno strumento) — to play (an instrument)
essere stonato — to be out of key
sognare — to dream
approvare — to approve
rendersi conto — to realize
crescere — to grow
informarsi — to get information on
farsi un'idea — to get an idea about
fare sport — to practice sports
chiacchierare — to chat
recitare (un ruolo) — to play (a role)
giocare (un gioco) — to play (a game)

MISCELLANEOUS

per niente — for nothing
davvero? — really?
non è il mio forte — I'm not good at . . .
come mai... ? — how come?
gradisce una tazza di tè? — would you like a cup of tea? (1)

HOW TO SAY IT

1. SPEAKING OF SPORTS

Mia figlia fa nuoto — My daughter goes swimming. *(2)*
La mia figlia maggiore fa danza — My oldest daughter takes ballet.
Mio marito è un appassionato di sci — My husband loves skiing.
Mia sorella gioca a tennis — My sister plays tennis.
Mio fratello fa vela — My brother is into boating.
Io non so sciare (nuotare, giocare a tennis, ecc.) — I do not know how to ski (swim, play tennis, etc.)
I miei figli fanno molto sport — My kids do a lot of sports.

2. PLAYING SPORTS

Fa qualche sport? — Do you play any sports?
Lei fa dello sport? — Do you play any sports?
Che sport fa? — Which sports do you play?
Quale sport preferisce? — Which sport do you prefer?

3. SPEAKING OF HOBBIES

Il mio hobby è la musica (la lettura, la fotografia) — My hobby is music (reading, photography).
Suono il violino (il piano, la chitarra, la tromba) — I play the violin (piano, guitar, trumpet).

4. LEISURE TIME

Che cosa farete questo fine-settimana? — What will you be doing this weekend?
Per le vacanze, che cosa fate? — What are you doing for the vacation?
Che programmi ha per la vacanze, signora? — What plans do you have for your vacation, madam?

5. WHAT TO DO FOR YOUR VACATION

Se farà bel tempo andrò al mare (3) — If the weather is nice, I'll go to the sea.
Come al solito andremo in montagna (in campagna) — As usual, we're going to the mountains (to the country).
Non abbiamo ancora un programma preciso — We haven't made definite plans yet.
Ci piacerebbe fare un viaggio — We'd like to take a trip.
Noi volevamo andare in Sicilia — We wanted to go to Sicily.

REMARKS...   *REMARKS...*   *REMARKS...*   *REMARKS...*

(1) "Gradire" means literally "to enjoy." — (2) For possessives without the article, see Grammar, D. 1. — (3) In this kind of sentence, the two verbs are either both in the present or in the future.

1. THE IMPERFECT

👂👂 LISTEN

Che cosa facevi quando eri giovane? - giocare a tennis
* *Quando ero giovane giocavo a tennis*
Che cosa facevi ieri alle 5? - bere il tè
* *Ieri alle 5 bevevo il tè*

Continue answering the questions as in the model.
Che cosa facevi quando eri giovane? - giocare a tennis — Che cosa facevi ieri alle 5? - bere il tè — Che cosa faceva la signora Rizzi quando era giovane? - fare danza — Che cosa faceva Marco quando era piccolo? - andare in piscina — Che cosa facevano Claudio e Filippo ieri alle 8? - cenare — Che cosa facevi ieri alle tre? - leggere il giornale — Che cosa facevate quando eravate bambini? - suonare il violino.

(See Grammar, L. 9.)

2. PRESENT PROGRESSIVE

STARE + GERUND

👂👂 LISTEN

Io-mangio
* *Sto mangiando*
Lui-legge
* *Sta leggendo*

Put the verb in the present progressive.
Io-mangio — Lui-legge — Noi-finiamo — Tu-scrivi — Voi-guardate la televisione — Io-scherzo — Loro-bevono il tè — Lei-fuma una sigaretta — Noi-facciamo colazione — Tu-dici la verità — Lei-chiacchiera con una signora.

(See Grammar, L. 13.)

3. "SE"

👂👂 LISTEN

Se fa bel tempo vado al mare
* *Se farà bel tempo andrò al mare*

Put the sentences in the future.
Se fa bel tempo vado al mare — Se ho tempo vengo da te — Se posso ti telefono alle 8 — Se vieni ti diverti sicuramente — Se piove non usciamo — Se fa brutto tempo restate a casa.

(See Grammar, L. 8.)

4. POSSESSIVES

WITH FAMILY MEMBERS

👂👂 LISTEN

Sorella
* *Questa è mia sorella*
Genitori
* *Questi sono i miei genitori*

Form sentences as in the model. Pay attention to the article used before the possessive adjective.
Sorella — Genitori — Marito — Moglie — Fratello — Padre — Figli — Madre — Figlie — Sorelle — Fratelli — Figlio.

(See Grammar, D. 1.)

5. I'D LIKE TO . . .

👂👂 LISTEN

Fare un viaggio
* *Mi piacerebbe fare un viaggio.*

Continue saying that you would like to do the following things.
Fare un viaggio — Andare a sciare — Uscire con te — Suonare uno strumento — Visitare Firenze — Andare in Sicillia — Conoscere bene l'Italia — Giocare bene a tennis.

6. SAYING THE OPPOSITE

👂👂 LISTEN

Mio figlio è sportivo
* *Il mio, invece, non è per niente sportivo*
Mia moglie è stonata
* *La mia, invece, non è per niente stonata*

Continue as in the model.
Mio figlio è sportivo — Mia moglie è stonata — Il mio appartamento è grande — La mia macchina è veloce — La mia camera è spaziosa — La mia cucina è moderna — I miei genitori sono severi.

(See Grammar, I.)

LEISURE TIME

These days, free time does not necessarily mean leisure time. Many Italians, despite a reduction in their official work hours, work more than ever. Everyone seems to hold down at least a couple of jobs. This phenomenon of "secondo lavoro" (moonlighting), where one might perform work as a mason, electrician, accountant, etc.—work that has nothing to do with what one does "officially"—appears to affect about 40 percent of the Italian work force.

Let's Play Soccer!

But do not think for a moment that all this extra work leaves no time for leisure activity. Italians are known for their ability and desire to have a good time, particularly with respect to their beloved soccer and the various festivals that occur throughout the year.

"La partita di calcio" (soccer match), which takes place every Sunday, is one of the most favorite pastimes of Italians. Essentially a masculine event, "il calcio" constitutes a way of organizing weekends and getting together with friends, and needless to say, a good way of letting off steam. In an old popular song, a woman is heard lamenting "La domenica, mi lasci sempre sola . . ." ("On Sundays, you always leave me alone"), alluding to her husband's going to the soccer match and leaving the family behind. The match always has an enthusiastic crowd of "tifosi" (fans), cheering for one team or another. Emotions frequently spill over, should the home team fall behind, or the referee give a penalty at an inopportune time. Whether it is watched on television, listened to on the radio, or seen at the stadium, the ritual of "la partita" sets the tempo for every Sunday afternoon in Italy.

The Sunday match also makes possible a different kind of leisure activity—gambling! Even if you do not like soccer, you can always bet on the outcome by playing the nationwide lottery known as the "Totocalcio," an extremely popular activity.

Now Let's Go to the Festival!

But soccer, other sports, and all the other amusements are no substitute for the innumerable festivals that take place throughout the peninsula. "La festa," especially the religious kind, is perhaps the most traditional form of leisure-related activity in Italy. There is the Carnival of Venice, the Palio of Siena, and the Sagra del Pesce in Camogli (on the Ligurian Riviera), to name but a few.

All these festivals, be they traditional or relatively new, always ring with the utmost liveliness and gaiety. Everyone participates with ardent enthusiasm! Without a doubt, these high-spirited festivals bear witness to the fact that even after a hard day's (or night's) work, Italians have no difficulty in having a good time.

N° 1 • • LISTEN

Check off all the sports mentioned in the taped conversations.

EQUITAZIONE

SCI

JUDO

PALLACANESTRO

CALCIO

NUOTO

SCHERMA

VELA

CICLISMO

DANZA

TENNIS

PATTINAGGIO

Match each drawing with the missing object. 1. *Racchetta* **2.** *Pallone* **3.** *Sci*
4. *Fioretto* **5.** *Cavallo* **6.** *Pattini* **7.** *Bicicletta* **8.** *Vela*

A ☐

B ☐

C ☐

D ☐

E ☐

F ☐

G ☐

H ☐

PROVERBIO ◉◉ LISTEN

L'ozio è il padre dei vizi
(lit., Idleness is the father of all vices).

The Devil finds work for idle hands.

(See solutions of page 28 of the booklet.)

LISTEN

AT THE TRAVEL AGENCY

L'impiegato : *Guardi questo giro della Sicilia, per esempio : è molto vario. Eccole il dépliant dettagliato.*

Signora Rizzi : *Grazie, me ne dia due, per cortesia.*

Signora Gili : *Vediamo... sì... Il primo giorno nel pomeriggio c'è una visita alla zona archeologica a Segeste e a Selinunte.*

Signora Rizzi : *Oh! Si visita Agrigento e c'è anche una visita ai monumenti illuminati, dopo cena...*

Signora Gili : *Non è male! Si visita anche Taormina, che deve essere splendida!*

Signora Rizzi : *Ma la cosa che mi attira di più, è l'escursione all'Etna.*

Signora Gili : *Ah sì! Ho sentito dire che è impressionante!*

Signora Rizzi : *Insomma, che cosa ne pensa? Mi sembra un viaggio magnifico!*

Signora Gili : *È un po' caro, però...*

L'impiegato : *No, non lo è, se lei considera che gli alberghi in cui soggiornerete sono tutti di prima categoria, con piscina e aria condizionata, e il prezzo è per la pensione completa.*

Signora Rizzi : *In effetti è vero.*

Signora Gili : *Comunque grazie, Lei è stato molto gentile. Rifletteremo e torneremo per prenotare, eventualmente.*

LISTEN AND REPEAT

You will find the translation on page 28 of the booklet.

GIRO DELLA SICILIA

1° giorno : Arrivo a Palermo. Sistemazione in autopullman. Visita di Segeste e Selinunte. Nel pomeriggio visita della zona archeologica. In serata si raggiunge Agrigento. Pernottamento in hotel.

2° giorno : Visita della Valle dei Templi. Escursione panoramica lungo la costa nel pomeriggio. Dopo cena visita ai monumenti illuminati.

3° giorno : Partenza per Catania. All'arrivo visita della città. In serata partenza per Taormina.

4° giorno : Visita di Taormina e del teatro. Nel pomeriggio partenza per l'Etna, dove si potranno ammirare la zona dei crateri e i campi di lava.

5° giorno : Siracusa. Visita della città e pomeriggio a disposizione.

6° giorno : Proseguimento per Messina. Giro della città. Nel pomeriggio partenza per Palermo.

7° giorno : In mattinata visita del chiostro di Monreale. 2ª colazione in albergo e trasferimento all'aeroporto.

Mrs. Rizzi and Mrs. Gili have an appointment at a travel agency to get some information on an organized tour of Sicily.

L'impiegato : *Viaggi organizzati in Sicilia? Ma naturalmente! Abbiamo diverse formule, da una settimana o da 15 giorni, o anche di più se vuole.*

Signora Rizzi : *No, no. Una settimana va bene. Però non vorrei rimanere fissa in un posto. Vorrei visitare un po' di tutto...*

Sicily:
1. A religious ceremony in Capizzi
2. The Taormina Beach
3. Greek ruins in Selinante
4. Agrigento

NOUNS

l'agenzia di viaggi — travel agency
la formula — type
il dépliant — flier/pamphlet
la visita — visit
la sistemazione — arrangement
la zona archeologica — archeological site
il pernottamento — stopover
l'escursione (f) — excursion
la costa — coast
il monumento — monument
il cratere — crater
la lava — lava
il proseguimento — follow-up/sequence
il giro della città — tour of the city
il chiostro — cloister
il trasferimento — transfer
l'aria condizionata — air conditioning
la pensione completa — room and full board

———————

la guida — guide
il circuito — circuit/tour
l'itinerario — itinerary
la cartina geografica — map
la piantina della città — city map
il vulcano — volcano
l'isola — island
la penisola — peninsula
la mezze pensione — room and partial board
l'autopullman (il pullman) — bus

il campeggio — camping
l'ufficio del turismo — tourism office

ADJECTIVES

diverso — different/diverse (1)
uguale — the same
vario — various
dettagliato — detailed
illuminato — well lit
splendido — splendid
impressionante — impressive
magnifico — magnificent

VERBS

rimanere fisso — to remain (in one place)
raggiungere — to reach
ammirare — to admire
considerare — to consider
soggiornare — to stay over
riflettere — to reflect

MISCELLANEOUS

anche di più — even more
me ne dia due — give me two (of them)
non è male! — it's not bad!
di prima categoria — first class/six-star
a disposizione — available
in serata — during the evening
in mattinata — during the morning
in giornata — during the day
nel pomeriggio — during the afternoon
1ª colazione — breakfast (2)
2ª colazione — lunch (2)

HOW TO SAY IT

1. SAYING WHEN AND WHERE ONE IS LEAVING

Vorrei andare in Sicilia — I'd like to go to Sicily.
Vorrei visitare la zona archeologica — I'd like to visit the archeological site.
Vorrei partire durante le vacanze di Natale (di Pasqua) — I'd like to leave during Christmas (Easter) vacation.
Vorrei partire d'estate (d'inverno, in autunno, in primavera) — I'd like to leave in the summer (winter, fall, spring). *(4)*
Vorrei restare a Taormina per 15 giorni — I'd like to stay 15 days in Taormina.

2. ASKING QUESTIONS ABOUT TRIPS

Che cosa comprende il prezzo? — What does the price include?
Di che categoria è l'albergo? — What kind of hotel is it?
Sono previste delle escursioni? — Are excursions included?
I trasferimenti sono in treno o in pullman? — Do you get there by train or by bus?

3. AT THE TOURISM OFFICE

Mi può dare una piantina della città? — Can you give me a map of the city?
Quali sono gli orari dei musei? — What are the hours of the museum?
Qual è il giorno di chiusura dei musei? — On what day are the museums closed?

4. LOCATING PLACES

L'albergo è a 10 chilometri dall'aeroporto — The hotel is 10 kilometers from the airport.
Siracusa è nel sud della Sicilia — Syracuse is in southern Sicily.
Enna e Caltanisetta sono nell'interno — Enna and Caltanisetta are in the interior.
Taormina è sulla costa — Taormina is on the coast.

5. GIVING ONE'S OPINION

Mi sembra un itinerario magnifico — It seems to be a magnificent itinerary.
Sono posti bellissimi — They are beautiful places.
È un'escursione interessantissima — It's a very interesting excursion.

REMARKS...   REMARKS...   REMARKS...   REMARKS...

(1) This means both "different" and "several." — (2) You will hear these terms mainly in hotels. "Lunch" is normally expressed by the word "pranzo." — (3) This is a time expression that constitutes a speech formula: "during. . ." — (4) Note that "estate" is a feminine noun.

1. QUANTITY

(● ●) LISTEN

Mi dia un dépliant, per cortesia
* *Me ne dia uno, per cortesia*
Mi dia una piantina, per cortesia
* *Me ne dia una, per cortesia*

Continue as in the model.
Mi dia un dépliant, per cortesia — Mi dia una piantina, per cortesia — Mi dia due cartoline, per cortesia — Mi dia 10 francobolli, per cortesia — Mi dia una busta, per cortesia — Mi dia due pacchetti di sigarette, per cortesia.

(See Grammar, E. 3.)

2. ACCEPTING SOMETHING

OBJECT PRONOUNS

(● ●) LISTEN

Le do un dépliant?
* *Si, me lo dia*
Le do una piantina?
* *Si, me la dia*

Continue answering in this way.
Le do un dépliant? — Le do una piantina? — Le do i francobolli? — Le do le buste? — Le do il giornale? — Le do gli orari dei musei? — Le do la cartina dell'isola? — Le do l'orario dei treni? — Le do i nomi degli alberghi? — Le do la ricevuta?

(See Grammar, E. 4.)

3. IN FRONT OF . . .

(● ●) LISTEN

Dove'è la spiaggia? — albergo
* *La spiaggia è davanti all'albergo*

Continue answering in this way.
Dov'è la spiaggia? - albergo — Dov'è la fermata dell'autobus? - tabaccaio — Dov'è il museo? - ufficio del turismo — Dov'è la casa? - farmacia — Dov'è l'albergo? - stazione.

(See Grammar, F.)

4. FAR AND NEAR

(● ●) LISTEN

L'albergo è vicino al centro?
* *No, è lontano dal centro*

Continue answering in this way.
L'albergo è vicino al centro? — L'albergo è vicino alla stazione? — Il museo è vicino all'ufficio del turismo? — La casa è vicino al mare? — La spiaggia è vicino al campeggio? — L'albergo è vicino alla fermata dell'autobus?

(See Grammar, F.)

5. INDEFINITE QUANTITIES

(● ●) LISTEN

Ho passato alcuni giorni a Taormina
* *Ho passato qualche giorno a Taormina*

Change the sentences by replacing "alcuni" with "qualche."
Ho passato alcuni giorni a Taormina — Ho comprato alcune riviste — Ho visitato alcuni musei — Ho conosciuto alcune persone — Ho spedito alcune cartoline — Sono andato in alcune agenzie — Ho chiesto alcune informazioni — Ho visitato alcune città.

(See Grammar, I.)

6. THE SUPERLATIVE

(● ●) LISTEN

Il pullman è moderno?
* *Si, è modernissimo!*
L'escursione è interessante?
* *Si, è interessantissima!*

Answer the questions by using the superlative, as in the model.
Il pullman è moderno? — L'escursione è interessante? — Il viaggio è bello? — La formula è cara? — La guida è brava? — I trasferimenti sono corti? — Le spiaggie sono belle? — La ragazza è giovane? — Gli italiani sono simpatici?

(See Grammar, H. 2.)

TRAVELING THROUGHOUT ITALY

Italians have always been great travelers and explorers. It is true of their past—such memorable names as Marco Polo, Cristoforo Colombo, and Amerigo Vespucci (who kindly bequeathed his name to the New World) inevitably come to mind. And it still holds true today. Italians travel more outside their borders than any of their European neighbors. In addition, Italians travel extensively within their own country. There always seems to be a constant stream of Italians in transit, and on Sundays, the inns throughout the countryside are always full.

This enthusiasm for getting to know one's country is facilitated by the extensive network of highways, one of the oldest (originally Mussolini's idea, who saw it as a strategic advantage) and densest in all Europe. The Po Valley, in particular, is crossed in every direction by a veritable spider's web of highways, which reduces significantly the distances between the different regions of the country.

Nature, Culture, History— All in One

What is it about Italy that compels one to travel it from one end to the other? For starters, Italy is a country of natural splendor surrounded by beaches, blessed with several mountain ranges (the Alps, Apennines, and Dolomites), and dotted with breathtaking plains and valleys.

Traveling throughout Italy is also like going back through time. If you are a student of history, try, for example, a visit to Rome. Here, you can start with prehistoric sites, work your way through Classical Roman architecture, continue on to Medieval and Renaissance architecture and areas, and end up in an ultramodern district on the outskirts of the city. There is also Pompeii and Herculaneum, ancient cities in southern Italy, that were completely buried by the eruption of Mt. Vesuvius in A.D. 79; the region of Tuscany, home of the Etruscan civilization (twelfth century B.C.); and the magnificent complex of paleo-Christian and Medieval churches and chapels of Santo Stefano in Bologna. And no lover of the Renaissance can afford to miss Florence. Oh yes! Don't forget Venice, Assisi, Siena, Urbino . . .

Sicily, and southern Italy in general, offer sumptuous mixtures of the past. Due to its insularity, its climate, and its history, Sicily can certainly make you feel as if you are in a different world. It is an island that boasts Greek, Byzantine, Arab, Norman, and other influences. Here you will see Greek temples blending with Arab mosques and Norman fortresses, and Baroque churches alongside palaces of Spanish influence. Agrigento, Selinonte, Segeste, Ragusa, Taormina, Palermo, Syracuse—the list goes on and on.

Geographic diversity, an immensely rich culture, and a complex history are what beckon you to experience the various Italys that make up the country as we know it today. Italy is a "must" for every traveler.

Write down the dates/time periods chosen by the travelers in the taped conversations.

A
GIOVEDI 25 DIC NATALE

1 ☐

B
MARTEDI 2 FEB MARTEDI GRASSO

2 ☐

C
DOMENICA 10 APRILE PASQUA

3 ☐

D
LUNEDI 1 NOVEMBRE TUTTI I SANTI

4 ☐

166.   *centosessantasei*

Weather report! Examine the following weather map of Italy, and then . . . circle each statement as either true or false.

1. *Al nord la temperatura massima è di 21 gradi*   V   F

2. *Il mar Ionio è mosso*   V   F

3. *Nelle regioni settentrionali (al nord) il*   V   F

4. *Il cielo è coperto con piogge abbondanti*   V   F

5. *In Sicilia il cielo è nuvoloso*   V   F

6. *In Sicilia la temperatura massima è di 27 gradi*   V   F

CIELO
sereno
poco nuvoloso
(coperto/pioggia icon)
coperto/pioggia
MARE
(calmo icon)
calmo
(mosso icon)
mosso
(agitato icon)
agitato
VENTI
(deboli icon)
deboli
(forti icon)
forti

21°

25°

26°

27°

PROVERBIO   🔊 LISTEN

Rosso di sera bel tempo si spera
(lit. A red sunset indicates good weather.)
Good things can be predicted on the basis of favorable signs.

(See solutions on page 29 of the booklet.)

4.3 DIALOGUE

◉◉ LISTEN

RELATING WHAT HAPPENED

Upon returning home, Mr. Rizzi tells his wife what happened to him that afternoon.

Lei : *Come mai ritorni così tardi? Hai l'aria sconvolta! Che cosa è successo?*

Lui : *Non me ne parlare! Sai che oggi dovevo andare dall'avvocato. Ho preso l'autobus perché in centro è impossibile parcheggiare e mentre ero sull'autobus mi hanno rubato il portafoglio...*

Lei : *Oh, accidenti! C'erano molti soldi dentro?*

Lui : *No, per fortuna avevo solo 40.000 lire, ma c'erano tutti i documenti...*

Lei : *Ma come è successo?*

Lui : *Guarda, non te lo so dire : era l'ora di punta. Come al solito l'autobus era molto affollato. A un certo punto qualcuno mi ha dato una spinta mentre l'autobus frenava, ma io non ci ho fatto caso. Mi sono accorto che non avevo più il portafoglio solo dopo.*

Lei : *Dove lo avevi messo?*

Lui : *Nella tasca dei pantaloni, come sempre. Mi sono accorto che non c'era più solamente quando sono sceso. Sono andato a prendere un caffè con l'avvocato, e al momento di pagare... non ti dico il mio imbarazzo! Il portafoglio : sparito!*

Lei : *Ma non hai visto il ladro?*

Lui : *Ma no, se ti dico che non mi sono reso conto di niente! Con tutta la gente che c'era... e poi probabilmente il ladro è sceso subito.*

Lei : *Hai sporto denuncia, almeno?*

Lui : *Naturalmente, anche se penso che non serva a molto.*

Lei : *Speriamo che il ladro ti restituisca i documenti. A volte capita.*

Lui : *Ah! che rabbia!*

Lei : *Non ti arrabbiare, dai! Sono cose che capitano! In fondo non è grave.*

Lui : *Hai ragione, però è talmente sgradevole subire un furto, soprattutto in un modo così stupido!*

Lei : *Ma sei sicuro di non averlo dimenticato a casa? Ora che ci penso mi sembra di averlo visto sul mobile dell'ingresso...*

Lui : *Ma no! È impossibile...*

Lei : *E questo che cos'è?*

Lui : *Santo cielo! È proprio il mio portafoglio! Ero così sicuro di averlo perso...*

◉◉ LISTEN AND REPEAT
You will find the translation on page 30 of the booklet.

1. The Gilli bar (Florence)
2. Bell tower by Giotto
3. Rooftops
4. A bar in the Piazza della Signoria
5. A typical Florentine scene
6. On the Ponte Vecchio

4.3 VOCABULARY

NOUNS

l'esperienza — experience
l'aria — air
il portafoglio — wallet
l'ora di punta — rush hour
la tasca — pocket
i pantaloni — pants
l'imbarazzo — embarrassment
il ladro — thief
la denuncia — report
il furto — theft
il modo — way, mode
il mobile — piece of furniture
l'ingresso — entrance

———————

il borsellino — small purse
la rapina — robbery
il rapinatore — robber
lo scippo — pickpocketing
la polizia — police
la questura — police station
il poliziotto — policeman

ADJECTIVES

sconvolto — upset
affollato — crowded
grave — grave, serious
gradevole/sgradevole —
pleasant/unpleasant
stupido/intelligente — stupid/intelligent

VERBS

raccontare — to tell
succedere — to happen
parcheggiare — to park
rubare — to rob/steal
dare una spinta — to give a shove/push
farci caso — to notice
accorgersi — to realize
sparire — to disappear
rendersi conto — to realize
sporgere denuncia — to report
restituire — to give back
capitare — to happen
arrabbiarsi — to get angry
subire — to undergo
dimenticare — to forget

MISCELLANEOUS

così — so
mentre — while
accidenti! — heck!
per fortuna — luckily
che rabbia! — I'm so angry!
dai! — come on! *(1)*
probabilmente — probably
almeno — at least
a volte — at times
in fondo — in the end
talmente — so
Santo cielo! — Dear Heavens!
proprio — really

HOW TO SAY IT

1. ASKING WHAT HAPPENED

Che cosa è successo? (che cosa è capitato?) — What happened?
Che cosa ti è successo? (che cosa ti è capitato?) — What happened to you?

2. SAYING WHAT HAPPENED

È successo questo — This happened.
Non è successo niente — Nothing happened.
Mi è capitato un fatto strano — Something strange happened to me.
Mi hanno rubato il portafoglio — They stole my wallet.
Ho subito un furto — I experienced a theft.

3. LETTING OFF STEAM

Che rabbia! — I am angry!
Accidenti! — Heck!

Non me ne parlare! — Don't talk to me!
Che sfortuna! — What bad luck!

4. CALMING SOMEONE DOWN

Non ti arrabbiare, dai! — Come on, don't be angry!
In fondo non è grave! — In the end, it's not serious!
Sono cose che capitano! — These things happen!

5. LEADING SOMEONE ON. . . .

E poi? — And then?
E allora? — And so?
Ma come è successo? — How did it happen?

Quando è successo? — When did it happen?
Dove è successo? — Where did it happen?
Come è finita? — How did it end up?

6. EXPRESSING YOUR POINT OF VIEW (2)

Penso (credo) di sì — I think so.
Penso (credo) di no — I think not.
Penso che non serva a molto — I think it is useless.
Credo che sia vero — I believe it is true.

REMARKS...   *REMARKS...*   *REMARKS...*   *REMARKS...*

(1) This is used only in familiar speech. — (2) Verbs that express opinion/point of view require the subjunctive. See Grammar, L. 11.

1. SAYING WHAT HAPPENED

🔊 LISTEN

Rubare il portafoglio
- *Mi hanno rubato il portafoglio*

Continue saying what happened.
Rubare il portafoglio — Rubare la valigia — Accusare di furto — Seguire per strada — Ritirare la patente — Dare una spinta — Dire che non c'è posto — Dare l'orario sbagliato.

(See Grammar, L.)

2. BEING POLITE

WITH DOUBLE PRONOUNS

🔊 LISTEN

Non te lo so dire
- *Non glielo so dire*

Change these sentences by using the polite form.
Non te lo so dire — Non te lo so spiegare — Non te lo so precisare — Non te lo so descrivere — Non te lo so indicare — Non te lo so raccontare — Non te lo so dire.

(See Grammar, E. 4.)

3. OFFERING TO HELP

POLITE FORMS

🔊 LISTEN

Chi mi da la valigia?
- *Gliela do io*

Chi mi indica l'albergo?
- *Glielo indico io*

Continue offering your help.
Chi mi da la valigia? — Chi mi indica l'albergo? — Chi mi apre la porta? — Chi mi da il libro? — Chi mi compra i biglietti? — Chi mi prenota le camere? — Chi mi offre una sigaretta? — Chi mi indica la fermata dell'autobus?

(See Grammar, E. 4.)

4. ORDERING

NEGATIVE FORMS

🔊 LISTEN

Compra il giornale!
- *Non comprare il giornale!*

Spedisci la lettera!
- *Non spedire la lettera!*

Continue ordering people in this way.
Compra il giornale! — Spedisci la lettera! — Leggi il libro! — Prendi il treno! — Bevi il caffè! — Attraversa la strada! — Fai le valigie! — Dì la verità! — Va' a teatro!

(See Grammar, L. 10.)

5. THE PRESENT SUBJUNCTIVE (essere/avere)

🔊 LISTEN

È vero?
- *Penso che sia vero*

Ha ragione?
- *Penso che abbia ragione*

Continue saying what you think, using "pensare" followed by the subjunctive.
È vero? — Ha ragione? — È italiano? — Ha 20 anni? — È interessante? — È giovane? — Ha l'aria condizionata? — È faticoso? — È sposato? — Ha la macchina? — È avvocato?

(See Grammar, L. 11.)

6. EXPRESSING NEED

"BISOGNA" + SUBJUNCTIVE

🔊 LISTEN

Mi dia un documento!
- *Bisogna che Lei mi dia un documento*

Mi ascolti!
- *Bisogna che Lei mi ascolti*

Change the sentences as in the model.
Mi dia un documento! — Mi ascolti! — Mi dica la verità! — Mi faccia un favore! — Mi accompagni alla stazione! — Mi telefoni alle 9! — Mi compri il giornale! — Mi dia un consiglio! — Mi capisca!

(See Grammar, L. 11.)

TRAFFIC!

Once you have encountered the traffic in a city like Milan, Turin, Rome, or Naples, "chaotic" will most likely be the first word that comes to mind. All those Fiats seem to have minds of their own, and how they avoid continually running into each other defies rational explanation!

To many Italians, "la macchina" is sacred. Considered a statement of social standing during the fifties and sixties, the automobile has now become commonplace. Fiat (an acronym for Fabbrica Italiana Automobili Torino), belonging to one of the great industrial dynasties of Europe, the Agnelli family, has played a major role in the economic development of the country by creating thousands of jobs and by recruiting its work force from all over the peninsula. Fiat, which now also builds trucks, is a powerful industry throughout all of Europe. Also, don't forget that Italy is home to such luxury cars as Bugatti, Alfa-Romeo, Lancia, and Maserati.

Autos, Autos, Everywhere!

But let's get back to the subject of traffic. A rush hour in Rome or Naples is worthy of a place in Dante's Inferno. Traffic rarely flows smoothly at any point during the day since, as in all large cities, everyone seems to be leaving at the same time. What's more, Italian eating habits add to this congestion by creating not two but four rush-hour periods during the day! And then there's the parking! Where can you find a spot? Try anywhere that looks feasible. It is not unusual to see double, triple, even quadruple parking in Rome or Naples. Just make sure to leave your door unlocked so that your triple-parked car can be maneuvered into a position to allow the other cars out.

Unfortunately, you are also bound to experience another problem that is common to all large cities. Dramatic increases in traffic are creating serious pollution problems in Italy's cosmopolitan areas. To deal with this, the government has initiated a program whereby, periodically, drivers are allowed to drive within the city only according to their license plate number. For example, those with even-numbered plates can drive one day and those with odd-numbered plates another day. All this traffic has inevitably led to a crackdown on speeding and illegal parking, too. Traffic police constantly patrol the highways using radar, and fines can reach over $1000 for speeding! Seat belts are now mandatory.

The Unwritten Rules of the Road

What is often missed in this scenario is that most Italians are essentially very good and considerate drivers, even though in Rome the traffic lights and stop signs seem purely decorative, and the horn the proof of one's existence. There is a kind of intuitive feel among Italian drivers, allowing for much more flexibility in the driving patterns of motorists, but at the same time ensuring respect for the other driver. All drivers may not stop at the red light, but they are ever mindful of the cars around them. Perhaps this explains why most people, including tourists, generally feel reasonably safe on the road in Italy.

4.3 TAKE-A-BREAK

N° 1 LISTEN

Check off all the things that were stolen from Mr. Cammelli's apartment.

DENUNCIA DI FURTO

COGNOME E NOME : ....

DATA DEL FURTO : .... 1999 ....

ORA (APPROSSIMATIVA) IN CUI È AVVENUTO IL FURTO ....

OGGETTI RUBATI :

- Argenteria ☐
- Elettrodomestici ☐
- Mobili ☐
- Quadri ☐
- Tappeti ☐
- Pellicce ☐
- Gioielli ☐
- Impianto Stereo ☐
- Dischi ☐
- Televisore a colori ☐
- Televisore bianco e nero ☐
- Vestiti ☐
- Libri ☐
- Macchina fotografica ☐
- Altri ....

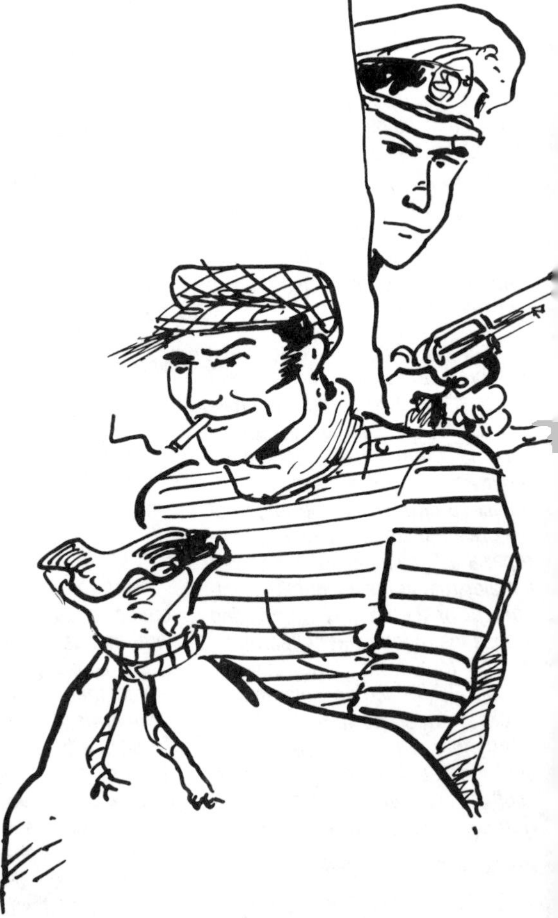

Anagram. *By rearranging the letters of the following words you will get the name (first and second) of a famous international thief.*
LUI, NIRO, PENSA...

. . . .

Rebus.

S

CA

PROVERBIO   ●● LISTEN

La casa nasconde ma non ruba
(lit. A house hides, but it does not steal.)

(See solutions on page 31 of the booklet.)

🔊 LISTEN

COMMON MYTHS ABOUT ITALIANS

The Rizzi's are at a cocktail party. They meet people from all over the world and get into a conversation about different peoples and cultures.

Signora Rizzi : *E così Lei è convinto che gli italiani siano pigri... è questa dunque la reputazione che abbiamo all'estero!*

L'inglese : *Non solo pigri! Nel mio paese si pensa che gli italiani siano tutti romantici, espansivi e un po' mafiosi... Naturalmente si tratta solo di luoghi comuni, e immagino che in Italia ci siano altrettanti luoghi comuni sugli inglesi...*

Signora Rizzi : *In effetti, prima di andare in Inghilterra credevo che tutti gli inglesi fossero freddi, seri e portassero la bombetta e l'ombrello in tutte le stagioni.*

L'inglese : *E adesso ha cambiato idea?*

Signora Rizzi : *Diciamo che ho imparato a non generalizzare, anche se penso che ci sia sempre un fondo di verità in tutti i luoghi comuni...*

Il tedesco : *E che cosa si dice dei tedeschi? Sono curioso di saperlo.*

Signora Rizzi : *Oh! I tedeschi hanno la fama di essere disciplinati, alti, biondi e con gli occhi azzurri, e appassionati di musica.*

Il tedesco : *Da noi si pensa che gli italiani, invece, siano tutti piccoli di statura, bruni, con gli occhi neri e la carnagione scura e mangino solo spaghetti...*

Il francese : *Scusate se mi intrometto nella vostra conversazione, ma l'argomento mi interessa : mi piacerebbe sapere che cosa si dice sui francesi...*

Signora Rizzi : *Sui francesi... non saprei dirLe. Chiediamolo a mio marito, che li conosce bene.*

Signòr Rizzi : *Forse sono un po' meno espansivi di noi, però hanno la fama di essere simpatici, raffinati e buongustai. Io credo che in realtà siamo molto simili, e se potessi vivrei volentieri in Francia.*

Signora Rizzi : *E che cosa faresti senza la tua mamma?*

Signor Rizzi : *Mia moglie mi prende in giro perché qui in Italia siamo tutti un po' mammoni, ma la Francia è un paese che mi attira molto...*

🔊 LISTEN AND REPEAT
You will find the translation on page 32 of the booklet.

1. Florence, Ponte Vecchio
2. Palazzo della Signoria
3. David and Perseus
4. A Florentine
5. The Neptune Fountain,
Piazza della Signoria

NOUNS

i luoghi comuni — common myths
la reputazione — reputation
l'estero — abroad
la bombetta — derby
l'ombrello — umbrella
la stagione — season
la fama — reputation/fame
la statura — height *(1)*
la carnagione — complexion
la conversazione — conversation
l'argomento — topic
il buongustaio — gourmet
la mamma — mother
il mammone — ''mama's boy''

---

il papà — dad
l'ambiente — environment
il popolo — people/population
la caratteristica — characteristic
le parti del corpo umano — parts of the human body
la testa — head
gli occhi — eyes
la bocca — mouth
i denti — teeth
le orecchie — ears
i capelli — hair
la mano — hand *(2)*
il braccio — arm *(3)*
la gamba — leg
il piede — foot
il petto — chest
la vita — life

la pelle — skin
il peso — weight

ADJECTIVES

pigro — lazy
romantico — romantic
espansivo — expansive
serio — serious
disciplinato — disciplined
alto/basso — tall/short
grasso/magro — fat/thin *(4)*
biondo, bruno, rosso, castano — blond, brown-haired, red-haired, auburn-haired
scuro/chiaro — dark/light
raffinato — refined
simile — similar

VERBS

trattarsi — to deal with
immaginare — to imagine
cambiare idea — to change one's mind
generalizzare — to generalize
imparare — to learn *(5)*
avere la fama (di) — to have the reputation
intromettersi — to join in
prendere in giro (qualcuno) — to pull someone's leg
attirare — to attract

MISCELLANEOUS

altrettanto/a/i/e — as well, as many
in realtà — in reality

1. DESCRIBING PEOPLE

I tedeschi sono alti, biondi e con gli occhi azzurri — Germans are tall, blond, and blue-eyed.
Gli italiani sono piccoli, bruni e con gli occhi neri — Italians are small, dark, and dark-eyed.
I tedeschi hanno la carnagione chiara — Germans have a light complexion.
Gli italiani hanno la carnagione scura — Italians have a dark complexion.

2. MORE WAYS OF DESCRIBING

Quella ragazza è magra — That girl is thin.
È bionda, con i capelli lunghi — She is blond and has long hair.
È un uomo abbastanza alto e robusto — He is a fairly tall and robust man.
È un regazzo con gli occhiali — That boy wears glasses.
Ha dei bellissimi occhi verdi — He/She has very beautiful green eyes.

3. DESCRIBING CHARACTER

È una persona intelligente e dinamica — He/She is an intelligent and dynamic person.
È un ragazzo simpatico e espansivo — He is a nice and exuberant boy.
Non è una persona molto seria — He/She is not a very serious person.

4. ASKING ABOUT OTHERS

Che cosa si dice dei tedeschi? — What do they say about Germans?
Che reputazione hanno i francesi in Italia? — What reputation do the French have in Italy?
Che fama hanno gli italiani all'estero? — What reputation do Italians have abroad?

5. "SE . . ."

Se potessi, vivrei volentieri in Francia! — If I could, I'd live in France! *(6)*
Se volessi, potrei partire domani — If I wanted to, I could leave tomorrow.
Se dovessi farlo, lo farei — If I had to do it, I would.

REMARKS...   *REMARKS...*   *REMARKS...*   *REMARKS...*

(1) "Altezza" can be used as a synonym. — (2) Note that this is a feminine noun (pl.: "le mani"). — (3) Plural: "le braccia" (f.) — (4) These words do not have negative connotations. They simply describe physical appearance. — (5) The word for "to teach" is "insegnare." — (6) See Grammar, L. 12.

1. EXPRESSING YOUR POINT OF VIEW

(• •) LISTEN

Gli italiani sono comunicativi

● *Credo che gli italiani siano comunicativi*

I tedeschi amano la musica

● *Credo che i tedeschi amino la musica*

Continue expressing your point of view in this way.
Gli italiani sono comunicativi — I tedeschi amano la musica — Gli inglesi portano sempre l'ombrello — I francesi sono buongustai — I russi bevono tutti la vodka — I napoletani mangiano ogni giorno la pizza. (See Grammar, L. 11.)

2. THE IMPERFECT SUBJUNCTIVE (essere/avere)

(• •) LISTEN

Credo che lui sia inglese

● *Anch'io credevo che fosse inglese*

Credo che abbia la patente

● *Anch'io credevo che avesse la patente*

Continue changing the sentences as in the model.
Credo che lui sia inglese — Credo che abbia la patente — Credo che sia ricco — Credo che abbia la macchina — Credo che sia in Francia — Credo che abbia gli occhi azzurri — Credo che sia una persona seria — Credo che abbia due figli. (See Grammar, L. 12.)

3. IMPERFECT SUBJUNCTIVE

(• •) LISTEN

Pensavi che venisse?

● *Sì, pensavo proprio che venisse!*

Pensavi che lo facesse?

● *Sì, pensavo proprio che lo facesse*

Continue answering the questions.
Pensavi che venisse? — Pensavi che lo facesse? — Pensavi che tornasse? — Pensavi che capisse? — Pensavi che arrivasse subito? — Pensavi che dormisse ancora? — Pensavi che dicesse la verità? (See Grammar, L. 12.)

4. "SE . . ."

(• •) LISTEN

Usciresti volentieri?

● *Sì, se potessi uscirei*

Lo faresti volentieri?

● *Sì, se potessi lo farei*

Continue answering the questions.
Usciresti volentieri? — Lo faresti volentieri? — Partiresti volentieri? — Ritorneresti volentieri? — Dormiresti volentieri? — Resteresti volentieri? — Continueresti volentieri?

(See Grammar, L. 12.)

5. DESCRIBING PEOPLE

(• •) LISTEN

Quel ragazzo pesa 100 chili

● *È grasso*

Quella ragazza misura 1,80 m

● *È alta*

Describe each person in this way.
Quel ragazzo pesa 100 chili — Quella ragazza misura 1,80 m — Lui non ha mai voglia di fare niente — Loro fanno molto sport — Voi siete vestiti molto bene — Loro mangiano solo cose buone — Tu segui sempre gli ordini — Lei pesa solo 45 chili.

6. COMPARING

(• •) LISTEN

Sono più espansivi gli italiani o gli inglesi?

● *Gli italiani sono più espansivi degli inglesi*

Continue comparing in this way.
Sono più espansivi gli italiani o gli inglesi? — Sono più disciplinati gli spagnoli o i tedeschi? — Sono più buongustai i francesi o i tedeschi? — Sono più romantici gli italiani o i frencesi? — Sono più alti gli svedesi o i siciliani?

(See Grammar, H. 1.)

BUT WHO ARE THE ITALIANS?

As we all know, all cultures have to put up with common misconceptions and stereotypes that others have about them. And as we have seen, Italians are not exceptions to this rule. All Italians are often thought of only as spaghetti lovers, happy-go-lucky romantics, and members of big families. Let's look at some of the most common myths regarding Italians and Italy.

The More Things Change . . .

In the political arena, it is often thought that Italy has an unstable government. Too many changes and upheavals, and an inability to form new governments are cited as proof. This impression could not be further from the truth. Since the Second World War, Italy has experienced remarkable political stability, resulting from rearrangements within the government and realignments within the political parties. Thus, in spite of the changes, the same politicians have been in power for a long time. If you studied Italy's political history since the War, you will find that the same familiar names remain important throughout the entire period.

The Italian Family—Myth and Reality

From the social point of view, there is one main myth to dispel. Because Italians are predominantly Catholic, one always pictures large, six-children families as the norm. Actually, modern Italy has one of the lowest birthrates in the world—less than two children per family! Yet they still consider the family as one of the most important values in life.

Who Doesn't Love Pasta?

Do Italians eat nothing but spaghetti? Indeed, pasta is a main staple in an Italian's diet. But then, pasta has become a main ingredient in the cuisines of other countries as well. And as we have seen, Italian cuisine is as varied as the people of Italy. Wherever you go in Italy, you are bound to experience a significant change in diet and cooking.

It is because of these surprising realities that Italians are such a fascinating people. Italy is a modern country in every sense of the word. Far from being happy-go-lucky romantics, Italians have made Italy's standard of living one of the highest in the world. And this cannot be achieved without hard work. Their reputation of being unproductive is ill-deserved.

One area in which Italians are perhaps among the most productive in the world is in the making of all kinds of luxury items. Cars by Lamborghini, clothes by Armani and Gucci, art books, furniture, and a host of other items are sought after by the whole world, no matter what the price! Indeed, if productivity is to be measured in terms of excellence, Italy would be second to none. As a last word about Italy's undeserved reputation, the latest figures show that Italy has one of the world's lowest unemployment rates. And it has had this rate for nearly a decade!

N° 1 LISTEN

Who is the surgeon? Listen to the event and then try to figure out who the surgeon is.

Here's another crossword puzzle for you.

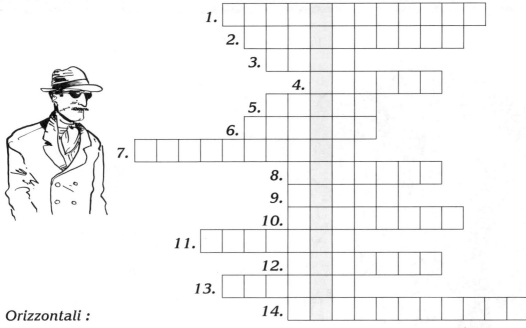

Orizzontali :

1. Rispettano le regole.
2. Colore della pelle.
3. Contrario di bassi.
4. Fuori del proprio paese.
5. Persona che ride poco.
6. Capelli chiari.
7. Amano la buona cucina.
8. Lo sono spesso gli occhi chiari.
9. Amano il dolce far niente.
10. Tipico cappello portato dagli inglesi.
11. Non possono vivere senza la mamma.
12. Individuo compromesso con la mafia.
13. Quasi uguale.
14. Fama.

Verticali :

Senza frontiere.

PROVERBIO • • LISTEN

Paese che vai, usanze che trovi
(lit., Every country has its customs.)

When in Rome, do as the Romans do.

(See solutions on page 33 of the booklet.)

● ● LISTEN

A VISIT TO FLORENCE

The Rizzi's are giving Mario (a visiting relative) advice on where to go sightseeing in Florence.

Sig.ra Rizzi : *Per prima cosa, per quanto tempo ti fermi?*

Mario : *Mi trattengo per due o tre giorni al massimo.*

Sig.ra Rizzi : *In così poco tempo non potrai visitare tutto. Firenze è talmente ricca di cose da vedere!*

Sig. Rizzi : *Secondo me innanzi tutto dovresti visitare Piazza della Signoria.*

Sig.ra Rizzi : *Sì, Piazza della Signoria con le sue statue e poi il Palazzo Vecchio, e naturalmente gli Uffizi.*

Sig. Rizzi : *Gli Uffizi vanno visitati con calma, e con delle scarpe comode...*

Mario : *E dov'è il famoso Ponte Vecchio?*

Sig. Rizzi : *Oh, guarda è proprio lì vicino, a pochi passi.*

Sig.ra Rizzi : *Vedrai è bellissimo! Pensa che dal '500 il ponte è sempre stato occupato dagli orefici e ancora oggi gode per questo di una vasta fama...*

Mario : *E la cattedrale?*

Sig. Rizzi : *Beh, la cattedrale va visitata assolutamente!*

Sig.ra Rizzi : *Vi si trovano marmi, ceramiche, affreschi e mosaici di diversi periodi e poi la cupola è del Brunelleschi.*

Mario : *Ah, sì, il celebre architetto del XV° secolo.*

Sig. Rizzi : *Ma tu che sei un appassionato di letteratura italiana dovresti andare a vedere la casa di Dante. È solo una curiosità, ma le stradine intorno alla casa sono molto caratteristiche.*

Mario : *Non c'è anche la sua tomba?*

Sig. Rizzi : *Eh no! La tomba di Dante non è a Firenze perché è morto in esilio a Ravenna.*

Sig.ra Rizzi : *Però nella chiesa di Santa Croce ci sono le tombe di alcuni dei più famosi scrittori, pittori e poeti italiani.*

Mario : *Ho capito! Due giorni non mi basteranno mai...!*

● ● LISTEN AND REPEAT
You will find the translation on page 33 of the booklet.

1. The famous Duomo (Florence)
2. The Bargello Museum
3. A Botticelli painting
in the Uffizi Gallery
4. Detail: door to the
Baptistry
5. Traditional/Festive clothing

3

5

NOUNS

la piazza — square
la statua — statue
il ponte — bridge
l'orefice (m) — goldsmith
la cattedrale — cathedral
il marmo — marble
la ceramica — ceramics
l'affresco — fresco
il mosaico — mosaic
la cupola — cupola
l'archittetto — architect
la stradina — small street/lane
la letteratura — literature
la curiosità — curiosity
la tomba — tomb
l'esilio — exile
la chiesa — church
lo scrittore — writer
il pittore — painter
il poeta — poet

———————

l'arte — art
lo stile — style
il Medio Evo — Middle Ages
il Rinascimento — Renaissance

ADJECTIVES

comodo/scomodo — comfortable/
uncomfortable
famoso (celebre) — famous/renowned/
well-known
vasto — vast
caratteristico — characteristic

VERBS

fermarsi (trattenersi) — to stay over (1)
visitare — to visit
godere di — to enjoy
morire — to die
nascere — to be born
crescere — to grow
bastare — to be enough
capire — to understand
consigliare — to advise

MISCELLANEOUS

al massimo — maximum
al minimo — minimum
in così poco tempo — in such a short time
talmente — so
innanzi tutto — above all
con calma — calmly
a pochi passi — a few paces away
intorno a — around
alcuni — some
il secolo — century
il XV° secolo — 15th century
il '400 — the 1400s (15th century)

HOW TO SAY IT

---

1. DIFFERENT WAYS OF SAYING "YOU MUST . . ."

La cattedrale *deve essere visitata*
La cattedrale *va visitata*
La cattedrale *è da visitare*
La cattedrale, *bisogna visitarla*

— You must visit the cathedral.

---

2. HISTORICAL PERIODS

Il Ponte Vecchio è del '200 (del XIII° secolo) — The Ponte Vecchio was built in the 13th century.
Dante è un poeta del '300 (del XIV° secolo) — Dante is a poet of the 14th century.

---

3. STYLES

È una chiesa romanica — It's a Roman church.
È una chiesa gotica — It's a Gothic church.
È un palazzo rinascimentale — It's a Renaissance palace.
È una statua barocca — It's a baroque statue.

---

4. IT WAS WRITTEN/PAINTED BY . . .

La Divina Commedia *è stata scritta da Dante Alighieri* — The Divine Comedy was written by Dante Alighieri.
La Gioconda *è stata dipinta da Leonardo da Vinci* — The Mona Lisa was painted by Leonardo da Vinci.

---

5. WHAT'S IT MADE OF?

Questa statua è de marmo bianco — This statue is made of white marble.
La parete è di ceramica — The partition is made of ceramic.
Il Ponte Vecchio era di legno — The Ponte Vecchio was made of wood.

| REMARKS... | REMARKS... | REMARKS... | REMARKS... |

(1) This verb means literally "to stop oneself."

1. EXPRESSING NEED

(• •) LISTEN

La cattedrale deve essere visitata
* *Va visitata assolutamente!*
Le lettere devono essere scritte a macchina
* *Vanno scritte a macchina assolutamente!*

Change the sentences by using "aller" followed by the past participle of the verb, as in the model.
La cattedrale deve essere visitata — Le lettere devono essere scritte a macchina — I documenti devono essere spediti domani — L'esercizio deve essere fatto — L'appuntamento deve essere preso per domani — La cassette devono essere ascoltate.

(See Grammar, L. 15.)

2. EXPRESSING NEED

(• •) LISTEN

Il libro è da comprare
* *Bisogna comprarlo*
Le cassette sono da ascoltare
* *Bisogna ascoltarle*

Change the sentences by using "bisogna" and replacing the noun with the appropriate pronoun.
Il libro è da comprare — Le cassette sono da ascoltare — La lettera è da spedire subito — Il film è da vedere — La città è da visitare a piedi — Gli esercizi sono da finire — La cena è da preparare.

(See Grammar, L. 15.)

3. CENTURIES

(• •) LISTEN

Dante è un poeta del XIV° secolo
* *Dante è un poeta del '300*

Continue as in the model.
Dante è un poeta del XIV° secolo — Caravaggio è un pittore del XVI° secolo — Alberto Moravia è uno scrittore del XX° secolo — Brunelleschi è un architetto del XV° secolo — Alessandro Manzoni
è uno scrittore del XIX° secolo — Antonio Vivaldi è un compositore del XVIII° secolo — Michelangelo è uno scultore, pittore e architetto del XVI° secolo.

(See Grammar, K. 3.)

4. THE PASSIVE VOICE

(• •) LISTEN

Dante ha scrito «La Divina Commedia»
* *«La Divina Commedia» è stata scritta da Dante*
Vivaldi ha composto «Le Quattro Stagioni»
* *«Le Quattro Stagioni» sono state composte da Vivaldi*

Continue putting the sentences in the passive voice.
Dante ha scritto «La Divina Commedia» — Vivaldi ha composto «Le Quattro Stagioni» — Leonardo da Vinci ha dipinto «La Gioconda» — Brunelleschi ha progettato la cupola della cattedrale di Firenze — Umberto Eco ha scritto «Il Nome della rosa» — Marcello Mastroianni ha interpretato molti film di Fellini.

(See Grammar, L. 14.)

5. SUPERLATIVES

(• •) LISTEN

«La Gioconda» è un famoso quadro di Leonardo da Vinci
* *«La Gioconda» è il quadro più famoso di Leonardo da Vinci*
Il Ponte Vecchio è un ponte antico di Firenze
* *Il Ponte Vecchio è il ponte più antico di Firenze*

Continue as in the model.
«La Gioconda» è un famoso quadro di Leonardo da Vinci — Il Ponte Vecchio è un ponte antico di Firenze — «La Divina Commedia» è una grande opera della letteratura italiana — Milano è una grande città del nord dell'Italia — Il calcio è uno sport diffuso e amato in Italia.

(See Grammar, H. 2.)

FLORENCE

Florentines are quite proud of their city, and for good reason. Not only has Florence given Italy its literary language (that of Dante, Petrarch, and Boccaccio), but it has always been a symbol of what Italian civilization stands for.

From 1865 to 1871 Florence was chosen over Rome to be the capital of the unified Italy. The reasons for this lie in Florence's cultural heritage. In the area of the visual arts, there is no city quite like Florence. It is the birthplace of Michelangelo, Botticelli, Donatello, Cellini, and Uccello, whose masterpieces helped create this Renaissance city. Here you will find, to name but a few, the famous Duomo and the Battistero, the Uffizi Gallery, and the Piazza della Signoria. And on every street corner you will see statues or monuments reminding us of Florence's rich past.

There is More to Florence Than Museums . . .

Florence has also always been a center for scientific theory and philosophy. Macchiavelli, the formidable political theorist, wrote The Prince there in 1532. The Medici family of Florence became prototypes of great politicians and planners during the Renaissance. And of course, Leonardo, from the neighboring town of Vinci (whence his family name) left the world his incomparable paintings and his groundbreaking thoughts ranging from natural history to experimental science. What's more, Florence was the first great modern state to abolish capital punishment (a daring move made by Leopold II, grand duke of Tuscany) in the eighteenth century.

Florence has also played a major role in the area of gastronomy. Florentines claim to have taught Europeans how to cook meat correctly, and to this day the famous "bistecca alla fiorentina" serves as proof. Think of all the recipes using spinach that bear the name "alla fiorentina."

Despite the endless lines of tourists at museum entrances and droves of visitors in the piazzas or on the Ponte Vecchio, Florence does not rely that heavily on tourism as a source of revenue; in fact only two percent of its income is derived from visitors. You need only take a walk outside the tourist centers and look in the shop windows. Yet its chic clothing boutiques, shoe stores, and leather goods stores are among the most famous in Europe, and certainly add to its appeal as a place to visit. Florence also boasts the largest bookstores in Italy, and offers an infinite program of art expositions and classical and jazz concerts. No, Florence is not just a city of museums: it is a vibrant city buzzing with activities that suit everyone's taste, which explains its popularity among travelers—both foreign and Italian.

●● LISTEN

Nel blu, dipinto di blu (Volare)
(D. Modugno - F. Migliacci)
Sung by Domenico Modugno
© Edizioni Curci

In the Blue, Painted Blue (Flying)

Penso che un sogno così non ritorni mai più
Me dipingevo le mani e la faccia di blu
Poi d'improvviso venivo dal vento rapito
E incominciavo a volare nel cielo infinito...

I think that such a dream will never return
I was painting my hands and face blue
Then all of a sudden I was taken away by a gust of wind
And I started to fly in the infinite sky . . .

Volare... oh, oh!... cantare... oh, oh, oh, oh!
Felice di stare lassù, nel blu, dipinto di blu,
E volavo, volavo felice più in alto del sole
                              [ed ancora più su
Mentre il mondo pian piano spariva
                              [lontano laggiù
Una musica dolce suonava soltanto per me...
Volare... oh, oh!... cantare... oh, oh, oh, oh!
Nel blu, dipinto di blu, felice di stare lassù

Flying . . . oh, oh! . . . Singing . . . oh, oh, oh, oh!
Happy to be up there in the blue sky, painted blue,
Happy flying higher than the sun
(and even higher)
While the far away world was
slowly disappearing below me
Flying . . . oh, oh! . . . Singing . . . oh, oh, oh, oh!
Happy to be up there in the blue sky, painted blue.

Ma tutti i sogni nell'alba svaniscono perché
quando tramonta, la luna li porta con sè
Ma io continuo a sognare negli occhi tuoi
                              [belli
che sono blu come un cielo trapunto di
                              [stelle

But all dreams disappear at
sunrise, because the disappearing
moon takes them with her.
But I continue to dream in your
beautiful eyes, which are as blue
as a starlit sky.

Volare... oh, oh!... cantare... oh, oh, oh, oh!
nel blu degli occhi tuoi blu
felice di stare quaggiù
E continuo a volare felice più in alto del
                              [sole ed ancora più su
mentre il mondo pian piano scompare
                              [negli occhi tuoi blu,
la tua voce è una musica dolce che
                              [suona per me...
Volare... oh, oh!... cantare... oh, oh, oh, oh!
nel blu degli occhi tuoi blu
felice di stare quaggiù
Con te!

Flying . . . oh, oh! . . . Singing . . . oh, oh, oh, oh!
in the blue of your blue eyes
happy to be down here with you
And I continue to fly higher than the sun
(and even higher)
while the world slowly disappears
in your blue eyes.
Your voice is sweet music which
is playing for me.
Flying . . . oh, oh! . . . Singing . . . oh, oh, oh, oh!
in the blue of your blue eyes
Happy to be down here
With you!

"FIGURES" OF SPEECH

AVERE IL DENTE AVVELENATO
(lit., to have a poisoned tooth)
To be a malicious gossiper

ATTACCARE BOTTONE
(lit., to sew on a button)
To force someone to listen to a long and boring talk

PRENDERE QUALCUNO PER IL NASO
(lit., to take someone by the nose)
To lead someone astray

ANDARE CON I PIEDI DI PIOMBO
(lit., to go with lead feet)
To proceed with caution

4. WRITTEN PRACTICE

4.1

FILL IN THE BLANKS WITH THE APPROPRIATE POSSESSIVE : *Signor Verdi, Le presento*
. . . . moglie. — Carlo ha una sorella: . . . . sorella si chiama Giulia. — Marco e Claudio
hanno un negozio di abbigliamento : . . . . . . negozio è in centro. — Io ho molti amici : . . . . . .
amici vivono in Italia. — Laura ha due fratelli : . . . . . . fratelli sono ancora piccoli.

TRANSLATE : *Le signore stanno prendendo il tè. — Come al solito andranno in campagna per il fine*
settimana. — Mi piacerebbe fare un viaggio all'estero.
He plays the guitar very well. — My children play tennis. — We don't know how to swim. — It's a
difficult choice.

4.2

ANSWER EACH QUESTION USING
me, lo, la, li, le AS REQUIRED BY EACH CASE : *Mi presti la piantina? — Mi racconti il*
tuo viaggio? — Mi scrivi una cartolina dalla Sicilia? — Mi racconti le tue vacanze? — Mi prendi un
dépliant all'agenzia? — Mi dai il tuo indirizzo?

TRANSLATE : *Nell'albergo c'è l'aria condizionata. — La formula comprende la pensione completa. —*
Qual e l'orario di chiusura dei musei?
We'd like to leave for the Christmas holidays. — Are there any organized trips to Sicily? — It's a very
beautiful place. — He would like to spend a few days at a seaside resort.

4.3

ANSWER EACH QUESTION IN THE AFFIRMATIVE, USING THE FORM te, lo, la, li, le OR glielo/la/li/le, ACCORD-
ING TO THE SENSE ("tu" OR "Lei") : *Mario, mi racconti la storia del furto? — Signor Verdi, mi racconta la*
storia del furto? — Antonio, mi ripeti il nome di quella persona? — Signor Neri, mi ripete il nome di
quella persona? — Sandro, mi porti i documenti? — Signor Santi, mi porta i documenti? — Giacomo,
mi dai le riviste nuove? — Signor Rossi, mi da le riviste nuove?

TRANSLATE : *Non ti preoccupare! — Può succedere . . . — Sull'autobus c'era molta gente.*
What happened? — I was aware of nothing. — I reported it to the police. — What bad luck!

4.4

PUT THE VERB IN PARENTHESES IN ITS APPROPRIATE SUBJUNCTIVE FORM, ACCORDING TO THE MEANING :
Credo che Marco (essere) . . . . . a Londra. — Penso che la mamma (arrivare) . . . . . domani. — Penso che
Giulio (avere) . . . . l'appuntamento alle 8. — Credo che loro (prendere) . . . . l'aereo. —
Penso che tu (essere) . . . . soddisfatto. — Credo che voi (capire) . . . . un po' l'italiano.

TRANSLATE : *Pensavano che gli italiani fossero tutti romantici. — Credevo che tu fossi a Roma in*
vacanza. — Se potessi, lo farei volentieri.
Northerners have light eyes and blond hair. — Italians have the reputation of being short and brown-
haired. — These are only common myths.

4.5

FILL IN THE BLANKS WITH
"va" OR "bisogna," AS EACH CASE REQUIRES : *La cattedrale . . . . . visitata assolutamente. —*
Il museo, ... visitarlo di mattina. — La grammatica . . . . studiata. —
I biglietti dell'autobus, ... comprarli dal tabaccaio. — La città . . . . girata a piedi. —
I mosaici . . . . vederli assolutamente.

TRANSLATE : *Nella basilica si trovano meravigliosi affreschi. — Firenze è una delle città italiane più*
visitate dai turisti.
It is a book written by a famous author. — It is a beautiful marble statue. — It's the oldest church in
Rome. — It's a Renaissance palace.

(See the answers on page 36 of the booklet.)

MORE VOCABULARY

WEATHER

acquazzone — pouring rain
afa — mugginess
brina — frost
cielo — sky
clima — climate
fulmine — bolt
ghiaccio — ice
grandine — hail
inondazione — flood
lampo — lightning
luna — moon
nebbia — fog
neve — snow
nuvola — cloud
pioggia — rain
siccità — dryness
sole — sun
stella — star
temporale — storm
terremoto — earthquake
tuono — clap of thunder
umidità — humidity
vento — wind

A BIT OF GEOGRAPHY

mare — sea
lago — lake
fiume — river
affluente — tributary
torrente — rapid river
monte — hill
montagna — mountain
collina — small hill
pianura — plain
altopiano — highland
golfo — gulf
foce — mouth
delta — delta
estuario — estuary

le Alpi — Alps
gli Appennini — Apennines
le Dolomiti — Dolomites
la pianura padana — Po Valley
la frontiera — frontier
il confine — border
il Mar Mediterraneo — Mediterranean Sea

il Mar Tirreno, Ionio, Adriatico
— Tyrrhenian, Ionian, Adriatic
Seas
l'oceano Atlantico, Pacifico, Indiano — Atlantic, Pacific, Indian
Oceans

GAMES

giochi di società — social
games
giocare a carte — to play cards
picche — spades
fiori — clubs
quadri — diamonds
cuori — hearts
fare un solitario — to play solitaire
giocare a dama — to play checkers
giocare a scacchi — to play
chess
giocare a dadi — to play with
dice

FAMILY MEMBERS

padre — father
madre — mother
genitori — parents
parenti — relatives
nonno/a — grandfather/grandmother
bisnonno/a — great-grandfather/grandmother
figlio/a — son/daughter
fratello — brother
sorella — sister
zio/a — uncle/aunt
cugino/a — cousin
nipote (m/f) — nephew/niece/grandchild
cognato/a — brother-in-law/sister-in-law
suocero/a — father-in-law/mother-in-law
genero — son-in-law
nuora — daughter-in-law
fratellastro — half-brother
sorellastra — half-sister
patrigno — stepfather
matrigna — stepmother

THE ITALIAN SCHOOL SYSTEM

asilo nido — kindergarten
scuola materna — nursery
school
scuola elementare — elementary
school
scuola media inferiore — lower
middle school
scuola media superiore —
higher middle school
liceo classico — high school
liceo scientifico — technical high
school
liceo linguistico — languages
high school
liceo artistico — art high school
instituto tecnico — technical
school
scuola magistrate — teachers'
college
università — university

AT THE UNIVERSITY

facoltà — faculty
di ingegneria — engineering
di medicina — medicine
di economia e commercio —
business and commerce
di legge — law
di scienze politiche — political
science
di lettere — arts
lingue straniere — foreign languages
di chimica — chemistry
di fisica — physics
di biologia — biology
di farmacia — pharmacy
di agraria — agriculture
di architettura — architecture

DIPLOMAS/CERTIFICATES

licenza elementare — elementary school diploma
licenza media — junior high diploma
maturità liceale — high school
diploma
laurea — university degree
diploma di istituto tecnico —
technical school diploma

TEST YOURSELF

1. COMPLETE WITH DOUBLE PRONOUNS AS REQUIRED BY EACH CASE

Maria vuole il mio libro e io . . . . presto.
Se vuoi un caffè, io . . . . offro volentieri.
Signora, non ho capito il Suo nome! . . . . può ripetere, per cortesia?
Ho visto una commedia divertente e . . . . racconto, Mario.
Il signor Verdi ha bisogno dei documenti e io . . . . do.

2. CHANGE THE FOLLOWING INTO HYPOTHETICAL STATEMENTS

imperfect subjunctive + conditional
Se posso, vengo con voi . . . .
Se fa bello, vado al mare . . . .
Se vado a Roma, visito la fontana di Trevi . . . .
Se ho tempo, gioco a tennis . . . .
Se ci sono 4 giorni di vacanza, parto . . . .

3. MAKE THE FOLLOWING SENTENCES PASSIVE

Tutti gli italiani seguono il calcio . . . .
Umberto Eco ha scritto Il Nome della rosa . . . .
Il direttore ha chiamato la segretaria . . . .
Cristoforo Colombo ha scoperto l'America . . . .
Gli americani hanno inventato la pop-art . . . .

4. WHAT WOULD YOU SAY IF YOU WANTED TO . . .

ask someone if he/she is involved in sports . . . .
ask someone what he/she is doing for the weekend . . . .
ask someone what happened . . . .

say that someone stole your wallet ....

ask what one thinks about the French in Italy ....

say that this place is from the 1400s ....

5. ONLY ONE SENTENCE IN EACH SET IS CORRECT. CAN YOU FIND IT?

A. *Mi piacerei andare in Sicilia* .... ☐
B. *Piacerebbemi andare in Sicilia* .... ☐
C. *Mi piacerebbe andare in Sicilia* .... ☐

A. *Vuole una cartina? Sì, mi dia una* .... ☐
B. *Vuole una cartina? Sì, me ne dia una* .... ☐
C. *Vuole una cartina? Sì, mi ne dia una* .... ☐

A. *Bisogna che voi andiate all'agenzia* .... ☐
B. *Bisogna che voi andate all'agenzia* .... ☐
C. *Bisogna che voi andaste all'agenzia* .... ☐

A. *È il quadro il più famoso di Leonardo* .... ☐
B. *È il quadro più famoso di Leonardo* .... ☐
C. *È il quadro più famosissimo di Leonardo* .... ☐

6. MATCH EACH QUESTION TO ITS ANSWER

A. *Non abbiamo ancora un programma preciso.*
B. *Grazie, volentieri!*
C. *Nella tasca dei pantaloni.*
D. *Per fortuna avevo solo 40.000 lire.*
E. *Mi trattengo per due o tre giorni.*

1. *C'erano molti soldi nel portafoglio?*
2. *Dove avevi messo il portafoglio?*
3. *Gradisce ancora una tazza di tè, signora?*
4. *Per quanto tempo ti fermi a Firenze?*
5. *Che cosa fate per le vacanze?*

(Check your answers on page 37 of the booklet.)

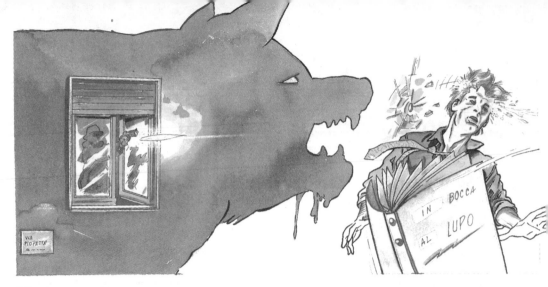

IN THE MOUTH OF THE WOLF

The light hadn't changed all day. It stayed a uniform gray and barely brightened the streets. From dawn to dusk all the lights stayed lit in the office, and when he went out into the twilight of the streets Ambrose' eyes started tearing. He was more tired than usual, so it was easy to accept Lucia's invitation. He recalled the same dull light in Milan. He felt out of sorts; he didn't know why, but an old story came to mind. Doubtless it was the melancholy of the moment. Sitting in an armchair at Lucia's, he told it to her.

"You know, when I lived in Milan, I often had breakfast at the bar at the corner of Pioppette Street and Porta Ticinese. It was a funny place at the time. In the evening, one rubbed elbows with the "in" crowd, petty drug dealers, or Heaven knows what. In the morning it became a normal place again, a bar like all the others. The croissants there were excellent. To make a long story short, every morning at the same time I passed a couple. There was nothing special about them; they were still young, ordinary. The man appeared somewhat pale, somewhat haggard, as if he had a secret illness or as if a fever consumed him. They always sat at the same table at the end of the room, near the bathroom door, and they never stopped talking in subdued voices, almost a murmur. They spoke French; that's what struck me. Besides this habit of keeping to themselves, of not being interested in what was going on around them, there was nothing remarkable about them. Yes, one thing maybe: their nonchalance. They arrived promply at eight-fifteen, and yet they didn't seem rushed, even though it was rush hour when people drank their coffee on the run without taking the trouble to sit down before running off to the streetcar stop across the street. And then, one fine day, they both disappeared. I didn't see them anymore for a month or so."

"E allora?"

"And then, one morning, I found them at the same table as though nothing had happened. The man seemed a little paler, a little sicker than before, but their manner hadn't changed a bit. But when he got up to go pay the cashier, I saw that he no longer had his left hand. Only a stump."

"Ma è straordinario," exclaimed Lucy. "È proprio la stessa storia che ho letta nel libro che interessava alla Aiguement!"

Ambrose paled. The ground tilted under his feet again and he gripped the arms of the chair. "No. Non è possibile."

"Ma sì, te lo giuro. Una storia così morbosa, non potevo fare a meno di notarla. Aspetta che vado a cercare una copia del libro."

And as she came back, triumphantly

waving a copy of In the Mouth of the Wolf in the air, the phone rang. She handed him the book, said "Scuza un attimo" and went to answer it. Ambrose looked at the page she'd opened to; again it was the chapter "Gelsi in via Pioppette." He didn't have time to see more—Lucy was already calling him.

"C'è un tizio che ti vuole parlare. Non ha detto il nome. Te lo passo?"

Ambrose grabbed the phone. His hand was sweating. He already knew whose voice he was going to hear.

"Pronto, Ambrogio? Hai letto il libro che ti ha gentilmente consigliato la signora Aiguement? Avresti tante cose da dimenticare. Purtroppo, temo che sia ormai un po' tardi. Mi spiace."

They'd hung up. Ambrose rushed to the window. The street was white with snow. A couple with their arms around each other was walking along the sidewalk across the street. A car came around the corner at full speed and disappeared at the intersection.

Ambrose came back. Lucy looked at him, uneasy. "Cosa ti succede? Guarda che sei pallidissimo. Cosa ti ha detto quell'uomo?"

She took his hand. He pulled it away. He hesitated, stammering: "Forse...forse mi conviene lasciarti. Sarebbe anche meglio per te. Credo proprio di essere nei guai."

"Non dire stupidaggini. Vedrai che passerà."

Without listening to her, he picked up the book and continued to read where he'd stopped just that morning. The story of the one-handed man was there, just as he'd told it to Lucy. The couple wasn't named, but Mr. S. mentioned a witness to whom he gave the initial A.:

"...Ero proprio lo stesso A. che aveva visto dalla finestra del suo appartamento in via Pioppette l'assassinio del banchiere Gelsi. Questo non mi avrebbe per nulla disturbato se i miei clienti non avessero richiesto un lavoro pulitissimo. Quindi non potevo lasciare in vita un testimone. Dovetti rintracciarlo perché, nel frattempo, si era trasferrito all' estero."

Ambrose felt his strength draining from him. He rapidly skimmed several lines.

"...certi delitti rimangono impuniti perché sono inspiegabili. Mi era facile eliminarlo nella città straniera dove viveva: mai nessuno avrebbe scoperto un qualsiasi collegamento tra la fine del banchiere Gelsi e la morte di questo giovanotto perbene. Nel mio mestiere, l'improbabile è l'unica cosa sicura. Dovevo giocare questa carta anche con A. Non era uno del giro degli affari, della finanza; non aveva niente da nascondere, tranne le solite cose: tresche di cui tutti sanno sempre tutto, piccoli vizi che fanno piuttosto tenerezza. Quasi una vita da impiegato."

Ambrose continued to skim hurriedly through the book. With a glance he still had the time to grasp: "...mi rincresce una cosa: e morta anche la ragazza con cui stava. Peccato non aver avuto più tempo a disposizione, ma l'ultimo treno partiva dalla gare de Lyon unʼ ora dopo; non potevo rimanere di più a Parigi..."

And he fell alongside Lucy. The impact of two bullets had smashed the windowpane into smithereens.

THE END.

Be a well-informed traveler!
The following brief guide will help you discover all of
Italy, from A to Z.

PRACTICAL INFORMATION

APERITIFS

In most cases, Italians like to get together for a drink in public rather than in their own homes. When you order a drink in a bar, you are usually served olives, chips, marinated onions, crackers, peanuts, and sometimes even a small portion of pasta. Usually, an Italian will order a glass of dry or sparkling white wine, such as a Pinot Grigio. But since Italy is the home of vermouth wines, including the famous Martini, cocktails are also popular. Some advice: try a Negroni, which is a mixture of sweet vermouth, gin, and Campari. You won't be disappointed! And, as the natives say, "Cicin!"

ART

Italy is a melting pot of various art forms as well as a kind of immense museum. In Italy, almost everyone finds the art that interests them: protohistoric ruins of Sardinia's nuraghi, examples of Etruscan art, Greek (especially in Sicily), Roman, early Christian (St. Apollinare Nuovo and St. Vitale in Ravenna), Romanesque (the Cattedrale di Torcello, in the Venetian lagoon, or Cefalu in Sicily), Norman-Arabic in Sicily (the cathedral of Amalfi or Saint John of the Hermits in Palermo), and Gothic (Castel del Monte, the palace of Frederick II in Puglia, the Piazza del Campo in Siena, the Doges Palace in Venice, the cathedral of il Duomo in Milan) and on and on. Don't forget the beauty and classicism of the Renaissance (oh, the lovely villas of Palladio, such as the Villa Rotunda) and the emotional Baroque period (Bernini's insane stone baldacchino at St. Peter's or the Trevi fountain, also in Rome, or the very Hispanic-American architecture of Lecce). There is neoclassic art (with Canova's Pauline Bonaparte), plus romantic, realistic, symbolistic, futuristic, abstract—you'll find it all!

AUTOMOBILE

Gasoline costs more in Italy than in many other countries and the Italian government has devised a voucher system. Foreigners, or expatriot Italians who own a car registered abroad, can buy discounted books of gas coupons and free toll tokens at Italian tourist offices or at border crossings. There are different discounted prices depending on your destination (all of Italy, the south, or the islands). These coupons must be purchased with foreign currency and when you buy one you automatically become a member of the ACI (Automobile Club of Italy). Remember that most highways are tollways, although certain ones, such as in Calabria or Sicily, are free. Italy's 3,780 mile (6,086 km) highway network is one of the best in Europe.
• To get your gas coupons, see a travel agent before your departure.

BOLOGNA

Nicknamed "Red Bologna" for its brick monuments (the Church of Saint Petronius) as well as for its left-wing politics, Bologna is a friendly city, known for the good humor of its citizens, its famous tomato sauce, called ragu (which we think of as spaghetti sauce), and for its more than 45 km of porticos which protect pedestrians from the sun and rain. Among the principal curiosities are the two leaning towers of Asinelli and Garisenda and the magnificent community of early Christian and Romanesque churches of Saint Stephen.

BREAD

Bread is one of the basic elements of Italian food. One can easily find, especially in the country, fat round loaves called micche or pagnotte. But what is truly fascinating is the enormous variety of panini, or little breads, each one having a different name and shape depending on its region of origin. The taste also varies, from breads without salt to breads with oil. The panifici (bakers) offer other typical products, such as the grissini, the breadsticks found on restaurant tables. They're wonderful to eat while waiting for your meal. Another bread product is focaccia from Liguria, which is a kind of soft pancake (watch out: the dough can be very greasy!), usually garnished with basil, anchovies, olives, or onions. Also in Liguria, you can find farinata, an ancient recipe made from chick-peas.

CAFÉS

Italy's large cafés are an integral part of its culture. Among the best known are the Florian and the Quadri, both in Venice's St. Mark's Square, with their magnificent interior salons and their Viennese orchestras playing outside. Rome's Greco, on the Via Condotti, is one of the most fashionable spots in the city and is frequented by many of Europe's intellectuals. Padua's Caffe Pedrocci, just off the Piazza Cavour, is a sort of neoclassical, Greek-Egyptian monument, founded in 1831. It was the French novelist Stendhal's favorite Italian café. Both the Doney and the Rivore are important watering spots for Florence's rich and famous. The Florio on the Via Po in Turin is a lovely café and also the best place to buy ice cream in the city. The Calfish is well known in Naples and the Sant'Ambroeus, on the Corso Matteotti in Milan, is particularly celebrated for its chocolates.

CULINARY SPECIALTIES

Since we will discuss pastas below, we'll mention here all the other variations of Italy's exquisite cuisine. First, let's discuss two or three characteristic dishes. Polenta originated in the poor sections of Venice. It's a simple mixture of cornmeal, salt, and water, and it forms the basic food of certain regions. No longer restricted to humble kitchens, it's now available in many modern supermarkets. Risotto, which is flavored with anything from saffron to seafood, is typical of the region of the Po River plain, where rice has been grown since the time of Napoleon. Finally, pizza, the famous and immensely popular pie covered with almost any ingredient imaginable, is a purely Neapolitan creation—it was originally created by the dock workers of Naples.

Let's discuss a few of the specialties you are likely to find in restaurants. Saltimbocca alla Romana is a sauteed veal scallop wrapped in ham and flavored with Marsala wine. Other Roman recipes include tripe with mint sauce and abbachio, a roasted spring lamb. Pasta al pesto is any type of pasta covered with a delicious sauce of basil, garlic, olive oil, and pine nuts. In Venice, besides fish and seafood dishes, one should try the fegato alla veneziana (pork liver sliced very thin and sauteed with onions), risi e bisi (rice and baby peas cooked in a beef bouillon), and Pasta e fagioli (a hearty soup containing pasta and red beans). In Liguria, a region between the mountains and the sea and, therefore, not traditionally a region where one eats much meat, there are several wonderful vegetable dishes, including stuffed or batter-fried vegetables (verdure fritte). It should be noted that breaded and deep-fried foods appear in all sections of Italy, from the famous Veal Scallopine Milanese to the scampi fritti, or fried scampi, very fat shrimp fried in oil. To finish, let's try carpaccio, very fine slices of raw meat served with a lemon slice, or melanzanne alla parmigiana (eggplant parmesan), or stracciatella, a soup made of parmesan cheese and eggs. But, there are still so many more local dishes we couldn't begin to mention them all!

FLORENCE

Florence is the capital of Tuscany, birthplace of the Renaissance, and considered by many to be the most beautiful city in Italy. Watch out for the affliction called "Stendhal's syndrome" which leaves the visitor in a dazed and confused state, overwhelmed by the city's beauty. There are too many things to see in Florence to mention them all here, so be sure to arm yourself with a good guidebook.

Tourist office: The one at the central station is open every day from 9:00 AM to 9:00 PM. There is also one on the Via Manzoni.

FOLK FESTIVALS

There are numerous festivals, fairs, and celebrations each year. Here are a few:
• January 6: Festival of the Befana (Epiphany) in Rome.
• January 17: In Sardinia, the procession of the Maimoiada with Mamutone masks, a tradition that is slowly fading.
• February: Many pre-Lenten carnivals take place, including one in the Piedmont town of Ivrea (famous for its battle of the oranges), the world-famous one in Venice, and one in Viareggio, Tuscany near Lucca, with its floats and political satires.

- First of March: In Oristano, Sardinia, the Sarti-glia—a horse race and Sixteenth Century tour-nament in authentic costumes.
- March or April: At Piana degli Albanesi in Sicily, a Byzantine Easter celebration with lovely local costumes.
- May 15: At Giubbio, in Perugia, the Feast of the Candles.
- May 31: Also at Giubbio, a crossbow tourna-ment.
- The first Thursday in May: At Cocullo (in the province of Aquila) in Abruzzi, the villagers honor their patron saint, San Domenico, by parading with live snakes.
- During May: In Camogli, Genoa, the May Fish Fair.
- End of May, beginning of June: In Genzano, the feast of the Infiorata. The procession of Corpus Domini takes place on a street covered with depictions of scenes made of flowers.
- July 2: The first run of Siena's Palio (a horse race which pits riders from the 17 ancient dis-tricts of the city against one another).
- Third Saturday and Sunday in July: The Feast of the Redeemer in Venice—a great celebration marking the end of a devastating plague in 1576.
- August 16: The second run of the Palio in Siena.
- First Sunday in September: In Venice, the Regate Storiche (historical regattas) on the Grand Ca-nal.
- Beginning of September: At Marostica (Vicenza) the town square is turned into a giant chess-board with living chess pieces.
- End of October: At the Val d'Aoste, the finale of the "Battaglia di Regine," a cow fight.
- End of November: At Gorgonzola (province of Milan), the gigantic Polentata, during which po-lenta with Gorgonzola cheese is prepared and enjoyed.

GENOA

Genoa is so close to the French border that it is often overlooked by tourists heading into the more "Italian" parts of Italy. Still, it's full of charm and worth a stop. The magnificent palaces of the Via Garibaldi reminded us that long ago Genoa was a rich and powerful city. For many years the city was neglected, but today Genoa is cleaning itself up in preparation for the 500th anniversary of the discovery of America by its native son, Christopher Columbus. Among the structures undergoing res-toration is the house where Columbus supposedly was born (its authenticity, however, is doubtful). Genoa has two notable landmarks: the Lanterna (the lighthouse) which is the city's symbol, and the cemetery of Staglieno, one of the most interesting in Europe.

HOURS

Taking into consideration local differences, the most accurate opening and closing schedules are as follows:
- Banks: 8:30 AM–1:30 PM (and 3:00 PM–4:00 PM in large cities). Closed on Saturdays, Sun-days, and holidays.
- Post offices: 8:30 AM–2:00 PM. Closed at noon on Saturdays and the last day of each month. Central post offices in large cities are open in the afternoons and until 7:00 PM. Post offices at airports and such central post office services as telegrams and registered mail are available at any time.
- Pharmacies: Usual hours—8:30 AM–1:00 PM, 4:30 PM–8:00 PM; night hours: 8:00 PM–8:30 AM. At all pharmacies you will find a list of other stores (called di turno) that remain open nights and Sundays.
- Shops: Stores with continuous hours are rare. In the north of Italy, the hours are generally 9:00 AM–1:00 PM and 4:00 PM–7:30 PM; in the south they are usually 5:00 PM–8:30 PM. All stores are closed on Sunday and half a day dur-ing the week.
- Gas stations: Usually closed from 11:30 AM–4:00 PM and after 7:00 PM.

MILAN

Milan is a busy city, famous for having more public clocks than any other city in Italy. (As the saying goes, time is money.) Milan is surrounded by its tangenziali, or suburbs, and is in the middle of a web of highways. It is a very accessible city. It has also become the most fashionable Italian city in every possible sense of the word and its clothing designers are famous throughout the world. Any attempt to discover Milan's riches should start with its celebrated cathedral or its exalted opera house, La Scala.

MONEY

Watch out! All bank notes are not exchanged at the same rate. For example, a 100,000 lire note, which was prohibited from exportation many years ago—as was the 50,000 lire note—is exchanged at a lower rate in banks outside of Italy. It's better, therefore, to leave Italy with bills no larger than 10,000 lire, since those are exchanged at a more favorable rate. Also, be aware that banks are generally closed in the afternoon and that checks and credit cards are not used as widely in Italy as they are in the United States.

MUSEUMS

There are several museums in Italy that should not be missed:
- The Pinacoteca di Brera in Milan, 28 Via Brera: Open daily from 9:00 AM to 7:00 PM; closed Mondays. (It is closed on Tuesday if the preceding Monday is a holiday.) The museum is open Sundays from 9:00 AM to 5:00 PM.
- The Egyptian Museum of Turin, 6 Via Accademia delle Scienze: One of the richest in Europe. It's open from 9:00 AM to 2:00 PM; closed Mondays, the national holiday, and a Tuesday following a Monday holiday.
- The Galleria dell'Accademia in Venice, located on the Campo della Carita: One of the largest museums in Italy. Open daily from 9:00 AM to 2:00 PM, Sundays from 9:00 AM to 1:00 PM; closed Mondays.
- The Peggy Guggenheim Collection, Palazzo Venier dei Leoni, Calle San Cristoforo, in Venice: A magnificent collection of modern art. Open every day, April to October, from 12:00 noon to 6:00 PM, Saturdays from 2:00 PM to 9:00 PM. Closed Tuesdays.
- The Uffizi Gallery, 6 Loggiato degli Uffizi, Florence: Open from 9:00 AM to 2:00 PM daily, Sundays from 9:00 AM to 1:00 PM; closed Mondays.
- The National Archeological Museum, 35 Piazza Museo, Naples: One of the best in Europe. Open daily from 9:00 AM to 2:00 PM, Sundays until 1:00 PM; closed Mondays.
- The Capodimonte National Gallery and Museum, Parco di Capodimonte, Naples: Open daily from 9:00 AM to 2:00 PM, Sundays until 1:00 PM; closed Mondays.

As for Rome, truly the museum city par excellence, there are too many to mention.

NAPLES

Naples is a city of generosity and excess, a city that's both mythical and a bit absurd, and a city that completely defies logic. Naples attracts and repels at the same time. To discover it, leave your camera equipment and luggage at the hotel and stroll down the side streets of Spaccanapoli, old Naples. How can you resist the inimitable charm—playful and tragic—of the Neapolitan people?

In addition to its atmosphere and magnificent location, Naples—the quintessential baroque city—offers visitors numerous monuments and museums worthy of interest.

For more than two centuries, the surrounding area has also attracted those interested in antiquities (Pompeii, Herculanum).

And a "must" for all tourists: the incredible sight of Mount Vesuvius across the Bay of Naples!

Tourist Office: Piazza Gesu Nuovo, or Central Station.

PASTA

Pasta is a basic element of Italian civilization and there is a huge variety available, with evocative names and interesting shapes. We'll just mention the most easy-to-find ones.
- Long and cylindrical: spaghetti, spaghettini (thinner), bucatini, ziti.
- Short: maccheroni, penne (beveled), rigatoni (tubes), fusili (twists), farfalle (butterflies), conchiglie (shells).
- Flat: fettucine (also called tagliatelle) and lasagna.

When pasta is stuffed, it is called ravioli (or agnolotti), cannelloni, or tortellini (in the shape of a ring).

Finally, there are pastas such as capellini (angel hair) or occhi di pernice (partridge eyes), which are found mainly in soups.

ROME

It's hard to define Rome, since it is not only Italy's capital, but also the seat of the Catholic Church, a living museum, a film capital, an ancient, Renaissance, baroque, and modern city, where all the styles are inextricably mixed. It's impossible to list all the attractions—remember simply the Coliseum (Rome's symbol), the Via Vittoria Veneto (Rome's Fifth Avenue), Trastevere (the quarter on the other side of the Tiber), the Spanish Steps of the Trinita dei Monti, the Castel Sant'Angelo, the pyramid of Caius Cestius, the Piazza Navona, with Bernini's reknowned Fountain of the Four Rivers, and, of course, St. Peter's Square in Vatican City, and the Sistine Chapel, with Michelangelo's incredible ceiling. Read more about it below, under "Vatican."

There is also the area of the E.U.R., which is a colossal new neighborhood built during Mussolini's regime and which houses government buildings, exhibition, meeting, and concert halls, all surrounded by gardens.

• Tourist Office: 5 Via Parigi or at the Termini station.

SAN MARINO

The Italian peninsula is divided into three states: the Italian Repubic with 116,316 square miles (301,260 km^2), the Republic of San Marino with 23.4 square miles (60.57 km^2), and Vatican City with only .17 square miles (.44 km^2). The oldest of the three is the Republic of San Marino, established in the Fourth Century. The capital city, San Marino, lies atop a rock and is a haven for drinkers (there is no tax on alcohol) and philatelists (manufacturing postage stamps is the Republic's largest industry).

SHOPPING

We couldn't possibly try to list all the stores in Italy! Instead, we'll mention a few of the best places for shopping. In Rome, the Piazza Barberini (at the end of the Via Vittorio Veneto), Via del Corso, which joins the Piazza Venezia to the Piazza del Popolo, and the streets located between the Via del Corso and the Piazza di Spagna (the Spanish Steps), like the Via Condotti or Via Frattina. One of Italy's best known department stores is Rinascente and there are two stores in Rome—Piazza Fiume and Piazza Colonna.

The chic shopping area of Milan is the Brera neighborhood, where fashion fanatics can find whatever their hearts desire. Stores are located around the central axis of the Via Montenapoleone,

particularly in the Via Bigli, Via Sant' Andrea, Via della Spiga or the Corso Matteotti.

In Naples, you must head for the Via dei Mille, Via Filangieri or Via Carlo Poerio, all in the residential area behind the Cellamare Palace.

In Florence, avid shoppers will want to visit the area just southwest of the Duomo around the Piazza della Repubblica. This is a kind of square that corresponds to an ancient Roman city. At the western boundary is the Via de'Tornabuoni, to the north, Via de Cerretani, to the east Via de Calzaioli, where, as the name implies, shoes are still sold.

Venice is not a shopper's mecca, but there are several lovely boutiques. The nicest ones are located between the Piazza San Marco and the Teatro la Fenice, in the Calle Large XXII Marzo, the Salizada San Moise, the Calle Vallaresso, the Frezzeria San Marco, or the Ramo Fuserie. Remember, too, that there are two special products that are made on Venice's islands: glass from the island of Murano and lace from Burano. Watch out, though, for the tourist traps.

SITES

Let's choose a few places arbitrarily from the huge number of beautiful areas in Italy. In Venice, Torcello, the farthest island, is the ancient queen of the lagoon. There's little left, just a few churches in the middle of the tall grasses, yet it remains a mysterious, meditative place. To get there, take a boat at the Fondamenta Nuove (the trip takes about three quarters of an hour).

Since we're starting from Venice, you mustn't miss taking the boat from Venice to Padua along the Canal de la Brenta. This lovely canal is lined with magnificent villas—former country houses of the Venetian aristocracy—among which are many designed by Palladio, such as the Malcontenta (Villa Foscari).

In the general vicinity of Milan, Lake Maggiore is particularly charming, largely because of the Borromean Islands at its center. These islands can be reached from Stresa. Of the three islands—Isola Bella, Isola dei Pescatori, which as its name suggests, borders a fisherman's village, and Isola Madre, the latter is undoubtedly the most fascinating. It shelters a palace that's surrounded by a lovely garden and it is truly a dream-like spot.

On the Italian Riviera there are several enchanting stops, such as Portofino or Cinque Terre. Portofino, where the European jet set moors its yachts, is an incomparable place with its old well-

protected port, its promontory, its sailor's cemetery, and the lovely monastery of San Fruttuoso.
You can get there by boat, from either Santa Marg-
herita Ligure or Genoa. Cinque Terre—or Five
Lands—is actually five cliff-hanging villages:
Monterosso, Vernazza, Corniglia, Manarola, and
Riomaggiore, all located between Levanto and La
Spezzia. The trail that links them is a sort of lover's
lane. Astonishingly enough, these towns are also
served by a railroad line and can be reached as well
by car (you follow a strange route that uses some
of the train tunnels). The most pleasant way to
arrive, however, is by boat.

In Tuscany, the lovely city of San Gimignano,
with its brick towers, gives the visitor a good idea
of life in Italy during the Middle Ages. Less than 39
miles (100 km) from Rome, between Viterbo and
Orte, one must see Bomarzo and visit its famous
parco dei mostri (park of monsters). The Bosco
Sacro (sacred wood) was built by Prince Pierfran-
cesco Orsini in the middle of the Sixteenth Century,
and Bomarzo Park—where natural rock was used
to form grotesque figures—is a fascinating excursion into the world of ancient mythology. In the
middle of the park stands a terrifying, fantastic
dragon whose open mouth "welcomes" all visitors. This is truly one of the most magical places
on earth!

When visiting Naples one must see Herculanum (Ercolano) or Pompei, the two famous
Roman villages destroyed by an eruption of Mount
Vesuvius in AD 79. The volcano's human victims
can still be seen, their bodies preserved by lava.
These two villages also tell us a great deal about
life in ancient Rome. Visitors arrive by a private
railroad line, the Circumvesiana, which leaves from
Naple's central station.

There are too many extraordinary sites in Italy
to mention . . . but we'll talk about just a few more,
such as Alberobello, in the ancient province of
Apulia (now called Puglia), with its unbelievable
trulli—cone-shaped stone huts that are more rem-
iniscent of Turkey than Italy. Don't miss the
wondrous nature reserve on the island of Alcudi
(15 residents), one of the Aeolian Islands off the
northeast coast of Sicily, or the countryside of Sardinia, which is a natural jewel of rare beauty. On
the north side of the island, one can admire the
rocks of Capo d'Orso, which have been sculpted by
erosion, or elsewhere, the megalithic ruins of the
fortified villages called nuraghi.

SPAS

The popularity of spas dates back to ancient
Rome, although we don't intend to discuss here the
Roman baths of Caracalla or other monuments of
antiquity. Let's talk instead about the Italian spas
still operating today where one can find all the
traditional elements that have made these watering
spots so popular through the years—the orchestras, gardens, and colonnades.

Some spas, of course, have actually been in
use since the days of the Romans and the Etruscans. The best known are Albano Terme in Venetia
(province of Padua); Ischia, near the Bay of
Naples; Salsomaggiore in Emilia-Romagna (the
province of Parma); Montecatini (province of Pi-
stoia); and Chianciano (near Siena in Tuscany),
where the Etruscans went to cure their liver ail-
ments; and giuggi (province of Frosinone) in
Latium. If you celebrate Christmas and New Year's
in Italy, it might be useful to have these names
close at hand.

TELEPHONES

There are telephone booths in the streets, train
stations, bars, and some restaurants. Public
phones are indicated by a sign. These telephones
take money or tokens, called gettoni (today worth
200 lire). Gettoni have the interesting feature of
also being used as ordinary pieces of money
whose value actually increases with inflation—five
tokens worth 500 lire four years ago are now worth
1,000 lire.

THEATER

Certain Italian theaters have international reputations, the most famous being La Scala, Milan's
opera house (Teatro Lirico della Scala, Piazza dell
Scala). Also in Milan is one of the bright lights of
modern European theater, the Piccolo Teatro de
Giorgio Strehler (2 Via Rovanello). Venice is the
home of another famous lyric theater, Teatro La
Fenice (Campo San Frantin), the only opera house
that has canals on two sides . . . and don't forget
the famous Theater of San Carlo in Naples, which
is even older and more lavish than La Scala and La
Fenice.

In the summer, after the theater season has
ended, there are many ballet and opera festivals
throughout Italy. One is in Verona and lasts
through July and August (Arena di Verona, 28

Piazza Bra, Verona 37121). There are also several open-air productions, including one in Rome at the Baths of Caracalla and two in Sicily in the Greek theaters of Syracuse and Taormina. And don't forget the Rossini Festival in Pesara (in August and September in The Marches), and the famous Festival of Two Worlds in Spoleto (from April to July), or the Musical Weeks in Stresa (along Lake Maggiore, in the province of Novara).

Speaking of festivals, we must mention three very famous and popular ones: the Venice International Film Festival, which begins at the end of August and lasts into September, the International Festival of Italian Music in San Remo (province of Imperia), which is held in February, and in September, Naples's Festival of Neapolitan Music.

TRANSPORTATION

Each city has its own transportation system and tickets can generally be purchased at newsstands.

In Rome you'll find two subway lines and numerous bus lines. One ticket costs 700 lire and is good for one hour. You can also buy ticket books and a tourist pass called the Roma Pass. Milan also has two subway lines but there are buses, trolleys, and cable cars as well. A ticket is good for 75 minutes. In Naples there is a subway line, buses, and several funiculars that link the low parts of the city with the higher area. In Turin there are both streetcars and buses. In Genoa the long-awaited subway system is scheduled to open in 1992. Currently, there are buses, several street elevators, and funiculars. A ticket, which costs 700 lire, is good for 75 minutes.

For all cities, one ticket allows you to use all modes of transportation, at least for the specified amount of time.

Finally, a word about the very special form of transportation available in Venice. The famous vaporetti, or motorboats, are very useful for visiting the city and islands, offering possibilities for several short cruises. There are both express and local routes. You can buy one ticket but you can also get a ticket that's good for one day on all lines (the biglietto giornaliero). For crossing the Grand Canal there are also the traghetti, which are ferry boats or public gondolas. You pay when you get on and remain standing during the crossing. Gondolas, which aren't really a form of public transportation, are much more expensive: 50,000 lire for 50 minutes for no more than five people.

There are taxis in all cities, even in Venice where they are actually motor boats. Fares vary greatly from place to place.

TRAIN STATIONS

There are tourist information offices in all large stations where, for example, you can find and reserve a hotel room, obtain a map, and get all sorts of information. There are also currency exchange windows that are open much later than banks (usually until about 7:00 PM). Also, in addition to simple locker rooms there are the albergo diurno—or daytime hotels—where one can freshen up, shower, shave, and even take a nap.

TURIN

This large industrial city on the banks of the Po River is often called the Detroit of Italy (it's the headquarters of the Fiat auto makers), but it still has a certain charm. It was formerly the capital of Savoy and its streets, squares, and colonnades still have a regal appearance. There is a monumental grouping of buildings at its center: the Royal Palace, the Madamma Palace, the Carignano Palace, the Piazza San Carlo, with its twin churches, and the Mole Antonelliana, whose high slender tower is a symbol of the city. Its palaces and numerous bronze statues give Turin the air of a great European capital of the past.
• Tourist bureau: 226 via Roma or the Porta Nuova Station.

VATICAN

Although located at the heart of Rome, Vatican City is a true independent state with only .17 square miles (.44 km²) it is thé smallest state in the world—and one of the richest. It attracts both Catholics and art lovers from all over the world. St. Peter's, the largest church in the world, is a great artistic and architectural feat. As for the Vatican's museums, they are so rich in art that a day's visit is not sufficient. Hurried visitors must be content with the works of Raphael and the impressive Sistine Chapel of Michelangelo.

- St. Peter's Basilica: Open from 7:00 AM to 7:00 PM.
- The Vatican Museum: Open from 9:00 AM to 4:00 PM except Sundays and holidays.
- Papal audiences: Every Wednesday from 11:00 AM in the Paul IV Hall, near the south side of St. Peter's. (Those who wish an audience should write in advance to the Prefetto della Casa Pontificia.)

VENICE

Everything about Venice is a marvel—the monuments, the museums, the location. A French writer of the end of the Fifteenth Century, Philippe de Communes, described the Grand Canal as "the loveliest street in the world." This is still true and the visitor should travel up and down it in every direction, both on foot and by boat. The best way to discover Venice is to simply set off with no particular route in mind. No matter where you go—and Venice isn't that large—you will come upon signs giving directions. Also, the Venetians are generally very helpful. With its canals, bridges, and special spots that look different at every hour of the day and in every season, Venice is truly a city of miracles. As soon as you leave the main areas, which are full of people, and stroll toward the Fondamente Nuove or the Arsenal and the San Pietro neighborhood, along the little canals of the interior, or the Giudecca, you'll be able to meditate on the wonders of Venice. You may find whatever you're looking for since, in the words of the French writer Michel Tournier, "Venice is a palace of mirrors that reflects all our fantasies."

- Tourist office: Piazza San Marco (Calle dell'Ascenzione); Gare Santa Lucia; Piazzale Roma (for those who arrive by car).

WINES

Italy produces nearly 1,500 different wines, among which 200 or so earn the DOC (Denominazione di Origine Controllata), indicating a quality product. Among the fine wines, we must include, among the reds, Chianti of Tuscany (the best have a black rooster on the neck of the bottle), plus Barolo, Nebiolo, Barbera, Dolcetto, all from the Piedmont region. Valpolicella comes from the area near Verona. Among the white wines found there are the Bianco dei Castelli Romani from the Rome region, Soave from near Verona, the Lacrima Christi from Vesuvius, Cortesi di Gavi from the Piedmont, and Vernaccia de San Gimignano from Tuscany. There are also special wines such as Lambrusco, a light sparkling red from Romagna, the famous Asti Spumante, which is a kind of champagne from the Piedmont, and Marsala, a strong, heady fortified wine that is sometimes thickened with a beaten egg yolk.

For true wine lovers there is the Enoteca Italica Permanente, in Siena, which is a government-run wine-tasting establishment. Here one can discover, and savor, all the different wines of the peninsula.

ACI	Automobile Club of Italy
ANSA	National Press Association
BI	Bank of Italy
BR	Red Brigade
CAP	Postal Code
CGIL	General Confederation of Italian Workers (like our AFL-CIO)
CISAL	Italian Confederation of Independent Labor Unions
CISL	Italian Confederation of Union Workers
CIT	Italian Tourist Bureau
CP	Post Office Box
DC	Christian Democratic Party
DP	Democratic Proletariat Party
ENAL	National Worker's Assistance Office
ENEL	National Organization for Electric Energy
ENIT	Italian National Tourist Bureau
EPT	Regional Tourist Bureau
FI	Frequency Modulation (FM)
FIA	Audio Amplitude Modulation (AM radio)
FIV	Video Amplitude Modulation (AM video)
FS, FF, SS	National railroad system
G.C.	Jesus Christ
GR	News radio
F.U.	Official news
IACP	Independent Institute for Low-Income Housing
INPS	National Institute for Social Services
INT	National Transportation Office
IVA	Value-added tax (VAT)
MEC	European Common Market
MSI	Italian Social Movement, a neo-fascist party
PA	Air Mail
PCI	Italian Communist Party
PLI	Italian Liberal Party
PRI	Italian Republican Party
PSDI	Italian Social-Democratic Party
PSI	Italian Socialist Party
POLSTRADA	Highway patrol
PS	State Police
PT	Post office and telegraph
PTP	Public telephone booth
PU	Urban police officers
RAI	Italian Radio and Television
RR	Acknowledgment of receipt (of something)
SP	National highway
TG	Television news
TUT	Urban unit tariff
TVC	Color television
US	1. Press office
	2. Emergency exit
VU	Police officer

PRACTICAL INFORMATION

VOCABULARY

The glossary lists 1,500 words and idiomatic expressions used in the book. The entries are given in alphabetical order with English translations. Verbs are in the infinitive and adjectives in the masculine. For an explanation on how to form feminine adjectives, please consult the grammar section in the booklet.

VOCABULARY

A

abbastanza — enough, quite
abbigliamento — clothing
abbondante — abundant
abitare — to live (somewhere)
Abruzzo — Abruzzi Region
accappatoio — bathrobe
accettare — to accept
acciuga — anchovy
accomodarsi — 1. to enter 2. to seat oneself 3. to go to the next cashier/teller/etc.
accompagnare — to accompany
accorciare — to shorten
accorgersi — to realize
aceto — vinegar
acqua (minerale) — (mineral) water
aquavite — brandy
acquazzone — pouring (rain)
acquisto — purchase
adesso — now
adottivo — adoptive
aereo — airplane
aeroporto — airport
afa — heat
affettuoso — affectionate
affittare — to rent
affitto — rent
affluente — affluent
affollato — crowded
affresco — fresco
Afghanistan — Afghanistan
Africa — Africa
agente (immobiliare) — (real estate) agent
agenzia — agency
agiato — calm
aglio — garlic
agosto — August
albergo (hotel) — hotel
albicocca — apricot
alcoolici — alcoholic beverages
alcuni — some
Algeria — Algeria
allegro — happy
allevamento — raising kids, rearing
alloggiare — to stay (somewhere)
allora — then
allungare — to lengthen
almeno — at least
Alpi — (the) Alps
altitudine — altitude
alto — 1. high 2. tall
altopiano — plateau
altrettanto — as much as
altrimenti — otherwise
altro — other

amare — to love
amaro — bitter
ambiente — environment
America — America
americano — American
ammalarsi — to become sick
ammirare — to admire
amore — love
analcoolici — nonalcoholic beverages
ananas — pineapple
anatra — duck
anche — also, too
ancora — again, still, yet
andare — to go
andare a letto — to go to bed
andata — one-way ticket
Angola — Angola
anguilla — eel
anguria — watermelon
animale — animal
anno — year
annoiarsi — to become bored
Antarctico — Antarctica
antibiotico — antibiotic
Antille — Antilles
antipatico — unpleasant
anzianità — old age
aperitivo — aperitif
apparenza — appearance
appartamento — apartment
appassionato — fond of
appena — just (adverb), as soon as, hardly
Appennini — Apennines
appetito — appetite
approvare — to approve
appuntamento — appointment, date
aprile — April
aprire — to open
Arabia Saudita — Saudi Arabia
aragosta — lobster
architetto — architect
argenteria — silverware
argento — silver
Argentina — Argentina
argomento — topic, subject
aria condizionata — air conditioning
armadio — cupboard, wardrobe
arrabbiarsi — to become angry
arrivare — to arrive
arrivo — arrival
arrosto — roast
arte — art
artista — artist
ascoltare — to listen (to)

Asia — Asia
asilo nido — kindergarten
aspettare — to wait (for)
aspirina — aspirin
assegno — check
assistente — assistant
assistente sociale — social worker
attendere — to wait, to expect
attenzione — attention
attimo — instant, minute
attirare — to attract
attore — actor
attraversare — to cross (over)
Australia — Australia
Austria — Austria
autista — driver
autobus — bus
automobile — automobile
autunno — autumn, fall
avere — to have
aver intenzione di — to intend (to)
aver mal di gola — to have a sore throat
aver mal di testa — to have a headache
avere fretta — to be in a hurry
avere la fama (di) — to have the reputation (of)
avere un certo appetito — to be rather hungry
avere una fame da lupi — to be as hungry as a bear (lit. wolves)
avere voglia (di) — to feel like
avvertire — to warn
avvocato — lawyer
azienda — business, company
azzurro — blue

B

bagagli — baggage
bagno — bath, bathroom
balcone — large window (balcony)
ballare — to dance
ballerina — ballerina
bambino — child
banana — banana
banca — bank
bandiera — flag
bar — espresso bar
barbiere — barber
barella — stretcher
Basilicata — Basilicata region

basilico — basil
basso — 1. low 2. short
bastare — to be enough, to suffice
battere — 1. to knock 2. to hit
Belgio — Belgium
bello — beautiful, handsome
bene — well
bere — to drink
berretto — cap
bianco — white
bicchiere — drinking glass
bicicletta — bicycle
biglietteria — ticket counter
biglietto — ticket
biologo — biologist
biondo — blond
birra — beer
birreria — beer store, pub, brewery
bisnonno — great-grandfather
bisogna che — it is necessary
    that
bistecca — steak
blu — dark blue
bocca — mouth
bollito — boiled
bombetta — derby
borsellino — small change purse
bottiglia — bottle
bottoncino — small button
bottone — button
box — garage
braccio (pl. braccia) — arm
Brasile — Brazil
bravo — good
brilliante — brilliant
brina — frost
bruno — brown
brutto — ugly
bue (pl. buoi) — ox, oxen
buio — dark
Bulgaria — Bulgaria
buonasera — good evening/
    afternoon
buongiorno — good morning/day
buongustaio — gourmet
buono — good

cabina — cabin
cacciagione — game
caffè — coffee
Calabria — Calabria
calamaro — squid
calcio — soccer
caldo — 1. heat 2. hot
calze — stockings

calzettoni — knee socks
calzolaio — shoemaker
calzoleria — shoestore
cambiare — to change, to
    exchange
cambiare idea — to change one's
    mind
cambio — exchange
camera (stanza) — room
camera da letto — bedroom
camera doppia — double room
camera matrimoniale — double
    bedroom
camera singola — single room
cameriere — waiter
camicetta — blouse
camicia — shirt
camicia da notte — night gown
Campania — Campania
Canada — Canada
canarino — canary
canottiera — undershirt
cantare — to sing
cantina — wine cellar
canzone — song
capelli — hair (on head)
capire — to understand
capitare — to happen
capo — head/chief
capolinea — terminal, end of the
    line
cappello — hat
cappotto — coat
cappuccino — cappuccino
capra — goat
capriolo — roe deer
capufficio — office manager
caratteristica — characteristic
carciofo — artichoke
carnagione — complexion
carne — meat
carnevale — carnival
caro — dear, expensive
carota — carrot
carpa — carp
carrozzeria — car body shop
carta d'identità — identification
    card/paper
carta di credito — credit card
cartina — map
casa — house, home
casa editrice — publishing house
casalinga — housewife
caso — case, chance
cassa — cashier
cassetta — box
cassetto — drawer
castano — nut brown, auburn

categoria — category
cattedrale — cathedral
cattivo — bad
causa — cause
cauzione — deposit, down
    payment
cavallo — horse
cavolo — cabbage
cece — chick-pea
Cecoslovacchia — Czechoslo-
    vakia
cena — dinner
cenare — to dine, to have dinner
centrale — central
centralinista — telephone
    operator
centro — center, downtown
ceramica — ceramic
cercare — to look for, to search
certamente — certainly, surely
certo — certainly, certain, sure
chi — who
chiacchierare — to chat
chiamarsi — to be called
chiaro — clear
chiave — key
chiesa — church
chilo — kilogram
chimico — chemist, chemical
chirurgo — surgeon
chitarra — guitar
chiudere — to close
Ciad — Chad
cibo — food
ciclismo — cycling
cielo — sky
Cile — Chile
ciliegia — cherry
Cina — China
cinema — movies, cinema,
    movie theater
cinghiale — boar
cintura — belt
cioè — that is
cipolla — onion
circuito — circuit
citofono — intercom
città — city
classe — class
classico — classic, classical
clima — climate
cocktail — cocktail
cognac — cognac
cognato — brother-in-law
cognome — surname, family
    name
colazione — breakfast, early lunch
colletto — collar

collina — hill
collo — neck
Colombia — Colombia
colore — color
coltello — knife
comico — comical, funny
cominciare — to begin
commedia — comedy
commercialista — business expert, business consultant
commerciante — dealer, trader, businessman
commesso — clerk
commissario — commissioner, chief of police
comodo — comfortable
compilare — fill out
completo — complete
complimento — compliment
comprare — to buy
compressa — tablet
compromesso — compromise
comunque — however, in any case
con — with
concerto — concert
condimento — seasoning
condizione — condition
confine — border
coniglio — rabbit
conoscere/conoscersi — to know (someone)/to know one another
consegna dei bagagli — baggage pickup
considerare — to consider
consigliare — to advise
contare — to count
continuare — to continue
conto — bill, account
conto corrente — current account
contorno — side dish
contrario — opposite
contratto d'affitto — rental contract
controllare — to check, to control
conversazione — conversation
coperto — cover charge
Corea — Korea
correre il rischio di — to run the risk of
còrridoio — corridor
corsista — enrolled student
corso — course
corto — short (in length, distance, etc.)
cosa — thing
coscia — thigh

così — so, thus
Costa d'Avorio — Ivory Coast
costume da bagno — bathing suit
cotone — cotton
cottura — cooking
cratere — mixing bowl, crater
credere — to believe
crescere — to grow
crudo — raw
cuccetta — sleeping berth
cuchiaino — teaspoon
cucchiaio — spoon
cucina — kitchen, stove
cugino — cousin
cuore — heart
cupola — dome, cupola
cura — cure, treatment
curare — to cure, to treat
curiosità — curiosity
curioso — curious

D

Danimarca — Denmark
danza (classica, moderna, jazz) — dance (classical, modern, jazz)
dare — to give
dare (darsi) del Lei — to use the polite form
dare (darsi) del tu — to use the familiar form
dare una spinta — to give a push
datore di lavoro — employer
davanti (a) — in front of
davvero — really
decentrato — out of town
decidere — to decide
decimo — tenth
delta — delta
denaro — money
dente — tooth
dentista — dentist
dentro — within, inside
dépliant — brochure, pamphlet
depresso — depressed
desiderare — to desire, to want
destinazione — destination
destino — destiny
destra — right
dettagliato — detailed
di — of
dicembre — December
dieci — ten
dietro — behind

difficile — difficult
digestivo — digestive, liqueur
dimenticare — to forget
dimostrare — to show
dimostrare l'età — to show one's age
dinamico — dynamic
Dio — God
dipendente — employee
dipendere (da) — to depend (on)
diploma — diploma
dire — to say, to tell
direttore amministrativo — administrative director/manager
direttore delle vendite — sales manager
dirigente — manager, executive
disciplinato — disciplined, orderly
disco — record
discoteca — disco
disegnatore industriale — industrial designer
disoccupato — unemployed
disoccupazione — unemployment
disonesto — dishonest
disponsible — available
disporre — to have at one's disposal
distratto — distracted
dito (pl. dita) — finger
ditta — firm, company
divano (sofà) — sofa
diventare — to become
diverso — different
divertente — enjoyable
divertirsi — to enjoy oneself
divorziare — to divorce
divorzio — divorce
documento — document, piece of identification
dogana — customs
dolce — sweet, dessert
dollaro US — US dollar
Dolomiti — Dolomites
domanda — question
domandare — to ask a question
domani — tomorrow
domenica — Sunday
donna — woman
dopo — after
doppi servizi — double bathroom
dormire — to sleep
dottore — doctor
dove — where
dovere — to have to
dramma — drama
drammatico — dramatic
dritto — straight ahead

drogheria — grocery store
droghiere — grocer
dunque — thus, therefore, so

ecco — here is/there is
eccolo — here he/it is
economico — economical, cheap
effettivamente — in effect, actually
Egitto — Egypt
elegante — elegant
elenco telefonico — telephone book
elettricista — electrician
elettrodomestico — appliance
elevato — elevated, high up
entrare — to enter
eppure — and yet
equitazione — horseback riding
eredità — inheritance
esclamarsi — to exclaim
escursione — excursion
esempio — example
esilio — exile
esistere — to exist
esitare — to hesitate
espansivo — expansive
esposizione — exposition
essere — to be
essere indeciso — to be uncertain/undecided
essere matto — to be crazy
essere pronto — to be ready
essere stonato — to lack a musical ear
est — east
estate — summer
estero — abroad
estuario — estuary
età — age
Etiopia — Ethiopia
etto — hectogram
Europa — Europe

fabbro — blacksmith
faccia — face
facile — easy
facoltà — faculty
fagiano — pheasant
fagiolino — string bean
fagiolo — bean
falegname — carpenter

falso — false
fama — fame, reputation
famiglia — family
famoso (celebre) — famous, well-known
fantascienza — science fiction
farci caso — to notice, to pay attention to
fare — to do, to make
fare colazione — to have breakfast/early lunch
fare il biglietto — to buy a (travel) ticket
fare in tempo — to arrive on time
fare sport — to practice a sport
fare un solitario — to play a game of solitaire
farfallino — little butterfly
farmacia — pharmacy
farmacista — pharmacist
farsi un'idea — to have an idea
fascino — charm
fatica — fatigue, tiredness
fattorino — bellboy
febbraio — February
febbre — fever, (body) temperature
felice — happy
ferie — holidays, vacations
fermarsi (trattenersi) — to stop/ stay over
fermata (dell'autobus) — bus stop
fiammifero — match
fico — fig
fidanzato — fiancé
fidarsi (di) — to trust
fiero — proud
figlio — son
figlio maggiore — older son
figlio minore — younger son
filla — lineup
filetto — filet
fine — end
fine-settimana — weekend
finestra — window
finire — to finish
Finlandia — Finland
fino a — until
finocchio — fennel
fiore — flower
fisico — physicist
fiume — river
foce — river mouth
foglio paga — paycheck
fondo — bottom
fontana — fountain
forchetta — fork
formaggio — cheese

formazione — formation
formula — formula/pattern
forno — oven
forse — maybe
forte — strong, loud
fortunato — fortunate, lucky
fotografo — photographer
fra — between, among
fragola — strawberry
francese — French
Francia — France
franco — franc
frase — phrase, sentence
fratellastro — stepbrother
fratello — brother
freddo — cold
fritto — fried
fronte — forehead
frontiera — frontier, border
frutta — fruit
frutti di mare — seafood
fruttivendolo — fruit vendor
fulmine — bolt of lightning
funghi — mushrooms
fuori — outside
furto — theft

gabinetto — toilet
galleria — gallery, shopping mall
gallina — chicken
gamba — leg
gamberetto — shrimp
gambero — shrimp, prawn
gassosa — carbonated soft drink
gatto — cat
gelateria, gelataio — ice cream parlor/vendor
generalizzare — to generalize
genero — son-in-law
genitori — parents
gennaio — January
geologo — geologist
Germania — Germany
gessato — striped
gestione — management
ghiaccio — ice
già — already
giacca — jacket
giallo — 1. yellow 2. mystery novel/movie
Giappone — Japan
ginecologo — gynecologist
ginnastica — physical exercise
ginocchio — knee

VOCABULARY

giocare (con un gioco) — to play (a game)

giocare a carte — to play cards

giocare a dadi — to shoot dice

giocare a dama — to play checkers

giocare a scacchi — to play chess

giochi di società — parlor games

gioco — game

gioielleria, gioielliere — jewelry shop/jeweler

Giordania — Jordan

giornalaio — newspaper vendor

giornale — newspaper

giornalista — journalist, newspaper reporter

giornata — day

giorno — day

giovane — young, youth

giovedì — Thursday

girare — to turn

girocollo — neckline

giro della città — tour of the city

giubbotto — jacket, windbreaker

giugno — June

goccia — drop

godere — to enjoy

gola — throat

golf — pullover sweater

golfo — gulf

gomito — elbow

gonna — skirt

gradevole — pleasant

grammo — gram

granchio — crab

grande — big, large, wide

grande magazzino — department store

grandine — hail

grappa — Italian brandy

grasso — fat

grave — grave, serious

grazie — thank you

grazie mille — a million thanks

Grecia — Greece

grigio — gray

guanti — gloves

guardare — to look at, to watch

guarire — to cure, to get better

Guatemala — Guatemala

guida — guide

idea — idea

idraulico — plumber

ieri — yesterday

illuminato — full of light, illuminated

imbarazzo — embarrassment

immaginare — to imagine

imparare — to learn

impermeabile — raincoat, trenchcoat

impianto stereo — stereo system

impiegato — employee

importante — important

impossibile — impossible

in effetti — in effect

in fondo a — at the end of

in genere — in general

incidente — accident

incominciare — to begin

incredibile — incredible, unbelievable

indeciso — indecisive, undecided, unsure

indennità — indemnity

India — India

individuo — individual

Indonesia — Indonesia

indovinello — riddle

industriale — 1. industrial 2. (company) executive

influenza — flu

informarsi — to get information

informatica — computer science

ingegnere — engineer

Inghilterra — England

inglese — English

ingresso — entrance

inizio — start, beginning

innamorato — in love

inondazione — flood

inquilino — renter

insalata mista — tossed salad

insegnante — teacher

insieme — together

insomma — as a matter of fact

insonnia — insomnia

insopportabile — unbearable

intelligente — intelligent

intenzione — intention

interessare — to interest

internazionale — international

interprete — interpreter

intorna a — around

intraprendente — enterprising, entrepreneurial

intromettersi — to join in

invece — instead

inverno — winter

Iraq — Iraq

Iran — Iran

Irlandia — Ireland

iscriversi — to register

isola — island

Israele — Israel

istituto tecnico — technical/vocational school

Italia — Italy

italiano — Italian

itinerario — itinerary

Iugoslavia — Yugoslavia

Kenia — Kenya

labbra — lips

ladro — thief

lago — lake

lampo — lightning

lampone — raspberry

lana — wool

largo — large, wide

lasciare — to leave

lasciar detto qualcosa — to leave a message

lato — side

lattaio — milk vendor

latte — milk

latteria — dairy

laurea — university degree

lavorare — to work

lavoro — work

leggero — light

lei — 1. she 2. you (polite)

lenticchia — lentil

lepre — jackrabbit

lettera — letter

letteratura — literature

letto — bed

lì — there

Libano — Lebanon

libero professionista — professional

Libia — Libya

libretto di assegno — checkbook

libro — book

licenza elementare — elementary school certificate

licenza media — middle school certificate

licenziamento — firing

liceo (upper) — high school

Liguria — Liguria

linea — line

lingua — language, tongue
liquore — liqueur
lira italiana — Italian lira
litro — liter
Lombardia — Lombardy
lontano da — far from
luccio — pike (fish)
luglio — July
luminoso — well lit
luna — moon
lunedì — Monday
lunghezza — length
lungo — long
luogo — place
Lussemburgo — Luxembourg
lusso — luxury

ma — but
macchina — car
macchina fotografica — camera
macellaio — butcher
macelleria — butcher shop
Madagascar — Madagascar
madre — mother
maestro — elementary school
teacher, music teacher
maggio — May
maglietta — undershirt, T-shirt
magnifico — magnificent
magro — thin, skinny
mai — never, ever
maiale — pig
male — bad
maleducato — boorish, uncouth
malinconia — melancholy
mamma — mom
mancare — to lack
mancia — tip
mandarino — mandarin orange
manica — sleeve
mano (pl. mani) — hand
Marche — Marche (region)
marco — (German) mark
mare — sea
Mare Mediterraneo — Mediterranean Sea
marito — husband
marmo — marble
Marocco — Morocco
marrone — brown
martedì — Tuesday
marzo — March
massimo — maximum
matrigna — stepmother

matrimonio — matrimony,
wedding
mattina — morning
mattinata — morning
maturità liceale — high school
diploma
me — me
meccanico — mechanic
medicina — medicine
medico — doctor
Medio Evo — Middle Ages
meglio — better
mela — apple
melanzana — eggplant
melone — melon
meno — less, minus
mensa aziendale — company
cafeteria
menta — mint
mento — chin
mentre — during
menù — menu
meraviglioso — marvelous
merciaio — merchant
mercoledì — Wednesday
merluzzo — cod
messaggio — message
Messico — Mexico
meteorologico — meteorological
metro — subway
mettere piede — to put one's foot
in
mezza pensione — room and
partial board
mezzo — half
mezzogiorno — noon
mi — me
milanese — Milanese
minestra — soup
minimo — minimal
ministero — ministry
minuto — minute
mirtillo — blueberry
misura — measure, size
mobile — piece of furniture
modello — model, pattern
modo — way (e.g. of doing something)
modulo — form (to fill out)
moglie — wife
Molise — Molise (region)
molluschi — mollusks
molto — much, a lot, very
momento — moment
montagna — mountain
monte — hill
monumento — monument
morire — to die

morto — dead
mosaico — mosaic
moscato — muscatel
Mozambico — Mozambique
mucca — cow
muscolo — muscle, mussel
museo — museum
musica — music
mutandine — underwear, panties

napoletano — Neapolitan
nascere — to be born
nascondere — to hide
naso — nose
Natale — Christmas
naturalmente — naturally
nave — ship, boat
nazionalità — nationality
nebbia — fog
necessario — necessary
negozio — store
Nepal — Nepal
nero — black
neve — snow
Nicaragua — Nicaragua
niente — nothing
Nigeria — Nigeria
nipote — 1. nephew 2. grandson/
granddaughter 3. grandchild
no — no
noioso — boring
nome — 1. name 2. first name
non — not
non vedere l'ora (di) — can't
wait (to)
nonno — grandfather
nono — ninth
nord — north
Norvegia — Norway
notte — night
novembre — November
nulla — nothing
numero di telefono — telephone
number
nuora — daughter-in-law
nuoto — swimming
Nuova Zelanda — New Zealand
nuovo — new
nuvola — cloud
nuvoloso — cloudy

oca (oche) — goose (geese)

occhio — eye
oceano — ocean
odiare — to hate
oggetto — object
oggi — today
olio — oil
oltrepassare — to surpass
ombrello — umbrella
onesto — honest
operaio — (blue-collar) worker
operare — to operate
ora — 1. hour 2. now
ora di punta — rush hour
ordinare — to order
orecchio — ear
orefice — goldsmith
organizzare — to organize
organizzazione — organization
ormai — by now
oro — gold
orologiaio — watchmaker
orologio — watch, clock
ostrica — oyster
ottavo — eighth
ottobre — October
ovest — west
ozio — idleness

pacchetto — package, packet
padre — father
padrino — godfather
padrone di casa — house owner
paese — country
pagare — to play
paio — pair
Pakistan — Pakistan
palazzo — building
pallacanestro — basketball
panetteria — bakery
panettiere — baker
paninoteca — sandwich shop
panna — fresh cream
pantaloncini — shorts
pantaloni — pants
pantofole — slippers
papà — dad
parcheggiare — to park
parecchi — several
parenti — relatives
parlare — to speak
parola — word
parrucchiere — hairdresser
partenza — departure
Pasqua — Easter
passante — passerby

passaporto — passport
passare — to pass by
passeggero — passenger
passeggiata — walk
pasta — pasta
pasticceria — pastry shop
pasticciere — pastry maker, vendor
pasto — meal
patata — potato
patatine — French fries
patente — driver's license
patrigno — stepfather
pattinaggio — skating
paura — fear
pausa — pause
pavimento — floor, pavement
pazzia — folly, madness
pecora — sheep
pelle — skin
pelliccia — fur coat
penisola — peninsula
pensare — to think
pensionato — retired person
pensione — retirement, pension
pensione completa — room and full board
pepe — pepper
peperone — pepperoni
per — for, through, on account of
per caso — by chance
per cortesia — please
per fortuna — by luck, luckily
pera — pear
perbacco! — well!
perché — why, because
perfetto — perfect
periodo — period (of time)
però — however, but
persona — person
Perù — Peru
pesante — heavy
pesca — peach
pesce — fish
pescespada — swordfish
pescheria — fish store
pescivendolo — fish vendor
peseta spagnola — Spanish peseta
peso — weight
pettegolezzo — gossip
petto — chest, breast
piacere — to like
piacevole — pleasant
piano — floor (level)
piantina della città — city map
pianura — plain
pianura padana — Po Valley

piatto — plate
piazza — (market) square
picche — spades (cards)
piccolo — small, little
piede — foot
piega — pleat
Piemonte — Piedmont
pieno — full
pigiama — pajama
pigro — lazy
pioggia — rain
piscina — swimming pool
piselli — peas
pista — runway, path, route
pittore — painter
più — more, plus
piumino — down jacket
piuttosto — rather
poco — little, few
poeta — poet
poi — then
polizia — police
poliziesco — police (adj.)
poliziotto — policeman
pollo — chicken (cooked)
Polonia — Poland
polpaccio — calf (leg)
polpo — octopus
polso — pulse, wrist
poltrona — armchair
pomeriggio — afternoon
pomodoro — tomato
ponte — bridge
popolo — people, population
porro — leek
porta — door
portafoglio — wallet
portare — to bring, to carry
portinaio — doorman
portineria — porter's lodge, superintendent's office
Portogallo — Portugal
portoghese — Portuguese
posate — tableware
possibile — possible
possibilmente — possibly
posta — mail
posto a sedere — seat
portere — to be able to
povere — poor
pranzare — to have lunch
pranzo — lunch
preferibilmente — preferably
preferire — to prefer
prego — you're welcome, please
prendere — to take, to have (something)

prendere in giro — to pull some-one's leg, to make fun (of some-one)
prenotare — to rserve
prenotazione — reservation
prepararsi — to prepare, to get ready
prescrivere — to prescribe
presentarsi — to introduce oneself
presto — soon, quickly
prezzemolo — parsley
primavera — spring
prima — before
primo — 1. first 2. first dish
principale — principal, boss
probabilmente — probably
problema — problem
professione — profession
professore — professor
programma — program
pronto! — hello! (on phone)
pronto soccorso — emergency room
proporre — to propose
proprio — really, quite
prossimo — next
protagonista — protagonist, main actor
provare — to try
proverbio — proverb
prugna — prune
psichiatra — psychiatrist
psicologo — psychologist
Puglia — Puglia (region)
pullman — sleeping car on a train
punti cardinal — cardinal directions
purtroppo — unfortunately

Q

quadretto — 1. square 2. small painting
quadri — diamonds (cards)
quadro — painting
quaglia — quail
qualche — some
qualcosa — something
qualcuno — someone
qualità — quality
quando — when
quanto — how much
quarto — fourth
quasi — almost
quello — that
questione — issue, question
questo — this

questura — police station
qui — here
quindi — thus, therefore
quintale — quintal, hundredweight (¹/₁₀ of a metric ton)
quinto — fifth
quotazione — value (money)

R

racchetta — racket
raccomandarsi — to recommend, to advise someone to do some-thing
raffinato — refined
raffreddore — (a) cold
ragazza — girl
ragazzino — young boy
ragazzo — boy
raggiungere — to reach
ragione — reason
ragioniere — accountant, book-keeper
rapina — theft, holdup
rappresentante — representative
realtà — reality
recitare (un ruolo) — to play a part
recuperare — to recover
refurtiva — booty, stolen goods
reggiseno — brassiere
regione — region
regista — movie director
Regno Unito — United Kingdom
regola — rule
rendersi conto — to realize
reparto — department
Repubblica Democratica Tedesca — German Democratic Republic
Repubblica Federale Tedesca — German Federal Republic
Repubblica Sudafricana — South African Republic
reputazione — reputation
residenza — residence
responsabile — director, manager
restare — to remain
restituire — to give back
riattaccare — to start again, to put back on
ribes — currant
ricco — rich
ricetta — prescription, recipe
ricevere — to receive
ricevuta — receipt
richiamare — to call back

ricordarsi — to remember
ridere — to laugh
ridicolo — ridiculous, funny
riflettere — to reflect
riga — line, ruler
rimanere — to remain
rimanere fisso — to remain in place, to not move
rimettere a nuovo — to renovate
rimpianto — regret
Rinascimento — Renaissance
rinfrescare — to refresh
ringraziare — to thank
ripetere — to repeat
ripetere lettera per lettera — to spell out
riposare — to relax
ripostiglio — closet, storage room
riscaldamento — heating
rischiare — to risk
riservato — reserved
rispettare — to respect
rispondere al telefono — to answer the phone
risposarsi — to remarry
risposta — answer
ristretto — strong coffee
ritardo — lateness
ritorno — return
riunione — meeting
riuscire — to succeed
rivedere — to review, to look over
rivista — magazine
Romania — Rumania
romantico — romantic
romanzo — novel
rosa — rose, pink
rosso — red
rosticceria — takeout food store, caterer
rubare — to steal

S

sabato — Saturday
sala — hall
sala d'attesa — waiting room
salario — salary
sale — salt
salire — to go up
salmone — salmon
salone — salon
salotto — living room
salumeria — delicatessen
salumiere — delicatessen owner
salutare — to greet
sandali — sandals

sapere — to know
Sardegna — Sardinia
sardina — sardine
sbagliare — to make a mistake
sbrigarsi — to hurry
scaffale — bookshelf
scaloppina — scallop
scampo — shrimp
scarpe — shoes
scegliere — to choose
scellino — shilling
scelta — choice
scena — scene
scendere — to go down, to
  descend
scherma — fencing
scherzare — to joke
schiena — back (of the body)
sci — ski
scialle — shawl
sciare — to ski
sciarpa — scarf
scioglilingua — tonguetwister
sciopero — (worker's) strike
scippo — pickpocketing
sciroppo — syrup
scomodo — uncomfortable
scomparire — to disappear
scontrino — bill
sconvolto — shaken
scorso — last (week, month, etc.)
scrittore — writer
scudo portoghese — Portuguese
scuola elementare — elementary
  school
scuola materna — nursery school
scuola media inferiore — junior
  high school
scuola media superiore — middle high school
scuola media superiore — high
  school
scuro — dark
scusare/scusarsi — to excuse/
  excuse oneself
secolo — century
secondo — 1. second 2. main
  entree
secondo — according to
segretario — secretary
seguire — to follow
sembrare — to seem
sempre — always
senape — mustard
Senegal — Senegal
seno — breast
sentimentale — sentimental
sentire — to hear, to feel

senza — without
seppia — sepia
sera — evening
serata — evening
serie — series
serio — serious
servire — to serve
sesto — sixth
seta — silk
sete — thirst
settembre — September
settimo — seventh
sgradevole — unpleasant
si — 1. one (in general) 2. oneself
  3. himself/herself
sì — yes
siccità — dryness
Sicilia — Sicily
sicuramente — surely
signora — madam, Mrs.
signore — Mr.
signorina — young lady, Miss,
  Ms.
silenzio — silence
simile — similar
simpatico — nice
sindacato — labor union
sinistra — left
Siria — Syria
sito — place, site
socio — member
soffitto — ceiling
soffrire — to suffer
soggiornare — to stay over
soggiorno — living room
sogliola — sole (fish)
sognare — to dream
sogno — dream
soldi — money
sole — sun
solo (solamente, soltanto) —
  only
Somalia — Somalia
somma — amount
sorella — sister
sorellastra — stepsister
sottile — thin, delicate
Spagna — Spain
spagnolo — Spanish
spalla — shoulder
sparire — to disappear
spaventarsi — to become afraid
spazioso — spacious
spendere — to spend (money)
sperare — to hope
spese di amministrazione —
  administrative costs
spesso — often

spettacolo — show
spiaggia — beach
spinaci — spinach
sporgere denuncia — to report
  (a theft)
sport — sport
sportello — teller's window, ticket
  window
sportivo — sport (adj), sporty
sporsarsi — to get married
spostamento — move
spremuta d'arancia — orange
  juice
spremuta di limone — lemon
  juice
spumante — sparkling wine
squadra — team
stagioni — seasons
stanza — room
stare a casa — to stay at home
stare bene/male = sentirsi
  bene/male — to feel good/bad
stasera — tonight
Stati Uniti — United States
statua — statue
statura — height (of a person)
stazione — station
stella — star
sterlina inglese — English pound
  sterling
stesso — same
stile — style
stimare — to estimate
stipendio — pay, stipend
stivali — boots
strada — street, road
stradale — street (adj)
strano — strange
stretto — tight
stringere — to tighten
studente — student
studio — studio, professional office
stupido — stupid
stupire/stupirsi — to amaze/to be
  amazed
subire — to undergo
subito — right away
succedere — to happen
succo di frutta — fruit juice
succo di pomodoro — tomato
  juice
sud — south
Sudan — Sudan
sugo — sauce
suo — 1. his/her 2. your (polite)
suocero — father-in-law
suonare (uno strumento) — to
  play (an instrument)

suora — nun
superficie — surface
supposta — suppository
sveglia — wakeup call, alarm clock
svegliarsi — to wake up
Svezia — Sweden
Svizzera — Switzerland
svizzero — Swiss

— T —

tabaccaio — tobacconist
tacco — heel
taglia — size
Tailandia — Thailand
talmente — so much
tappeto — carpet
tardi — late
tasca — pocket
tassista — taxi driver
tavola calda — snack bar
tavolo — table
taxi — taxi
tè — tea
teatro — theater
tedesco — German
telefonare — to phone
telefonata — phone call
televisore — TV set
temperature — temperature
tempo — weather, time (in general)
temporale — storm
tennis — tennis
termosifone — radiator
terrazza — terrace, balcony
terremoto — earthquake
terribile — terrible
terzo — third
testa — head
tinca — trench (fish)
tinta unita — one color
tintoria — dry cleaners
tipico — typical
tomba — tomb
tonnellata — tonne
tonno — tuna
tornare — to come back, to return
toro — bull
torrente — rapids
Toscana — Tuscany
tosse — cough
tovaglia — tablecloth
tovagliolo — napkin
tra — between, among
traduttore — translator
traffico — traffic

traforo del Monte Bianco — Mt. Blanc Tunnel
tragedia — tragedy
tram — streetcar, trolley
tranquillo — peaceful, tranquil
traslocare — to move (house)
trasloco — moving
trattarsi (di) — to deal with
trattoria — restaurant
traversa — crossroad
tredicesima — 1. holiday pay 2. thirteenth
treno — train
Trentino Alto-Adige — Trentino Alto-Adige (region)
triste — sad
troppo — too much
trota — trout
trottare — to trot
trovare — to find
truccarsi — to put on makeup
trucco — makeup
Tunisia — Tunisia
tuono — clap of thunder
Turchia — Turkey
turismo — tourism
tutti — everyone, everybody
tutto — everything, all

— U —

uccidere — to kill
ufficio — office
uguale — same
ultimo — last
Umbria -- Umbria (region)
umidità — humidity
undicesimo — eleventh
Ungheria — Hungary
Unione Sovietica — Soviet Union
unità — unit, unity
università — university
uomo — man
uovo — egg
urgenza — urgency
usanza — custom
uscire — to go out
uva — grapes

— V —

va bene — OK
vagone letto — sleeping car
valere — to be worth
valigia — suitcase
Valle d'Aosta — Aosta Valley

valore — value
vano — room
vario — various, different
vasto — vast
vecchio — old
vedere — to see
vela — sail
venerdì — Friday
Veneto — Veneto (region)
Venezuela — Venezuela
venire — to come
ventesimo — twentieth
vento — wind
veramente — really
verde — green
verdura — vegetables
vero — true
versare — to pour, to deposit (money)
verso — toward
vestaglia — nightgown
vestirsi — to get dressed
vestito — dress, suit
vetrina — store window
viaggiatore — traveler
viaggio organizzato — organized trip
vicino a — near
Vietnam — Vietnam
vino (rosso, bianco, rosato) — wine (red, white, rosé)
viola — purple
violento — violent
violino — violin
visita — visit
visitare — to visit
viso — face
vita — 1. life 2. waist
vivace — lively
vivere — to live
vizio — bad habit, vice
voce — voice
vodka — vodka
volare — to fly
volere — to want to
volo — flight
volta — time (event)
vongola — clam
vulcano — volcano

— Z —

Zaire — Zaire
zero — zero
zio — uncle
zucchero — sugar
zucchino — zucchini

KEY TO PRONUNCIATION

CONSONANTS

ITALIAN LETTER(S)	SOUND IN ENGLISH	EXAMPLES
ci	chee (<u>chee</u>se)	cinema *(chEE-nay-mah)*, movies
ce	chay (<u>chair</u>)	piacere *(pee-ah-chAY-reh)*, pleasure
ca	kah (<u>c</u>ot)	casa *(kAH-sah)*, house
co	koh (<u>c</u>old)	cotto *(kOHt-toh)*, cooked
che	kay (<u>k</u>ent)	perché *(pehr-kAY)*, because
chi	key (<u>key</u>)	pochi *(pOH-key)*, few
gi	jee (<u>jee</u>p)	giro *(jEE-roh)*, turn
ge	jay (<u>g</u>eneral)	generale *(jay-nay-rAH-leh)*, general
gh	gh (spa<u>gh</u>etti)	spaghetti *(spah-ghAYt-tee)*
gli	ll (mi<u>lli</u>on)	egli *(AY-ly-ee)*, he bottiglia *(boht-tEE-ly-ee-ah)*, bottle
gn	ny (ca<u>ny</u>on)	magnifico *(mah-ny-EE-fee-koh)*, magnificent
qu	koo (<u>qu</u>iet)	àquila *(AH-koo-ee-lah)*, eagle
sce	sh (fi<u>sh</u>)	pesce *(pAY-sheh)*, fish
sci		sciòpero *(shee-OH-peh-roh)*, strike
z or zz	ts (ea<u>ts</u>)	pizza *(pEE-tsah)*, pizza zero *(tsEH-roh)*, zero

ITALIAN LETTER(S)	SOUND IN ENGLISH	EXAMPLES
a	ah (y<u>a</u>cht)	casa *(kAH-sah)*, house
è	eh (n<u>e</u>t)	lèggere *(lEH-jeh-reh)*, to read
e	ay (h<u>ay</u>)	mela *(mAY-lah)*, apple
i	ee (f<u>ee</u>t)	libri *(lEE-bree)*, books
o	oh (r<u>o</u>pe)	boccone *(boh-kOH-neh)*, mouthful
u	oo (c<u>oo</u>l)	tutto *(tOOt-toh)*, everything

The remaining Italian sounds and letters correspond, more or less, to English ones. For example:

<u>B</u>ologna *(boh-lOH-nyah)*

<u>F</u>irenze *(fee-rEHn-tseh)*

<u>N</u>apoli *(nAH-poh-lee)*

<u>P</u>isa *(pEE-sah)*

<u>R</u>oma *(rOH-mah)*

<u>T</u>orino *(toh-rEE-noh)*

PHOTO CREDITS